UNIFIED THEATRE COMMAND

Breaking Free of Military Silos

Brig Ashok Pathak

Vitasta

Published by
Renu Kaul Verma
Vitasta Publishing Pvt Ltd
4348/4C, Ansari Road, Daryaganj
New Delhi - 110 002
info@vitastapublishing.com

ISBN: 978-81-19670-28-4

First Edition 2025
MRP ₹695

Layout & Cover Design by Rohit Gautam
Printed by Vikas Computer and Printers, New Delhi

Contents

Preface

The bill for Inter-Services Organisations (Command, Control and Discipline) was introduced on 15 March 2023 in the Indian Lok Sabha (the lower house of Parliament). In the third week of June 2023, several mainstream newspapers in India reported near consensus (99%) among the three services on the number and structure of theatre commands. This consensus took more than seven decades to be arrived at, after the need was first felt for joint operations among the three services, four years after the first Chief of Defence Staff (CDS) was appointed by the government and three months after the bill was placed in the House. As per newspaper reports it may take three to four years (or even longer) before the biggest and long-awaited military reform can take place in one of the most threatened nations (attacked thrice by neighbours, constant insurgency since Independence, and substantial loss of territory in 1948-49—Pakistan Occupied Kashmir, Aksai Chin in 1959 when China occupied that part of Kashmir).

This chronology was the stimulus for undertaking this study. If 'change' is the eternal constant why does it take so long for

India to change—in the face of environmental factors screaming for change? Hence it was important to address this critical issue right in the beginning. The comfort we seek and enjoy in status quo (monumental inertia) is baffling. Even if we discount the delay on account of the inherently slow pace of democracy, India's case must be unique in deliberately sleeping over a problem for decades—which may be due, as Dr S Jaishankar suggests, to a 'theory of insanity'. Though the Minister of External Affairs labels this tendency as a 'hesitation of history', we can describe it in a less diplomatic way as a crippling inertia in decision making in India. This is due to a number of other factors. Utter lack of confidence in one's own capabilities and hence propensity to ape the West, low levels of sincerity of purpose and honesty in accepting 'process defects', transactional approach in bringing about organisational efficiencies and avoiding hard decisions even when these are overdue. Though it may seem out of place to say so, the author thinks that our propensity for maintaining the status quo needs to be analysed since it will affect the implementation and operationalisation of reforms.

Military reforms of this proportion should be of interest to all who take interest in national security. Hence a glossary of military terms is provided to get everyone on the same starting point. Those who have a military background will find it mundane and may skip the section.

The literature review and discussions with scholars at the Centre for Land Warfare System (CLAWS) on 19 January 2022, with scholars of the Centre for Air Power System (CAPS) on 8 February 2022 and with former Signal Officer in Chief (SO-in-C), Lt Gen Rajeev Sabherwal, provide some insight into the impact the affected environment has on the subject. I am extremely grateful to Lt Gen Vijay Kumar Ahluwalia, Director

CLAWS 2018-22, and Air Marshal Anil Chopra, Director CAPS for the time they spared for the discussions. It is the literature review that prompted other sections in the study. The literature review also includes the author's own analysis supported by relevant data/information.

Though the concept of theatre commands was actually operationalised during the closing months of WWI in the Battle of Somme and Amiens, the Navy and ground forces cooperated even before this period. However, it was only in WWII that both Allied and Axis powers conducted long campaigns following the concept of unified regional (theatre) commands. Surprisingly, the outcome of this centralised command varied from nation to nation based on the way the concept was operationalised by each one of them, acting jointly or severally. This brought us to the matrix or the levels at which theatre wars are conducted. This matrix becomes useful for identifying the fault lines that affect the performance of a theatre command.

While the Western experience is covered in brief, the Indian experience post-Independence required more detailed analysis. Several senior opinion leaders in this domain feel that, 'India has done so well in all the wars since 1947 without the formation of theatre commands, so why disturb the apple cart by imposing a foreign concept?' The section on the Indian experience highlights the bigger goals that could have been achieved given the immense human sacrifice involved. It emerges that the perceived victories hid some glaring shortcomings arising especially from the disjointed conduct of operations.

Relevant issues gleaned from the statecraft, military organisation, and war-fighting strategies adopted during ancient Indian history as also during the medieval period, indicate that the Indian military establishment needs to look inwards to absorb the basic principles and even the concepts of jointness in military operations.

In the final chapter, the oft-quoted US and Chinese theatre commands have been discussed in some detail, bringing out the major differences between these two and what India can learn from them. The example of the IDF (Israel Defence Forces) given in the study might be thought provoking for the reader. Here is a tiny country surrounded by big and hostile neighbours who were determined to annihilate it right from the beginning. Israel fought its way through all these decades and resolved all major issues using military power and diplomacy (from a position of strength but with a message of peaceful coexistence). The IDF does not talk of jointness, theatre command or even air-land battle (which the Americans declare to have learnt from the IDF). They just do it. Their doctrines do not smell of Western influence. They do not copy the British though they did raise two brigades while fighting alongside the British troops in WWII.

The IDF developed its own war fighting strategies and defeated the Arab League trained by the British in 'set piece battles, as per the plan, steamrolling the adversary with mass in slow moving plodding campaigns'. Against this the IDF employed an 'all-of-nation' approach, using sheer grit and audacity and throwing everything they had and fighting as per the terrain and enemy.

Finally the recommendations. I feel that the study would have been incomplete without seeking advice from someone who is leading this complex and long overdue transformation. I am extremely grateful to Lt Gen Rajesh Pant, former National Cyber Security Coordinator for setting up my interaction with Chief of Defence Staff Gen Anil Chauhan. The CDS was very generous in taking out almost an hour from his packed schedule on 4 September 2023. I could explain the issues I had addressed in the study and draw broad inferences based on the analysis. In response to my specific queries, the CDS expressed his satisfaction at the willing cooperation he was getting from the three service chiefs. He was also very clear that before the theatre structures are announced, all the issues pertaining to jointness and integration are to be resolved so that the theatre commanders do not have to wade through uncertainties. The CDS explained the basic tenets of jointness and integration and briefly touched upon the issues to be addressed in creating theatre structures. The relevant part has been included in Chapter 3. On my way back from the meeting, I realised the enormity of the task ahead in creating a culture of jointness in the armed forces.

I am grateful to Mahroof Raza for his valuable advice. He has been with the subject for more than three decades and has seen the relevant environment from the perspectives of cutting edge military leadership and at strategic levels. Mahroof's presence during discussions on national security in leading electronic media has always been intellectually stimulating and educative.

For obvious reasons, the study does not lay down any structure. It is not possible to be wiser than the illustrious professionals who are already on the job. The author made an attempt to visualise how the reformed armed force will look like once the job is completed. However, the efficacy of these reforms will depend on the organisational dynamics—a function of people at various levels. This study will help the reader to understand the relevant aspects of military reforms that are underway at the highest level in India and to participate in an informed debate on the subject.

★★★

The Challenge
Overcoming Inertia

IT MAY LOOK surprising to see military professionals and experts still debating an issue that a large number of military powers have already settled decades back. However, the current unwillingness to accept any change to the status quo would look very natural once we get familiar with the crippling inertia and propensity for maintaining the status quo in post-Independent India.

Inheritance of a Legacy of Inertia

The post World War II period from 1945 to 1960, saw three dozen countries becoming independent or attaining self-governed status. India was one of these with some unique distinctions. First, it was the only decolonised country in 1947 that was partitioned into two. Second, even after being declared an independent country, India opted to retain a British military commander and the last Viceroy, as their first governor general (virtual head of state), Lord Mountbatten, who retained this position for about ten months (15 August 1947 to June 1948) after independence. Third, British officers were retained to head the Indian Armed Forces on the premise that since the 'native Indian officers in the army had no experience of functioning at high ranks, they would need a few years of handholding. A British officer, Brigadier C H I Akehurst headed the Corps of Signals of the Indian Army till 1954. Fourth, British advice was sought and followed for all strategic decisions pertaining to nation building.

What did the British do to deserve this honour? In the year 1600, India's GDP in the prevailing international dollar rates was 74,250 million and British GDP was USD 6,700 million. When the British left, India's GDP was 2,55,852 million dollars and that of Britain was 3,14,969 million dollars. A total of thirty-four major famines occurred during a time window of 120 years during the British Rule. This was double the number of famines which India faced in 2000 years before the British rule. From 1765 to 1938, Britain drained $45 trillion from India—17 times the current GDP of the UK. Shashi Tharoor (*An Era of Darkness, 2016*) quotes British MP Dr Vickerman Rutherford 'In return for India's invaluable service during the war (WWI), we gave to the Indian nation such a discreditable, disgraceful and tyrannical constitution.' So what explains the propensity to follow the footsteps of such colonial masters? An inheritance of a legacy of inertia and a monumental resistance to change.

There are three major factors that explain the monumental inertia. First, the complex nature of India's 'freedom struggle' and the texture of India's indigenous political leadership that took over from the British colonisers. Second, the internal strife in India with a number of sub-national undercurrents. Third, an unrealistic, and ill-informed geopolitical visualisation by the Indian leadership in 1947 that made the armed forces redundant to start with.

The Indian National Congress (INC) that is credited with spearheading the struggle for independence and finally getting rid of the colonisers was established by a British civil servant in 1885. Many political commentators find this organisation a 'valve' providing for an outlet for letting off steam of unrest from the population through a non-violent movement that gave us nothing. After 50 years of this struggle, a dominion government was formed in 1935 under British rule. Members in this government could debate, make laws but the viceroy had the final word. The viceroy could change the decisions made by the house without ascribing any reason.

The British Indian army was inducted in WWII without consulting the Indian members in this dominion government. The Government of India Act was made by this government in 1935. Almost 90% of the existing Indian Constitution comprises of the Government of India Act 1935 made by the erstwhile colonial masters. Bulk of the judicial laws, police laws and the armed forces traditions flow from the 1935 dispensation or even earlier.

It is interesting to note that on the eve of Independence, Gandhiji was concerned about the rot that had set in the political parties. Some legislators were demanding money from businessmen to get them licences; they indulged in black marketing and subverting the judiciary and intimidating top officials to secure transfers and promotions for their protégés. He asked for the dissolution of the Indian National Congress as a political party and setting up of a Lok Seva Sangh. No one supported him. He felt isolated and used by his protégés. It was in this personal phase of disenchantment that he was assassinated. This was also the time when communal violence was at its peak.

We need to look at Gandhiji's theory and experiments with non-violence and non-cooperation more closely since these movements shaped the way independent India functioned long after Gandhiji left the scene. His close colleagues, including Jawaharlal Nehru and Maulana Azad, found it strange that he should abandon the

Chauri Chaura non-cooperation movement in 1920 because a few policemen were killed by the agitators in retaliation to what the police did to them. This was the time when the British were on the back foot (Durgadas, 1969, reprint 1981).

Maulana Azad was aghast when Gandhiji turned soft on Subhas Chandra Bose in the wake of the Japanese victory over the British during the first three years of WWII. Gandhiji suggested to Azad that if the Japanese win the war then India will get freedom. Shashi Tharoor while commenting on Gandhiji's thinking that the 'willing sacrifice of the innocent is the most powerful answer to the insolent tyranny', finds the concept, 'frighteningly unrealistic'. As per Tharoor, Nelson Mandela found Gandhiji's non-violence against tyrants 'useless'. Tharoor goes even further. Gandhiji's methods are being widely used by militants and other retrograde organisations in India post Independence to stall actions on militants or to block overdue reform processes.

India became a free nation in the wake of the communal divide that created Pakistan. The Indian political leadership was under the strong influence of communist China and Soviet Russia. This placed Indian people into the cauldron of subnational/communally charged movements and left wing propaganda. Both these aspects ensured politics with communal flavour and misplaced pursuit of socialism. Consequently, for the next twenty-four years, India became poorer and more illiterate than ever. Not taking a decision, stalling good decisions, extending state control over almost all citizen activities and getting accustomed to near stagnation became a dominant culture. Above all Indian political leadership and consequently a huge section of intelligentsia viewed nationalism, nationalistic ideology and patriotism through the prism of erstwhile colonial masters or through communist concepts.

Finally, let us look at the relationship between the political leadership, bureaucracy and the armed forces. The British ruled India on the strength of loyal British Indian Armed Forces that comprised very high proportion of native soldiers. Just before the 1857 war of independence the British Presidency Army had 3,13,500 Indian natives and 38,000 British troops (mostly officers). During WWI, the British Indian Army consisted of 39 Horsed Cavalry Regiments, 138 Infantry Battalions, and 12 Mountain Batteries (that had artillery guns). Some 74,187 Indian soldiers died in this war (Tharoor, 2016) and were forgotten by the British as well as by their own country, India.

The promise of freeing India after the war was broken. During WWII, the bulk of the 14th Army that was fighting in Burma (present day Myanmar) comprised of Indian men and officers. During this war, the British Indian Royal Air Force, and Navy also came into being. The strength of Indian officers and men in the British Indian Armed Forces was close to two million by the middle of 1945. Between 1 September 1939 to 28 February 1945, the Indians suffered 1,49,225 casualties (Tharoor).

In both these wars, the Indian troops fought to save the British Empire in almost all continents. Ironically, during WWI, the Indian troops (recruited with the help of Gandhiji against the wishes of the people) fought against the Ottoman Empire and helped in ending the rule of the Caliphate. Bulk of these troops (in the Egyptian Expedition Force) were Muslims. Once the Caliphate was removed, the INC under Gandhiji joined the Khilafat Movement to restore the rule of the Caliphate in 1920. By 1922, the Turkish leadership itself gave up the demand for the Caliphate.

When this force exhibited signs of anger and revolt against the British in the wake of the proposed trial of INA soldiers, the

British realised that they could no longer govern India. Such was the importance given by the colonial powers to the Indian officers and men who fought alongside the British soldiers and officers in the two great wars and even before this period in providing the British with military might. These very Indian officers and soldiers had turned nationalistic and were filled with patriotic pride such that the British had to leave post haste. Major General V K Singh in his book, *The Contribution of Jubbulpore Mutiny to India's Freedom* brings out the scale of the military revolt that took place when the prisoners of Azad Hind Fauj of Subhas Chandra Bose were being tried by the British. Tharoor has the same opinion 'when the sailors of the Royal Indian Navy mutinied and fired their own canons on the British Port installations, the British realised that the 'game was up'. In spite of all that it was propagated that India won her freedom through non-violent means through non-cooperation with the British.

Thus, when the first Commander-in-Chief of the Indian Army in independent India met Gandhiji (the tallest leader at that time) he was told that the Indian Army had been involved in killing fellow Indians under the British rule and that they should now atone for their sins by cleaning latrines and getting involved in other such nation building work. Nehru, the first Indian Prime Minister felt that India is a peace loving country hence army is not required. Most ironically, the Indian political establishment of 1947 exhibited more faith in the British officers who were retained after independence. Indian politicians were also apprehensive about the prospect of Indian army officers grabbing power through a coup.

The above factors not only made the nation a status quo community but converted the Indian Forces into an institution with inherent inertia and craving more for entitlement and position as against efficiency and performance.

Both, China to the East and Pakistan to the West exploited this ecosystem by creating internal turbulence and external aggressions on India. At the time of Independence, India had a formidable strength of men and material that had taken part in two world wars. But as discussed earlier, the dominant belief and carefully propagated narrative by the political leadership in Independent India, conveyed an impression that the armed forces were not that critical to national security. This feeling prevailed for the next fifteen years in the face of overwhelming evidence to the contrary.

The Chinese invasion was helpful to some extent. But the armed forces as an institution did not develop a sound mechanism of learning from experience in an objective manner. Hence, in spite of fighting several short duration wars with her neighbours, countering internal turbulence due to insurgency and terrorism there was no mechanism of maintaining official records of conflicts with a view to change the national approach, formulate new strategies and operational doctrines, restructure organisations and so on. This inculcated a feeling of 'all is well' and complacency. Though several eminent soldiers who took part in these wars did write excellent books bringing out the incidents of failure and how things could be improved, their suggestions and warnings were ignored. Besides, for the first six to seven decades, the cycle of taking decisions and implementing these remained excruciatingly slow and at times retrograde.

It is against this backdrop that India's journey for creating jointness in the armed forces needs to be discussed. Jointness in planning and execution, among the three services in India's Armed Forces was felt even before the 1962 war, may be right after Independence. Later in 1971, the spectacular military victory that led to the creation of a new nation, Bangladesh, brought the then government closest to appointing General (Later Field Marshal) SHFJ Manekshaw as Chief of the Defence Staff (CDS), thus paving the way for creation of the joint command structure.

Shri P N Haksar, the then Principal Secretary to the Prime Minister called Air Chief Marshall (ACM) P C Lal asking his views on appointing Gen Manekshaw as the CDS 'in recognition of the way he had directed the Bangladesh War'. Lal wrote back, stating, 'All the three chiefs and each service had contributed in the victory. Undoubtedly, the Army did a good job and Manekshaw as Chief of Staff Committee did coordinate well, but there was no case for a CDS'. This was a case of a wrong question getting a wrong answer. First, appointment of someone like Manekshaw as CDS, should not have been considered as an award for directing the war well. What the Bangladesh war taught was that synergistic application of the three services under a commander with sound judgment would result in high probability of resounding military outcomes in a short span of time with low cost in terms of men and material. Hence, the armed forces need to be so structured as to replicate this experience in any future military conflict.

Second, the question was asked of a wrong person. It is not for an Air Chief to decide whether he would consider functioning under a CDS from the Army. There is hardly any probability of the Air Chief saying 'yes' to the question. In fact service chiefs do not decide on whether there should be joint planning and execution. The cabinet committee on security formulates the national vision on all aspects related to the security and well-being of the nation. The military derives their own strategic vision from the national vision. The organisational structures and hierarchies follow.

Twenty-seven years later, India fought another war with

Pakistan on the Kargil heights. The way the war was forced on India, its execution, high rates of casualties and overall impact on the national security were studied by the Kargil Review Committee (KRC). The KRC recommended restructuring of national security management and apex decision making processes. It took another two decades for the Indian government after the Kargil war to take a bold and firm decision for paving the way for joint unified command.

Breaking Free of the Crippling Inertia

On 1 January 2020, the Government of India appointed General Bipin Rawat as CDS not as a reward but as necessity for a task. This time around they did not ask any of the service chiefs for approval or advice! The path to the desired jointness among the Indian Armed Forces was open, at least to the government. Work started on the project in mission mode. The outline of the structure of the joint command was firmly in place before Gen Bipin Rawat, the first CDS of the Indian Armed Forces passed away in an unfortunate air crash.

On 28 September 2022, the government decided to appoint Lt General Anil Chauhan as the second CDS to continue the project from where late General Rawat had left. On 4 October 2022, Air Chief Marshal V R Chaudhari reportedly said in the *Times of India,* dated 5 October 2022 that the IAF is not opposed to the creation of theatre command but the doctrinal aspects of IAF should not be compromised. Incidentally, the Indian Armed Forces made their first Tri-Service Doctrine in 2017. This doctrine includes the IAF doctrine. If the IAF doctrine is revised so would the Tri-Service Doctrine. But, the IAF doctrine cannot be at divergence from the Tri-Service doctrine.

On 15 March 2023, a bill for Inter Services Organisations

was placed in Parliament. Subsequently, sometime in July 2023 the Standing Parliamentary Committee cleared the Bill to be implemented without any dilution. The Bill was later passed by the Indian Parliament. The decks are now clear for the Bill to be discussed at the highest levels in the country and passed. The political leadership has finally taken up the responsibility to reform India's most respected institution.

★★★

The Basics of Nomenclature

WE NEED TO look at the relevant aspects of the existing set up of command and control in the armed forces in India. The basic units in the army are battalions (especially for infantry, army services corps,), regiments (for armoured, artillery, engineers, air defence, signals, special forces). The infantry, special forces and armoured regiments are involved in direct combat. Artillery, engineers, air defence, signals are combat support elements. The rest are for logistics support. Though all fighting units involved in direct combat do have combat and logistics support elements, additional combat support and logistics support are provided by the units designed and specialised for these roles.

It is only at the level of a division that ground-based fire support (artillery), armoured fighting capability, engineers support (engineers regiment), signal communications (signals regiment), logistics (services and ordnance units) are made integral to the organisation (divisions). Between the divisions and the basic fighting units are brigades generally comprising of three infantry units for infantry brigades, three armoured regiments for armoured brigades, and three artillery regiments for artillery brigades. There are Air Defence, engineers and para brigades on similar lines. Three brigades generally form a division. Similarly, three divisions form a corps and three corps form an army command. An Army Commander has the authority to decide on the overall operational objectives, tasks of organisations in his command. The operational control of the battles are generally with the corps commanders.

We may look little deeper into the way these organisations are formed, their capabilities, technological and people-centric aspects. Firstly, each of the arms (involved in direct fighting), combat support arm (involved in direct support of the fighting arm), and services units (for logistics) are highly specialised in their respective roles. Personnel and officers are recruited/commissioned into these specialised forces—infantry, armour, artillery, engineers, air defence, signals and so on. Their training, experience and internalisation of military knowledge is predominantly fulcrummed around their own arm or service. Though they pick up experiential learning about other components of their service (army), while serving in brigades and divisions.

The personnel and officers also undergo training courses to learn about the other components of the army. Once the officers reach the rank of a colonel they get ready to take over command of a formation that may include specialised components. A divisional commander (major general) is the first level of leadership where almost all components of the army are under command. It is here that the degree of difficulty increases manifold in commanding a force that has varied specialisation, culture, technological endowment, and the capability to influence the outcome of a battle. The organisational dynamics must ensure that the right type of leaders command divisions, those who have excellent 'people skill' to understand the nuances of such a force, keep the force fully motivated, technologically equipped, organisationally committed to the goals the division is set to achieve.

The leadership style here needs to be transformational since each commanding officer under the divisional commander comes with special expertise, work culture and understanding his role in war. At times the leadership needs to depend on collectivism and even delegation to someone who understands the battle situation better in that phase of operations. The complexity of this task is evident from the fact that synergistic application of all divisional resources in war is not very common. In all the wars that India has fought such examples where the intra service resources were optimised are rare.

The basic fighting element in the navy is task unit (3 to 5 ships). Further up are task groups (up to 10 ships), task force (comprising of 2 to 5 task groups), fleet (comprising of several task groups). The compositions, tasking and control of these units, groups, forces and fleets are with the naval commanders. The air force has total command of their flights, squadrons, wings and air bases and all air assets including those meant for air defence. Modern wars are fought with a number of other military and non-military assets like cyber space, political, economic, and psychological warfare components. These are commanded and controlled by their respective component heads.

In joint military operations, the complexity and hence the difficulty of leadership are multiplied. Here we place elements of other services like the air force or the navy under the jurisdiction of a theatre commander from one particular service—say army. Hence, besides dealing with his own highly specialised elements of ground forces other services come under his direct command. Our war time experience in tri-service operations is rather poor.

Modern wars go beyond the tri-service domain also. These are multidimensional, highly dynamic, continuous and fluctuating between the non-military and military domains. Commanders even at the highest level of a theatre or even a service find it extremely difficult to muster the national assets for fighting a war. Besides, since they get used to dealing with their respective command set ups their capabilities to optimise resources from other services or asset bases is extremely stunted even when these are allotted to them during war. Thus, if we wish to optimise the utilisation of national power during non-military and military conflicts, there are two essential requirements.

First, the requisite assets need to be placed in a unified command responsible for a geographical area or operation. Second, the task requires designing a command and control structure that facilitates unity of command without diluting efficiency of use of specialised forces or services. Thus, for example, while it will be essential to place air force components under a theatre commander, the actual operational employment, including tasking based on the overall theatre strategy, needs to be delegated to the air force commander who is well versed with the finer aspects of air power utilisation. This will also require a mix of formal structure and informal culture of mutual trust and respect for each other.

Glossary Used in Theatre Command

The glossary given below is derived primarily from American experience in WWII. Hence the terms used are contextual. Even among the allied forces, the interpretation and actual applications differed as per the national preferences. Besides, the personal traits of commanders also impacted the actual operationalisation of these concepts.

Integrated, Combined and Joint Operations

Dr Noel Sproles and Alex Yates of the Australian Government Department of Defence (Command and Control Division

Information Science Laboratory) in their paper, *A Historical Study of Operational Command: A Resource for Researchers* highlight salient aspects of these three terms in the context of multi-national forces that fight together as an alliance or as part of a coalition. Integrated command is primarily for an alliance force, 'when a single commander is appointed from one of the allied nations with a multinational make-up of the subordinate commanders and staffs. A staff in which one officer only is appointed to each post on the establishment of the headquarters, irrespective of nationality and Service'. Thus, in case an officer is appointed to coordinate air recce missions from one of the nationalities—say France, then this French officer will be coordinating air recce missions of all the other nations in the alliance. The air elements will be operating under their own national commanders. Thus there is no structural or operational jointness in integrated command.

The terms combined and joint are generally used interchangeably though 'joint operations' is a much better and in vogue term that denotes jointness of structure, planning and operations. While in the integrated command it is the objective or the military goal that is common and coordinated. In joint operation the command, resources, policies and processes are all common to the force. Integration is close to addition whereas jointness would imply a case where sum individual parts is less effective than the whole formed by jointness.

A Unified Theatre Command (UTC) means a single recognised command authority during an operation. We would define UTC as a military force in a given geographical area, under one commander-in-chief for a common objective, for a given campaign or series of campaigns against a threat.

The purpose of UTC is to ensure synergistic force application and economy of resource utilisation by preventing duplication of plans and resources for the same objective.

A UTC would have supreme commander and commander-in-chief (C-in-C) at the apex. The US Forces considered Army Group (two or more armies, an army being equivalent to a command in the Indian context) as the minimum force level under a C-in-C. He would have his own tactical air force under him. General MacArthur was the Commander-in-Chief South-West Pacific Area. He could take decisions without reference to joint chiefs at Washington. As a rule, the C-in-C was not expected to deal with the day to day operations and monitoring.

He had three major roles. First, to set principle objectives for the campaign; second, to regulate strengths of various commands as per the objectives and lastly, distribute logistics and supporting forces. The British kept C-in-C even below army groups. As an example they designated Royal Air Force (RAF) commander-in-chief in a theatre for all aspects pertaining to the force including operations, training, administration etc. The British C-in-C functioned under the overall supervision/direction of the High Command at London (Churchill). The Americans found this arrangement quite counter-productive and at times dangerous. Similarly, General Claude Auchinleck was C-in-C India command since 1943. He was responsible for maintaining training area in India for the entire South-East Asia Command.

The term, Supreme Commander was generally applicable when forces from more than one nation were to operate together. A supreme commander then had jurisdiction over the commanders of all the forces from different nationalities placed under him. A supreme commander was not expected to directly command the forces under him since, multi-national forces did not want their forces to be commanded directly by a general from a different nation.

UTC would have the apex, component elements, the force and staff. The apex would include the top politico-military decision makers at strategic levels. This apex would have subordinate commanders for actual conduct of operations.The component elements will include the service specific organisations like the air force, navy, cyber and so on. These are highly specialised branches and hence are given more autonomy to support the operational levels under the overall requirement set by the common objective.

Staff: For control and liaison with the force executing the task the apex body would need a suitable organisation. This is also necessitated keeping in view the complexity and multiplicity of responsibilities of the commanders. The primary role of staff in jointness is to create and sustain trust across the force. The commander's behaviour and attitude are critical in ensuring the right behaviour of the staff, who can act as a glue to keep the force together. It can also destroy the cohesiveness of the force.

Task Force: A temporary grouping of units, under one commander, formed for the purpose of carrying out a specific operation or mission. In order to maintain the spirit of joint operations supported by delegation of operational roles to the subordinate commanders, creation of task forces are generally kept to the minimum and for very short periods of time. However, there have been instances when theatre commanders created quasi permanent task forces to micro manage theatre operations, for example, MacArthur and Montgomery.

The Commander-in-Chief can either exercise his command function directly over the entire theatre or can even delegate some part of command to any of the component elements. Thus, the model can be either purely direct command or hybrid model (part direct part delegated). The critical aspects of UTC are unity of efforts, coordination and cooperation.

Supreme Commander: Two or more Commanders-in-chief of their respective theatres can be placed under a supreme commander. This term was more relevant during the World Wars where forces of different nationalities were included in UTCs.

Hybrid UTC: The theatre command can delegate command to a subordinate commander (generally for the component commander of a specialised service) the overall responsibility of command for their respective component forces without altering the overall mission of the campaign. Such UTCs are desginated to function under a hybrid system of the UTC.

Span of Control: This denotes the degree of freedom on types of decisions a theatre commander or even a supreme commander can take without approval from the designated authority for the decision. The most popular example of this case is denial of nuclear weapons against China by the president of the US to the supreme commander of allied forces in the Korean war (1951-54). Similarly, during the conduct of WWII General MacArthur had changed an Australian general. The Australian government intervened and the decision was revoked.

India-specific Terms and Historical Background

During the colonial era, the British kept the status of the Commander-in-Chief of the army next to the viceroy. He was part of the decision-making policy for the British colonial empire in India. There were occasions when they took over as viceroys. Wavell, Auchinleck and Mountbatten are few of the top military officers who held the positions of C-in-C; Wavell and Mountbatten later functioned as viceroys. They did this because the British ruled over India through the British Indian Armed Forces. As soon as they realised that the native soldiers were not with them, their days in India ended in a hurry.

Commander–in–Chief (C-in-C) Army: General Cariappa was appointed the first Commander-in-Chief in January 1949. He was tasked to Indianise the Indian Army into a nationalist army by inculcating an Indian ethos among the officers and men. However, he was known as a 'pucca British saheb' more English than the English themselves.

His regimental officer Lt Gen Nathu Singh was seeped in the Indian traditions and liked to be dressed in Indian attire. Cariappa never approved of it though he never questioned Nathu Singh. The Indian C-in-C had operational control over his forces. On a similar pattern, the Navy and the Air Force had their respective C–in-C Navy and C–in-C Air Force though initially junior in rank (equivalent to three star general) to the C–in-C Army. Later their ranks were also raised to that of four star generals.

Commander-in-Chief (C-in-C) Navy: Highest ranking naval officer with operational command of all naval forces and naval assets in India.

Commander-in-Chief (C-in-C) Air Force: Highest ranking air force officer with operational command of air power and air assets in India.

Chief of Army/Naval/Air Staff: The institution of COAS/CNS/CAS is a dilution in the powers of the C-in-C in that these appointments do not have direct commands over their respective forces. The operational command is with the General Officer Commander-in-Chief in each command. The Chiefs of Army/Navy/Air staff also do not have direct access to the PM, the Cabinet or the Raksha Mantri (Defence Minister). They are expected to reach out to the cabinet or the Raksha Mantri through the Defence Secretary. The Defence Secretary has authority but the responsibility and accountability are with the COAS/CNS/CAS.

Integrated Defence Staff (IDS)

During the Kargil war with Pakistan in 1999, lack of inter service coordination (primarily between the Army and the IAF) came under criticism. The Kargil Review Committee Report paved the way for integrated defence staff HQ at Delhi headed by a three star equivalent officer from the Army/Navy or the IAF. The staff comprised of officers and men from the three services. HQ IDS was primarily tasked with formulation of policies, doctrines and related coordination. However, due to lack of adequate authority, resources and rank structures, this HQ has not been able to substitute the creation of unified theatre commands.

In the next chapter, we will be able to analyse, through literature review, the thought processes of military professionals in India on the idea related to military reforms for creating unified theatre commands. The brief given above will help readers who do not have 'military service experience' to understand the literature review in a proper perspective.

★★★

Review of Literature

Responding to Theatre Commands

GIVEN THE GLOBAL trends and the undeniable need for these defence reforms, there should have been near unanimity on this decision in India. But there are more differences than points of consensus. Even at the top level in the Army there is a feeling that more time and discussion is required. 'It has to be a deliberate, thoughtful, and well considered implementation. Fruition will take many years,' said General Naravane as Army Chief. Two years after his retirement, General Naravane observed that the nation needs to first formulate its defence strategy before implementing restructuring into theatre commands.

Hence any discussion on the subject needs to take into account what the military professionals think of restructuring India's Armed Forces into Unified Theatre Commands (UTCs) and what is at the root of all this delay and resistance. Besides reviewing and analysing the literature on the subject, it was also necessary to interact with some relevant think tanks as part of an idea engineering exercise.

The general reaction to the government decision for creating UTC has been on predictable lines. Firstly, in the operational domain there is a feeling, 'We did so well in 1971 war without having theatre commands, so where is the need? It is a borrowed concept from the West, not suitable for India (Air Marshal Brijesh Dhar Jayal, *TOI,* 22 November 2021)'.

'In case of theatre commands how can troops in desert go and fight in the mountains/jungles and vice versa.'(Col DJS Chahal—Olive Greens Institute blog, 1 June 2020). 'Theatre Commands will be fighting battles rather than fighting a war.' 'China is three times the size of India. Hence switching of forces from one sector to another would have been difficult hence they opted for a big theatre command. In India switching of forces from one sector to another is relatively easy. Hence why go for UTC. Division of meagre resources will reduce combat efficiency at the point of decision.'

'I believe in Theatre Command India is one theatre,' Air Chief Marshal B S Dhanoa (Retd) reported in IDSA (https://idsa.in/system/files/jds/14-2-2020-achieving-jointness-in-war-asingh.pdf). Another Air Chief Marshal (Arup Raha) quotes Dhanoa in NDC publications (Force, 2020).

A second group of opinions is related to civil military relations. There are contradictory opinions on this issue. Some feel that creation of theatre command is being done to bring the military under political control as has been done in China. As per a USI paper, the opposite effect is envisaged in that 'it will improve civil-military relations especially by way of allowing the armed forces to have their voice heard by the government (under the garb of military control the armed forces are denied a say in decision making since 1950)'.

Third, aspects related to these changes pertain to resource-based capabilities both in terms of finances and material assets. Almost all senior military officers feel, 'Defence budget is much lower than what the World Bank figures show. It is around 1.6 to 1.8 per cent of the GDP. The bureaucracy has included defence pensions too in the defence budget. Earlier this was not part of the defence budget.' This was a reaction to the author's presentation at Centre for Land Warfare Studies (CLAWS) when the World Bank figures were shown to the attendees. India's expenditure on defence has been in sync with the global trends and countries that spent a higher percentage of GDP on defence did not gain much by way of winning in wars or securing their respective nations.

Fourth, there are people-centred misgivings. Cadre satisfaction may get affected adversely since the number of 'three star' generals/equivalent are likely to decrease; reduction of manpower in these reforms will decrease the fighting capability of forces; the need to harmonise rules and regulations and so on.

Fifth, those who favour the government decision feel that UTC will help in the conduct of operations especially in multidomain threats in fifth, sixth and seventh generation wars. There is also a view that the CDS be made responsible for defence of India and be made a permanent member of the Cabinet committee on Security.

Analysis

Operational Efficiency

The view, that the Indian military has done well without reforms related to theatre commands, is misplaced. Given the resources, the military could have done far better than what it did. One of the reasons for sub-optimal performance has been political naivety. However, military inefficiency especially due to utter lack of jointness has also been a major contributing factor. We will deal with this issue in more detail in subsequent discussions. As regards correlating size with creation of theatre commands there are smaller nations who have theatre commands. This is not about size; it is about mental efficiency through synergised efforts and leadership, capability to do more with less. We will see later that in all the wars India fought, 'resources' were never a constraint. This holds good even for the 1962 debacle where inspite of political bungling the military could have saved the day especially after Bomdi La.

Civil Military Integration/Synergy, Decision Making

The general perception about the concept of civil military relations and the impact of reforms on it is again due to deep distrust and bias. First, all major nations irrespective of the political system keep their respective military under political control. It needs to be that way. Even a brief look at countries where the military calls the shots will convince the reader the validity of this statement. Coming to the specific case of India where the perception that the bureaucrats call all the shots may not reflect the whole truth. Lt Gen Thakur Nathu Singh way back in 1947 opposed the then Prime Minister of India on the latter's suggestion to retain senior British officers in the Indian Army for leadership roles. The PM agreed. Gen Cariappa's intervention on refusing to recruit soldiers of INA in the Indian Army was against what the Government of India wanted.

The Indian Government agreed with the Army Chief. Lt Gen Sagat Singh refused to withdraw from Nathu La in 1965 against the Government decision. The then PM upheld Gen Sagat Singh's decision. Sam Manekshaw's intervention in Bangladesh operations when he wanted the then Government to wait till the winter for operations to liberate Bangladesh, was respected. Thus historical facts indicate that when the military top brass wanted to be heard they were heard and their decisions respected.

Even the decision for the creation of theatre commands—that could have come about in 1972—was kept hanging in the balance since the then Air Chief did not agree. Some senior military officers felt that the Ministry of Defence (MoD) being staffed by bureaucrats is slow in decision making and is not aware of military matters. There are a number of cases where the higher Headquarters of military establishments have been equally lethargic and took wrong decisions. One of the suggestions to improve the civil military cooperation is to make CDS responsible for defence of India. However, in 6th and 7th generation wars, the CDS may not have the required knowledge and resources for defending the nation from a large number of threats. The CDS needs to get direct access to the highest political leadership on critical issues related to the three services.

Budgeting and Finance, Resource-based Capability

Military scholars have opposing views on this issue. Some feel that theatre commands are necessary to cope with the dwindling defence budget. There is a contrarian view that restructuring the armed forces in theatre commands will entail increase in the defence budget due to duplication in distribution of resources. Another suggestion in this context is a reduction of troop strength by at least 1,50,000 so that money saved here can be used for capital expenditure. The entire subject of budget allocation, finance or macro or political economy needs to be looked at from a number of perspectives. First, it is important to take note of what the global institutes perceive of India's defence spending.

Second, the perception and satisfaction level of our commanders and, third, and most important, the impact on the soldiers. As per the World Bank data, India ranks fifth in terms of expenditure in percentage of GDP on defence after Saudi

Arabia (8.4%), Israel (5.6%), Russia (4.3%), US (3.7%), India (2.9%). China is way behind us at 1.7% of the GDP on defence. A comparison of defence spending, GDP and GDP per capita will highlight how much a nation can afford to spend on defence.

Country	**% of GDP on Defence**	**GDP in billion dollars**	**Per capita GDP in dollars**	**Remarks**
Saudi Arabia	8.4	700.12 (842.12)	20110	
Israel	5.6	407 (467)	44168	
Russia	4.3	1487 (1647)	10126	
US	3.7	(20893) 22939	63413	
India	2.9	2660 (2946)	1927	We still have very low GDP per capita. In 2023 this is well above $2000 but still lower than most countries by a big margin.
China	1.7	(14866)16862	13231	

Source: World Bank Figures, 2020

Global trends in defence spending compared to India, China and Pakistan and expenditure on defence since 1960 are given below:

Year	India (In %)	India GDP per capita (In USD)	Pakistan (In %)	Pakistan GDP per capita (In USD)	China (In %)	China GDP per capita (In USD)	Global Average (percent-age of GDP as defence budget)
1960	2.04	82.189	4.3	83.338		89.521	6.399
1965	3.87 rose to 4 in '63	119.319	5.9 (3.8 in 1964)	116.447		98.487	5.308
1970	3.1	112.4	6.15	172.446		113.163	4.7
1972	3.8	122.982	6.86	153.384		131.884	4.223
1987	4.2	340	6.9	339.332		251.812	3.788
1989	3.534	346	6.533	384.364	2.447	310. 882	3.444
1992	2.705	316	6.698	429.147	2.45	366	2.943
1999	2.9	441	5.19 (6.037 in 1996)	454.276	1.871	4873	2.213
2014	2.54	1573	3.4	1251	1.729	7636	2.25
2020	2.9	1927	4	1188	1.75	10434	2.361

Source: World Bank Reports

Based on the above data, it emerges that:

- India's expenditure on defence was irrationally low in 1960.
- There are wide fluctuations in defence expenditure incurred by India and Pakistan; China on the other hand has been steady.
- India's defence budget does not appear to be linked with any vision or strategic approach.
- Pakistan overspent on defence and did not gain much from it.
- China though spends much lesser percentage of GDP on defence but its GDP is three times that of India.

As regards the perception of military leaders, the allocation of 2.9 per cent of GDP on India's defence budget is highly exaggerated since it includes several other expenditures such as pension of defence personnel as well as the civilian staff that forms part of the MoD that bloats up the figure. If we exclude the revenue expenditure, then less than 30 per cent of defence budget is available for modernisation. The figure that is generally acceptable to the military scholars is around 1.6 per cent of the GDP. This assertion becomes credible if we look at the way defence budget is allotted and more importantly spent. There are four major flaws in the process of defence budgeting in India:

- The three services prepare their Long-Term Perspective Plans (LTPP) based on the threat and capabilities required by each service to meet these threats. These plans cover a period of five to ten years. These plans remain internal documents of each service and are not vetted/financially supported by the government.
- The three services send their budgetary demands to the defence secretary through their respective service channels. These demands may or may not be reflections of respective LTPP.
- Allotments are made by the Finance Secretary based on resources. Invariably arbitrary cuts are made by the finance department.

- The process of expenditure is so complicated that each service finds it very difficult to spend the allotted money in a logical and deliberate manner in the financial year. If the allotted funds are not spent within the financial year the allotment lapses.

Defence budget must be allotted based on the desired capability building. This capability, in terms of visualised threat, needs to be laid out in broad terms in the joint doctrine. The overall capability needs to be then divided into programmes with budget allotment for each approved programme and related objectives. The programmes will contain systems and define the capacity being acquired by it.

The litmus test of adequacy or otherwise of defence budget is the impact on the soldier during war. In 1962, 1965, 1971 and 1999, the man on the ground/in the cockpit or on board the ship went to fight with critical deficiency/limitation with respect to military resources. We will discuss this in more detail in the relevant section on Indian experience in these wars. Besides the current strategy to initiate a political economy that considers defence expenditure as defence investment by increasing the percentage of indigenous defence systems and enhancing defence export will be discussed in chapter 3.

People-centric Issues

Air Marshal Anil Chopra's views as expressed in Observer Research Foundation (ORF), USI and in some TV debates opine that, 'When we reduce 17 individual commands to seven commands then the number of high ranking military officers will reduce. This will have an adverse effect on the morale of the services.' The US has 40 four star generals as against four in the Indian Armed Forces. However, there is hardly any case where more number of generals resulted in winning a war or in ensuring high morale across the rank and file of the forces. While there are enough cases to prove the contrary, namely that militaries lighter at the 'top' did much better than the top-heavy forces.

Given the steep pyramidal hierarchy of the armed forces the number of officers who reach colonel and equivalent is far less. Bulk of the leadership is on the shoulders of officers who do not make it beyond colonel or equivalent. As per an Observer Research Foundation (ORF) paper by Laxman Behera for 65,707 officers of the ranks of Lt Cols and below and equivalent ranks in the other two services–which every commissioned officer reaches, there are only 145 slots for the rank of Lt Gen and equivalent in the three services. It is their morale that is equally important and Theatre Command structures will not change their fate on promotions.

The US had much higher officers-to-men ratio in Vietnam. Besides they had far too many generals and equivalent in their forces deployed in Vietnam. This did not help them in winning the war. Even in WWII their performance at operational levels was just about mediocre. Second assumption is 'numbers count'. We will see in various operations in the Indian and global context that numbers do not count. Smaller but more efficient forces employed synergistically achieve far superior results. The Israeli Defence Force (IDF) always had numbers against them. This did not stop them from defeating the Arab forces on all occasions. We will see the details in discussion over the wars Israel fought since 1948.

Think Tanks on Theatre Command

Gurmeet Kanwal and Neha Kohli in an IDSA publication in 2018, *Defence Reforms A National Perspective*, trace the history of India's defence reforms since Independence. A bulk of the findings in this publication are revealing and disheartening. The higher defence organisation in India was prepared by the last British Viceroy to India, Lord Mountbatten and Lord Ismay. What these two British lords handed over to the Indian political leadership in 1947 remained unchanged for the next 17 years. Post the 1962 debacle, some cosmetic changes were made to include defence planning as part of the five years plan. This was more to do with finance and budgeting than any organisational reforms. The Defence Secretary remained the boss for national security. After more than four decades, in 1990, the cabinet committee on security was formed.

The first serious attempt to reform the defence forces structure was made after the Kargil war in 1999. The recommendations of the Kargil Review Committee (Group of Ministers) were accepted in totality except (perhaps) for appointment of CDS. The IDSA publication also covers aspects related to training in the armed forces with a cursory glance. This part just lists out the training establishments of the three services with an 'all is well approach'. The major weakness this publication brings out in defence reforms in India is that while recommendations are accepted, implementation is tardy in most cases.

Other two authentic documents—a book sponsored by Manohar Parrikar Institute of Defence and Strategic Analysis (MP-IDSA) and a monograph published by the United Services Institute (USI)—suggest that the need for Theatre Command or jointness among the three defence services was felt right after Independence. The documents quote Lord Mountbatten writing to the then Prime Minister about its need. The PM concurred but the Defence Minister scuttled the proposal. Thereafter, there has been a list of periodic unsuccessful attempts through committees, review committees and so on. In

2014 a new government—with a good majority came to power. This government made it clear that there is need for structural changes in the defence forces and their management. The armed forces as well as the bureaucratic set-up continued to debate without coming to any conclusion—a well-established trend in India since 1947. In 2019 the same government came to power with a bigger mandate. This time the government did not wait for the 'intelligentsia' to decide. The government appointed a CDS and gave out clear instructions what they want in terms of reforms in armed forces. The IDSA and USI documents were presented in the wake of the government's decision to reform.

The IDSA document makes six broad assertions/ recommendations. First, India needs to learn from the American experience in this initiative since both the countries are democracies. They faced similar challenges and generated similar debates in their respective professional circles. Also the American initiative is based on their experience in WWII. Second, the creation of theatre commands will provide national strategic and security guidance. It will integrate, and indigenise the three services with greater cost efficiency. The document cites the example of the Army and the IAF buying exactly similar Apache helicopters at different costs from the same source. This will be prevented when one agency procures for all the three services.

Third, the structure will end bureaucratic control over armed forces by incorporating military professionals in the decision-making processes pertaining to the armed forces. Fourthly, the size of a theatre command will depend upon threat and geographical area. A theatre command will include component command elements such as Special Forces (SF), coastal, cyber, logistics, communication and training command besides army, navy and air force. However, resources from one theatre can be moved to the other theatre as per the changing operational requirements. In essence, there will be seven commands instead of the current 17. These will include a Maritime Command, Andaman and Nicobar Command, Air Defence Command, Strategic Force Command, Northern Command (as it exists today), Western Command (Pakistan-specific) and Eastern Command for the Chinese threat.

National Defence College Publication 2022

This publication is a compilation of articles by officers selected for the prestigious NDC course at New Delhi. Most of these officers rose to the top echelons of the three services. Two of the articles in this publication are of interest to our study—*Synergy in Higher Defence Organization* by the former Air Chief Arup Raha and, *Lessons for Jointness from the Andaman Nicobar Command Experience*, by former Chief of Staff ANC, Rear Admiral Sudhir Pillai. The former Air Chief made some very pertinent suggestions. First, creation of unified regional commands will increase efficiency. However, the 'rush to do so is misplaced'. Second, the air force and naval assets are limited and hence distributing these among the theatre commands—especially with the maritime and ground-based theatre will create conflict of interests.

Third, due to shrinking budgets, creating theatre commands in India will be economically unviable. Fourth, since world over, employment of air power follows the principle of centralised planning and decentralised execution, the force remains under a single commander. Fifth, geographical area of India is equal to the Chinese WTC, hence while it is prudent for China to create theatre commands, it may not be appropriate for India. India's resources especially with regard to air force and navy are much less compared to China and the US. To this end, serious efforts are being made to catch up. Besides getting Rafale for the IAF, fighter air craft for the navy (Rafale M) are being procured on priority. Besides, indigenous LCAs are being inducted. Procurement of defence systems for the three services has been accelerated during the last three years. As regards geographical size, Israel has four commands. IDF has always been a joint force.

Rear Admiral Sudhir Pillai (Retired) former Chief of Staff ANC, brought out critical issues that need to be resolved in the only tri-service command India has had for more than a decade. In the context of doctrinal approach to theatre command, he quoted Capt Robert C Rubel, former US Navy Fighter Pilot enumerating principles of jointness. Rubel observed that merging services in to unified organisations compensates for weakness of one service by leveraging the strengths of others as per principle of complementarity. Second, the principle of hierarchy states that jointness is inversely proportional to the length of hierarchy, flatter organisations exhibit better jointness.

Third, as per the principles of necessity, jointness at lower echelons tends to increase in the face of increased enemy threats. Also, at lower levels, military organisations synchronise much better. Fourth, disrupting unit cohesion is detrimental to jointness. Fifth, as per principle of integration, attaching elements of one service to another impairs the organisational efficiency despite the additive strength. Sixth, diversity helps enhance jointness. Lastly, joint organisations must be formed in a proactive manner.

If we look deeper into these principles, it will not be difficult to deduce that for all these principles, 'conditions apply'. The Germans synchronised much faster even when elements from other services were integrated during an operation. The Americans and the British took quite some time to adjust to each other. Also, the Indian forces did not get into joint operations mode even in the face of intense enemy threat (for instance at the Battle of Dograi in 1965, operations in Shakargarh in1971 and the Kargil War in 1999). However, these principles are useful in structuring the joint forces and formulating doctrines as per the cultural aspects of the forces deployed. These issues will be further elaborated while discussing experiences in WWII as well as in the Indian context.

★★★

Conversations with the Experts

DISCUSSION WITH NEW Delhi-based Army and Air Force Think Tanks–Centre for Land Warfare Studies (CLAWS) and Centre for Air Power Studies (CAPS) on 19 January and 8 February 2022 respectively:

Lt Gen Vijay Kumar Ahluwalia, Director CLAWS and eight scholars made four major suggestions on issues related to defence budgeting, battle field transparency, role of civilian experts in theatre commands and theatre commands in relation to China's Western Theatre Command. A very senior scholar felt that the actual budgeting for defence is less than 1.6 per cent of the budget and the MoD has included defence pensions in this budget. The defence pension includes a sizeable chunk for defence civilians. This anomaly needs to be removed. The Director CLAWS suggested that given the regional disposition of the geographical joint command, the type of platforms and weapon systems and dynamic battle field conditions, there will be need for precise battle field situational awareness. This would need a very robust surveillance system. As regards the role of civilian experts in theatre battle, the scholars suggested that given the nature of modern wars ranging from the first to the seventh generation warfare, there would be need for civilian experts to contribute in the circumstance of undeclared warfare. Lastly, the scholars also felt that the regional reorientation of theatre commands must take into account the fact that a single theatre command in China (WTC) addresses all Chinese military issues against India. In fact the WTC also incorporates a part of the Pakistani threat to India from the Gilgit Baltistan region.

CAPS – 08 February 2022

CAPS scholars published a number of papers that dealt with issues related to personnel, clarity of overall concept, dynamism in organisational structure, integration of communication systems of the three services, budgeting and finance, and evolving consensus:

- Personnel: Brigadiers (or equivalent) and above need to grow beyond their regimental affiliations and uniforms when they operate in the Theater Command (TC) environment. There is trust deficit among the senior ranks in the three services. There is need to understand the core traits of each domain. The Indian Armed Forces have come a long way in terms of technology adaption and evolution of operational doctrines.
- The theatre commanders need to internalise these aspects for the three services to optimise the utilisation of all components. They need to acquire highly complex knowledge, skills and leadership acumen to measure up to the task. There is need to harmonise the chain of command in theatre command. In the existing Andaman and Nicobar (ANC) tri-services joint command, there are issues within the theatre that cannot be resolved by the theatre commander due to lack of authority. The ANC commander being from the Indian Navy can also not take disciplinary action against personnel from other services.

- Civil military discord is overplayed; in any democracy the civilian set up has the final say. The armed forces need to operate under appropriate scrutiny. For smooth operations the personnel policies for the three services need to be harmonised.
- Clarity on what Theatre Command Would Entail: Need to bring out a white paper on the subject before implementing the concept. In a tri-service seminar conducted by the USI involving brigadier level officers of the three services, officers from all the services had apprehensions about viability of theatre command as envisaged by the Department of Military Affairs (DMA).
- Dynamism in Organisation Structure: The Unified Command Plan in the US is reviewed every two years. Hence there is a need for dynamism in our implementation plan. The concept of a separate Air Defense Command defies logic. If it is done to placate the IAF, the decision misses the crux of jointness.
- Integrate Communication System: There is a need to integrate the communication systems of the three services. At present the Army, Navy and the IAF have their own networks with no inter-operability. There is a need to study and improve the tri-service command in the ANC in detail before embarking on full scale implementation at the national level.
- Budgeting and Finance: We lack deep pockets like the US and totalitarian governments like China. In budgeting for defence, the pensions need to be separated. Also, under the current policy paradigm, there is excessive wasteful expenditure to meet deadlines of the financial year.
- Consensus: Our approach needs to be based on consultative consensus and be India centric. We need to adopt a 'whole of government' approach to national security.

Joint Communication Systems: Indian Context*

During General Bipin Rawat's stint as CDS, substantial ground was covered for creating communication systems that would facilitate jointness. To start with, each service had its own network. The Army had the Army Switched Communication Network (ASCON), for Navy it was 'Navy in', IAF had Airforce Net (AFNET). The first step to interconnect these separate networks was through voice switches at Delhi, Kolkata and Mumbai. The next logical step was to connect the data networks of the three services since modern wars use massive amounts of data.

While the Army and the Navy agreed to share their data networks through data switches, the IAF wanted to keep their data network separate since they thought that the IAF data network requires much higher grade of security. A compromise was then worked out by connecting the three service networks through email servers so that they could intercommunicate through emails. This resolved the data communication requirement to some extent.

In 2016, Defence Communication Network (DCN) was planned to be established as a tri-service strategic communication system. This network was completed by 2019. However, it suffered from some major drawbacks. First, it did not have any worthwhile application required for network centric war—situational awareness, decision support system, surveillance

---

* Gist of Discussion with a former Signal Officer-in-Chief who headed the panel for joint communication systems for UTC

systems integration and fire support network. Secondly, its reach was only to corps level whereas, actual fighting is done at battalion, airbase, ship level. Thus the troops in contact remained out of its reach. The next big step towards creating a common communication system was the project Network For Spectrum (NFS). In that the services offloaded part of their military specific spectrum for civilian use and the government provides them optical fibre-based media network for military use. This fibre-based network could be used for operational and strategic purposes (perhaps down to divisional/brigade headquarters).

While the Army and the Navy opted for the media (Optical Fibre) the IAF wanted a certain quantum of bandwidth which the BSNL was to provide free of cost. However, once all the ten NFS projects were completed the IAF was also asked to dehire bandwidth and use the media laid for them under NFS.

It appears that the three services as users of communication systems are more comfortable with voice and emails as compared to data. This limits the usefulness and speed that a communication system can provide. The communication systems as of now are bereft of useful applications that could have optimised its use.

It is interesting to note that the relevant environment in India appears to have ignored the global compulsion of joint operations conducted by theatre command. Another aspect that is missing in the Indian discourse is the political impact on operationalisation of jointness through theatre commands. Hence it will be prudent to go through some of the historical facts related to joint operations. Our primary focus will be on WWII though the concept came into being during the closing months of WWI and even before.

★★★

The Turning Point

There are times when services fight in total synergy without formal restructuring into theatre commands and there are instances when military commanders flout the spirit of theatre command even in a formal structure—the difference lies in the probability.

THE BRITISH GROUND forces (under Wolfe) and the British Navy (under Vice Admiral Charles Saunders) demonstrated the telling effects of inter service cooperation in 1759 in the Battle of Quebec. The essence of Uniform Theatre Command (UTC) was again exhibited much before the terms related to this concept became part of military lexicon, when the American Navy (under Admiral Porter) and the ground forces (under General Grant) performed in complete synergy in 1863 for capturing Vicksburg during the American Civil War.

Both these events demonstrated the impact of operational synergy borne out of willing cooperation and collaboration among the services involved without any formal restructuring of forces. Towards the end of WWI, the British and the French forces displayed extraordinary synergy among their infantry, engineers, newly introduced armour and a nascent Royal Air Force to defeat the Germans in the Battle of Amiens. India's Eastern Army during the liberation war of 1971, especially for the 101

Communication Zone Area under General Gurbaksh Gill and 4 Corps under General Sagat Singh, provide excellent examples in intra and inter service synergy. If this be so, why not leave it to the good cooperative instinct of the concerned commanders and avoid the painful job of reforms? The reason is simple. Such wilful cooperation among and within the services is more of an exception than the rule. Even when a formal structure for unity of command exists, senior military commanders are known to resist and at times flout the expected spirit of cooperation.

Early Experiences of Jointness

Quebec, 13 September 1759: During this operation against the French, the British ground forces under Maj Gen James Wolfe were supported by Vice Admiral Charles Saunders in successful amphibious landing upstream of River Saint Lawrence to draw the French Forces out in the open. The battle that followed culminated in decisive victory of the British Forces over the French. Before the Royal Navy came to the assistance of ground forces all efforts to draw out the French into the plains of Abraham near Quebec had failed. Incidentally, both Wolfe and Saunders coordinated the battle and cooperated to the fullest in its difficult execution without any one of them formally placed under the command of the other.

Vicksburg, 04 July 1863: A US Army War College Report of 2000 cites the Battle of Vicksburg of 1863 as the first joint operation conducted by the US Army, US Navy and the US Marine Corps. As per the research reports (Lt Col Bret D Daugherty) the battle was planned, coordinated and conducted jointly by these three military services. Though there was no formal structure of jointness, the subordinate commanders involved in the battle were authorised by their respective service heads General Ulysses Grant heading the Army, Rear Admiral David D Porter heading the Navy and Brigadier General Alfred W Ellett, commanding the Marines, to plan and conduct operations in a joint manner. Before this joint operation, the US Army had tried their best to capture the Vicksburg defences atop a hill feature along the Mississippi River. But they could not dislodge the defenders from the defences in the Vicksburg City. Thereafter the Navy and the marines joined the army in a joint operation. General Grant, when speaking of Admiral Porter at Vicksburg, noted that he had no more authority to command Porter than he (Porter) had to command him. But this was no bar to the two commanders cooperating with each other to capture Vicksburg. Incidentally, Rear Admiral Porter had a strong disliking for the US Army Generals who had graduated from West Point.

Before this joint effort a number of attempts to capture Vicksburg had failed due to inter service discord. The Secretary of Navy nudged Rear Admiral Porter to cooperate with the US Army. Fortunately for the federal forces, Porter got along well with General Grant and General Sherman of the US Army since 1862. This made a great difference in the successful conduct of the Vicksburg battle.

Experience During WWI—Somme, Battle of Amiens, 8 August 1918

Amiens happened to be a vital communication centre (rail junction) in the theatre of Somme where gruesome battles of attrition were being fought between the Germans and the Allied Forces (French, British, Australians and Canadians) since 1916. By May 1918, the Germans had pushed the Allied Forces to Amiens. At this time the defence of Amiens was extremely critical for survival of the Allied Forces.

Three major decisions helped the Allied Forces to avert annihilation and reverse the course of the entire war. First, Field Marshall Sir Douglas Haig of the British Army insisted that General Ferdinand Foch, Chief of the French Army, be appointed Generalissimo to command all Allied Forces in the theatre. Second, it was decided to commence a counter offensive though the Allied Forces were consistently beaten till that phase of war.

They had raw troops and the German defences along the three rivers (Somme, Avre and Ancre) were well fortified. Third, for the first time since the beginning of the war, the offensive was to involve tanks, combat aircraft, engineer resources and the infantry in a highly coordinated manner to break through the German defences in relentless, mobile operations taking risks and ensuring a deep push against the defenders. The air effort was to focus on supporting mobile operations. The tanks were to exploit speed, surprise and numbers to overwhelm the German defenders. Engineers were to breach enemy obstacles, improve trafficability for the follow up and logistics echelons and conduct demolitions where necessary. Infantry was to assault under immense cover of air force, artillery, tanks, and machine gun fire.

To all those who were accustomed to trench warfare fought from 1914 till early May 1918, this plan looked unreal and a work of fantasy. But the plan worked and changed the course of war, leading to an armistice and surrender of the German Forces. Ironically, the Allied Forces who had invented and used this approach to fight a mobile war forgot the lessons learnt by the time the WWII started about two decades later. The Germans who were on the receiving end in 1918 internalised the lessons and even improved upon it to humiliate the Allied Forces from 1939 to 1942 in WWII.

UTCs during WWII—Performance Analysis

The formal structuring, planning and conduct of operations based on UTCs over a sustained period during the war came around during WWII where vast geographical areas, massive force structures, complex and long range weapon systems and multinational forces made it mandatory for the participants to practise the concept as we know it today.

Allied Forces formed UTCs with the US, French, British and the Australian Forces. Their commanders were Americans and British except for the French General Maurice Gamelin who commanded the French Forces (in France). The Russians who were with the allies too had UTCs but these comprised of Russian Forces and were commanded by Russian generals. Similarly, the Germans and the Japanese had a theatre-based command system. While the Germans commanded multinational theatre command (with Italy, Spanish volunteers, Finns, etc) the Japanese had their own theatre commands. It will be interesting to note how the national culture, personalities of leaders and military competence differentiated the structure and more importantly impacted the performance of these theatre commands.

The Americans entered the war almost a year after the war had begun. They were initially not prepared for a war at this scale. But the US had the most elaborate industrial base and a highly skilled technical workforce. What they lacked in the strength of their armed forces during the initial stages was made up by their vast production base. The US Forces marched behind massive fire power and excellent weapon systems. They did not have a separate service for air power. The US Army had the US Army Air Force. However, this air force conducted independent bombing operations over Japan and in many other theatres. The amount of incendiary and destructive bombing done by the US

Army Air Force was excessively devastating and, at times, insane, even before they dropped the two nuclear bombs on Japan. The US had some of the best leaders especially suitable for theatre commands like Eisenhower and Marshall. Besides there were some who created disharmony across the theatre command and hence produced sub optimal results. These included General MacArthur, and Admiral Nimitz. Though both these senior military officers were effective in their own way, they were not the most suitable in creating and sustaining synergy. Among the self-centred and those who relied on showmanship, the most notable American commander was General Patton. An interesting fact about these top ranking officers was that all these were highly popular in their country thanks to the presence of a captive media. General Eisenhower's staff included thousands of media personnel to report on the American 'exploits' during the war.

As a rule, the Americans believed in full operational control over the campaigns in their respective theatres. They followed the principle of authority, accountability and responsibility at one point. Though in several cases their own theatre commanders (MacArthur and Nimitz) created problems in this unity of command. But, as a rule, the American lexicon avoided vague words like 'overall supervision', 'guidance' etc. while describing the role of their theatre commanders. As regards the military competence of American soldiers in the war, it was devoid of any spectacular performance or acts of uncommon courage in any sustained manner.

As discussed earlier, the American Forces had the best of the weapon systems, knew how to use and maintain these and relied on excessive firepower with complete disregard to collateral damage to the civilians and non-military infrastructure. Their appetite to 'destroy' with gay abandon was illustrated in the firebombing of Japan from January to 14 August 1945. The indiscriminate napalm bombing by the 21 Bomber Squadron (B-29) under Major General Curtis LeMay of the US Army Air Force razed sixty-seven Japanese cities to ashes. More people lost their lives due to the fire in Tokyo in just a six-hour period than at any time in the history of the war. Even after the Enola Gay (specially equipped B-29) dropped nuclear bombs on Hiroshima (6 August 1945) followed by Nagasaki (9 August 1945), LeMay continued with carpet bombing of napalm on the Japanese cities destroying hospitals, schools and homes that had no relevance to Japanese war fighting efforts.

Another dysfunctional trait of the US Forces was too many officers. As per Gabriel A Richard and Savage L Paul, in *Crisis in Command Mismanagement in the Army*, the strength of their officers (in Vietnam) bore no bearing on the operational requirement. Actual troops in combat always remained a very small fraction of the overall US Forces in the theatre.

The British too had their UTCs as part of multinational forces—primarily with the US, France and Australia. At the apex level the British generally followed a consultative and collective decision-making approach by achieving broad consensus. They were loath to place their forces under formal and direct control of commanders from other nationalities, However, there were occasions when they consented to work under 'direction' and not under control. Similarly, their approach to resolve inter service jointness among the British Forces was also based on a consultative approach.

The British military leadership was cautious, plodding, and was concerned more with conducting operations according to plan rather than fighting the enemy. During the period 1939 to as late as 1942, the British Forces could not withstand the

German blitzkrieg either in the European or the North African theatres. It was only at the Battle of El-Alamein that the British Eighth Army tasted victory. At this time Rommel's Afrika Korps was vastly outnumbered and Hitler had opened the ill-fated Russian campaign ignoring Rommel's demands.

There were occasions when the British commanders disregarded jointness to pursue their own service or career interests. As regards the Royal Air Force, they excelled more in air superiority operations or independent air wars (Battle of Britain) and less in ground support of their forces both in the European and North African theatres. The Royal Air Force spent considerable time and effort on counter air operations, carpet bombing of German cities and industrial bases. Like the Americans, the British too had little concern for civilian casualties while conducting carpet bombing of German cities.

The RAF destroyed Dresden, a small German town, killing 25,000 civilians in hospitals, schools and homes who were not related to German warfighting effort. This kind of insane bombing by the RAF was aimed at demoralising the adversary. The German Forces were not demoralised by this kind of bombing. None of these operations made any dent on the German capacity to conduct their air operations or maintain the required production capabilities for the war effort.

Norman Dixon in *Psychology of Military Incompetence*, describes the British officers as having 'crippling incuriousness' with, 'too much body and too little head'. These officers displayed 'snobbishness, exclusiveness and sense of honour coupled with lack of intellectual ability'. These were the officers who commanded the British Indian Army from 1752 till the end of WWII or perhaps till Independence in 1947.

The Russians had the best arrangement for their theatre

commands especially at the apex level where Stalin gave clear direction and complete freedom to his theatre commanders to lead their respective theatre campaigns. However, at the operational level, the Russians lacked the swiftness of decision-making, and innovative employment of their forces. It was their sheer number, and the vastness of the USSR as a country that defeated, the Germans who made massive strides into Russia with less than half the force level compared to the Russians. Even in their defeat, the Germans never lost balance and conducted orderly withdrawal against heavy odds.

Another aspect that differentiated the Russians from the rest was employment of their air arm. The Russian Air Force did not harbour any strategic goal or separate doctrine. Their air force existed to support the ground forces without harbouring any ambition to be distinguished as a separate 'war winning' force. The technical and fighting efficiencies of the Russian Air Force was primitive compared to the Luftwaffe in WWII.

The dynamics of German theatre commands were almost opposite of what the Russians had. The Germans excelled at the 'theatre force' level. Their theatre commanders were excellent leaders, leading their respective forces from the front. The German Army had the maximum ratio of 'generals to other officers' killed in the war. One of Rommel's ideas about leadership was, 'aggressive, dynamic, unpredictable and founded on the principle that the place of commander is at the front', as quoted by Ronald Lewin in his book on Rommel.

Their forces from different theatres, different formations and even different services assimilated and synergised very quickly when grouped together for a battle or campaign. They did not require long periods of familiarisation, joint training and mock battles before being launched together. German fighting formations included infantry, motorised and panzer divisions. The Waffen SS troops were taken from the infantry. It was common for men and officers to be shifted from one to the other division and even to the Luftwaffe—the German Air Force.

Thus a panzer division officer could be transferred to the Luftwaffe and vice versa. Generally top performing officers of panzer divisions were taken in Luftwaffe. Thus when an erstwhile panzer division officer was flying a sortie to support his ground forces, he knew exactly what he was doing and how the targets on the ground look like. The German Air Force even had special Stuka dive bombers to support the ground forces. The Messerschmitt 109 (Me 109) was a superior aircraft. Except for the Battle of Britain the German Air Force did not get involved in any strategic air war role. All their air efforts were strictly for the support of ground battles.

The German Armed Forces displayed a very high level of synergy in their ground and air components. First, the German force levels in any theatre were always much smaller than their respective adversaries in terms of sheer numbers. Against 138 French Infantry Divisions (including the British Expeditionary Force – BEF) the Germans had just 131. Against 3,173 tanks of the French (including 310 British tanks) the Germans had 2,445. In terms of combat air craft also, the Allied Forces had more than those of the Germans. Second, the quality of major equipment like the tanks, artillery pieces, aircraft also gave advantage to the Allied Forces.

The French tanks had higher calibre guns and better protection. Even with this disparity in the initial force levels the Germans advanced much faster through the enemy defences and inflicted much heavier casualties on the adversaries. Rommel's 7 Panzer Division advanced 150 miles (241-kms) in a single day against the French and British opposition in France in 1940. 7 Panzer Division suffered 412 tanks destroyed and 3,000 troops killed against 450 tanks, 300 guns, 7,000 transports of Allied Forces destroyed and 1,00,000 allied troops taken as prisoners in the initial advance in France through the Ardennes Offensive (16 June 1940). Third, both the German and Allied troops had experience of fighting in the same terrain just twenty years back. Fourth, the terrain favoured the defender. It had a river obstacle (River Meuse), an adjoining forested and mountainous terrain (Ardennes) and an artificial obstacle (Maginot Line).

In spite of all these advantages enjoyed by their adversaries, the German offensive burst through the French defences and humiliated the huge Allied Forces within a matter of two weeks, pushing them to the beaches of Dunkirk. What contributed to the synergistic application of lesser and at times inferior force to rout a superior force?

Similarly, in North Africa, the Germans hardly enjoyed the traditional superiority of the attacker against the defender during the entire campaign from Tripoli to El-Alamein (2,100 km) but they were always attacking, outwitting and winning against the Allied Forces whether at Al Agaila, Benghazi, Tobruk and even at El-Alamein. Montgomery's Eighth Army (total 11 divisions including four armoured divisions) had 900 guns, 1030 tanks, 530 aircraft against Rommel's Afrika Korps (10 divisions out of which only four were German including two Panzer divisions), including 500 guns, 300 tanks and 350 air craft. In ground troops, Montgomery was far superior to Rommel's troops. But it was Rommel who went on the offensive first.

When he realised the overwhelming strength of the opposition, he withdrew in an orderly manner all the way back to Tripoli. Montgomery's forces just followed the withdrawal without any serious effort to trap the withdrawing Afrika Korps. Keeping in view the fighting capabilities of the Italian troops, Rommel had less than half the force level compared to Montgomery's forces. Besides Rommel was in ill health.

In the Russian campaign, too, odds pertaining to the initial force levels were more or less evenly matched. When Operation Barbarossa commenced on 22 June 1941, the Germans had 120 infantry (including those of their allies), 19 Panzer and 16 Motorised divisions supported by 1945 combat aircraft. Against this the Russians had 121 infantry, 12 tank and 9.5 motorised divisions supported by 10,000 combat aircraft (only half of these were functional). However, the Russian formations were smaller with comparatively inferior weapon platforms, poorer communications and were ill trained.

By end September 1941, the Germans advanced 1,500 kms in comparatively flat riverine terrain ideally suited for mechanised war. At this time, they were getting ready to capture Moscow and Leningrad. But then the first snowfall occurred on 6 October 1941. The long Russian winter had commenced for which the Germans were not prepared since Hitler had imagined that Russia will fall within two weeks (like France) and hence no winter clothing was catered for.

The German Forces were never in a state of panic retreat. However their brilliance on the battlefield was done in by excessive interference from the high command (OKW). Towards the middle of 1942, Hitler started getting impatient and distrusting of his theatre commanders. His direct interference at the functional and operational levels reduced some of his best theatre commanders (Gerd Von Rundstedt, Erwin Rommel, Heinz Guderian) into squad leaders. This was a major and critical drawback of German UTCs that robbed them of their victory in war.

In Japan's case, the apex politico-military leadership was heavily biased towards the army. Hence their employment of Air Force and Navy was lopsided. Besides while the Japanese did extremely well in divisional battles, their overall strategy at the theatre level was out of sync with the overall goal. Also, the excessive brutality meted out to the prisoners of war by the Japanese Forces was entirely unnecessary and did not serve them well.

Lessons

At the core of successful joint operations are human factors. First, is the capability of commanders and men to rise above their parochial and self-serving interests to the larger good of the organisation. Second is a clear and unbiased understanding of strengths, limitations and nuances of sister services, component forces and other specialised elements with regard to their contributions for achievement of operational and strategic objectives. This is especially significant for the combatant commanders in the theatre. Third is, mastering the art of orchestrating controlled operationalisation of theatre plans through delegation and intervening only in supporting and handholding functions. Let the subordinate commanders at all levels bloom and be recognised. Inculcate a culture of 'we, us and ours' and dissuade the propensity of 'I, me and mine'.

At the organisational level, the historical evidence highlights a frame-work with five basic levels. The first level is that of the political leadership at the national level constituted by the top decision-makers in the nation such as the President, the Prime Minister, the Military or single party Dictator. It is at this level that vision-related questions are answered. What the nation stands for, where do the people aspire to place themselves in the global order, what civilisational sensibilities and values they have and what is precious to the country that must be preserved at all costs. Answers to these questions also bring out the relevance, strategic role and degree of operational freedom that the armed forces of the nation enjoy. During WWII, the general impression among the top generals about their political leadership was rather poor. A British General, Sir Henry Wilson in WWI had commented, 'politicians form a factor which the soldier must take as much into account as his enemy'.

Though the comments were made during WWI, several generals in the British Forces felt the same in WWII about Churchill. Hitler was the worst example who was not only unreasonable in dealing with his top commanders but was instrumental in murdering some of the best field marshals Germany had during WWII.

However, Hitler's case is on the extreme end. At the second level are the military commanders at the highest level. Their wisdom, calibre and courage as leaders translate national security vision into military strategies. At the third level is the force that includes operational commanders. The capability at this level is gauged by demonstrated performance in the battlefields—tenacity, raw courage, commitment and technological/system adaption.

The fourth level is the technological structure. This involves Intelligence, Surveillance and Reconnaissance (ISR), command, control, communication, logistics and information assurance (cyber) capabilities. At the fifth level, is the staff support that acts as a glue for the entire system. We can look at these factors in some detail with some relevant examples.

Political Leadership: At this level, there are five major functions that need to be performed with utmost care. At this level of leadership sufficient time and resources are available for taking decisions but the margin of error is very small. Any misjudgement or error in decision at this level has huge ripple effects down the chain. The major functions at this level include:

- **Clarity of shared national vision on national security:** Most of the nations involved in WWII erred in this function. Nations joined alliances and war without any clarity on what they wished to achieve in terms of their national vision. Italy first joined the war on the side of Axis Powers and later changed over to the Allied Forces. In either case there was no clarity. Similarly, it was futile for Germany to renege on their promise to the USSR on the 'no war' pact. Invading USSR when Rommel was so close to the oil fields of Egypt was a political blunder. Japan's attack on Pearl Harbour was also a monumental miscalculation.
- **Defining the role of armed forces in national security:** In case of a conflict of national interests that can threaten national security, the political leadership has several instruments of the state that can be activated to win the conflict. Military is one of these and has a limited role as well as the time window for employment. Both these aspects related to the role and the duration need to be very clearly decided by the political leadership. Countries like Germany and Japan overplayed the role and time window for employment of military power. Britain and even the US were ill-prepared to start with. We will discuss this issue in more detail in case of India.
- **Checks and balances in decision making:** A small error of judgement or resource allocation at the highest level results in very big setbacks down the chain. Hence the process of decision-making concerning the use of military power needs to have proper checks and balances. Germany paid a very heavy price for unbridled power with their Fuhrer. In case of Britain, some major setbacks were averted by checking Churchill's propensity to dictate terms to the combatant commanders. Wherever Churchill could get his way in influencing the field commanders' operational plans the results were sub optimal.

- **Decision on the span of control to the combatant commanders:** The Americans had a clearer strategy in delegating authority and accountability to a single commander. Wherever there were personal human failings amongst the commanders due to the factor of ego the state department stepped in to resolve the issue. It is here that Generals Marshall and Eisenhower played key roles.

Top Military Commanders: These are the combatant commanders (theatre commanders) and the component (functional) force commanders. They need to:

- Internalise the national vision on national security and translate this into military strategy.
- Have moral courage to stop unwise and disastrous decisions by political leadership that have a bearing on military operations. Hitler's decision to invade France through the narrow mountainous gap was debated in detail by the field commanders before they agreed to launch it. This time, Hitler was proved right. Later, Hitler's decision to open the Russian front was opposed by the field commanders but they gave in under pressure.
- Commanders at this level do not get involved in day to day conduct of the battle. Their role is resource allocation as per the threat and the goals. They are in the supportive rather than in commanding roles. During WWII several commanders (MacArthur, Montgomery) loved to control the conduct of battle at operational levels. Hitler controlled the battle at squad level in 1944. The results were poor.

The Force and the Operational Commanders: This is the level where battles are actually fought. In most armies it is the corps or division that gets involved in actual combat. In case of Israeli Defence Forces (IDF), the brigade battle groups conduct operations. At operational level, commanders need to:

- Make a very detailed plan with thorough knowledge of all factors but at the same time be prepared to change the plan as per the situation and the enemy. This demands a very clear and bold mind.
- There is no option for the operational commanders but to lead from the front. Information coming from the forward edge of the combat zone gets distorted at times. Hence commanders need to reach the trouble spot for taking appropriate decisions. The IDF tactical approach follows this dictum.
- Optimise resources: For this the operational commanders need to be thoroughly aware of the strengths and limitations of the resources under their respective commands—air, armour, engineers and other resources can multiply the impact if used in synergy.
- Create combined arms teams and joint services team. The IDF has integrated air support teams with battalion level forces for exfiltration and attack operations. Similarly, the Americans integrated the combat teams (based on an armoured squadron) with the US Navy (Hawk Eye) and US Air Arm (through data links from the combat aircraft).
- Fast pace of adaptation in changing battlefield situations. The German troops excelled in doing this and moved from one theatre to another and adapted quickly to the new battle conditions.
- Coupled with the fast pace of inter theatre adaptation, the troops need to master the art of quick launch, fast-paced engagements and recoup for launch elsewhere. The Israelis employed the same armour formations in Sinai followed by their application in the Golan heights within twenty-four hours in just six days of war in 1967.
- Given the modern technostructure available to the modern forces, troops need to be tech savvy as well as need to possess higher educational background.

The Technostructure will have:

- Modern networks for surveillance, command and control, fire support and logistics.
- The network will have to be robust, dynamic and secure.
- For speedy movements in inter and intra theatre regions, the surface logistics need to be modern—equipped with rail, road, maritime and air network. It will have to incorporate the modern technologies of Supply Chain Management through palletisation, coding, bulk handling and bulk breaking using Artificial Intelligence and robotics.

The Support Staff acts as enablers and glue in joint operations. Good supporting staff refrain from tying the commanders to the HQ. Since commanders need to be constantly in touch with the actual ground situation (and not totally dependent on what the staff feeds them). Staff in joint operations must:

- Understand and internalise the capabilities, limitations and sensitivities of each component element.
- Encourage and enable synergy.
- Inculcate supporting as against controlling behaviour.
- Must pass back objective feedback to the commanders.
- Be a small setup: The Germans had the smallest support staff and they were the best in this job. The Israelis also have miniscule support staff. Hence their operations were fast-paced. The British and the Americans have huge support staff. Their operations are not that precise and fast. Indian Forces have been learning from the British and the American setups.

Performance of theatre commands depends not on the discrete capabilities at each level but more on the synergistic application and operational interplay among these levels.

The Five Layered Model

Political leadership	Clarity, checks and balances, understand role of armed forces
Top Military leadership	Vision to strategies, allocate resources, morale courage
The Force and the operational commanders	Combined services, speed of ops, tech adaption
Technostructure	ISR, networks, logistics means and technologies
Support Staff	Understand complexities, support not control, synergise, avoid bureaucracy, smaller the better

The Germans for example excelled in the capabilities of their top military commanders, a highly disciplined, adaptable and agile force, and a competent General Staff. However, their crippling weaknesses at the political leadership level neutralised all the benefits. The Americans did not have much to show at the level of force capability and even the calibre of their generals but their political wisdom, and the sheer size of their technostructure (especially the American production bases and economy) tilted the balance in their favour.

In order to get an Indian perspective, we will now analyse the performance of the Indian Armed Forces with the above framework as a reference point. We will also examine whether the Indian Armed Forces could have learnt from the pre-colonial past.

★★★

Wars in India
Ancient and Colonial Eras

The Glorious Past the Indian Intelligentsia
Forgot for Political Correctness

MUCH BEFORE THE Roman and other western empires with armed forces came into being, Indian civilisation had witnessed some great wars. Since the time of the *Ramayana* (7,000 to 11,000 years ago), India had a mature polity, vibrant civilisation, and well documented treatises of efficient military systems. There is also well documented and scientific evidence of continuity of this civilisation from the times of the *Ramayana* to the time the great battle of *Mahabharat* was fought in 1198 BC (some historians put it at 3000 BC). Different dynasties of indigenous kings ruled India from this period to 1192 AD when invasions by Turco-Afghans commenced followed by the colonisation of India by the British. Even during the period of Mogul dominance and under British rule, a cumulative period of around 500 years, the Indian way of life and civilisation remained intact.

Though, in essence the British destroyed the Indian economy and created an Indian elite that became enamoured of British culture, it will be interesting to examine this wide canvas of time to find answers to the questions that are relevant to this part of our study. Specifically, we will attempt to answer four questions.

First, the political concept of national security and the relevance of war in ancient Indian civilisation. Second, the role and relevance of the military in a nation state. Third, the composition of ancient armed forces and how they synergised their efforts. Fourth, the hierarchies of military leaders and expectations from them in terms of their leadership qualities and expected outcomes from their performance.

The Indian kingdoms under different indigenous rulers were headed by people well-versed in the art and science of war. In fact, constant readiness for war and willingness to fight when the need arose was part of the survival instinct and maintenance of peace for a nation. In other words, war was a necessity even if some kings preferred to call it a 'necessary evil'. However, between wars and the psychological barrenness of peace (as perceived by the standing armies of the kings), the kings indulged in a number of non-military efforts for the prosperity, well-being, development and occasional expansion of their sphere of influence. This is evident from the enormous creation of knowledge, cultural richness, human awareness and wealth in ancient India. India remained the wealthiest, the most knowledge-rich and the most powerful and hence a sought-after nation for thousands of years.

The nation states generally fought for their way of life, honour and territorial integrity. These aspects were never compromised for the sake of peace on the aggressors' terms. Around 400 BC, the Indian kingdoms were sensitive to threats in their neighbourhood. Thus, the territorial integrity of the nation also included a favourable positioning of the adjoining states. Any neighbouring state that was likely to turn hostile towards the mainland was forced to fall in line.

To secure his empire, the monarch had non-military and military means. Generally the former were preferred. The military means were used only when the non-military means failed to bring about the desired outcome. The study of relevant literature on the subject indicates that national security during those times was the responsibility of the king (head of the state) who was advised by a council (of ministers), elders and other advisors not part of the council, spies, head of state treasury, head of foreign affairs, head of the military (*senadhyaksh* or *senapati* who headed all the wings of the military). Though the final decision rested on the king, it was seldom that the king ignored inputs by any of the groups enumerated above.

In all the campaigns, it is common to read about convening meetings of relevant experts or advisory groups. This practice had been in vogue from the days of the *Ramayana* to all the empires later on. The practice of collectivism in decision making was common. Once the major decisions were taken, each of the concerned wings shared the same vision and made their own strategies accordingly. Emperors generally had influence over smaller kingdoms in his empire.

Each kingdom, and even some important entitled nobles had their own armies. These armies fought under one banner and cooperated with each other. It was only when these smaller kingdoms or the armies ignored the principle of unity of effort or acted against the interests of the emperor that big empires started falling apart and ceded ground to the invaders. Thus, the common features of the concept of national security and its operationalisation in India for most of the period have been:

- A shared, clear vision of national security based on preservation of their way of life (civilisation), territorial integrity or impending threat through the adjoining states.
- Maintenance of honourable peace depended on strong military for internal as well as external security.

- Preferred means for maintaining peace at own terms was through non-military means. It was only when the non-military means did not suffice that military force was applied.
- The military force was applied in a manner that ensured minimal damage to own and adversary's non-military as well as military assets.
- Once the monarch extended his empire, the new territory captured in war was developed in terms of citizen-centric infrastructure and civilisational culture. This is how remnants of Indian culture are found in countries such as Afghanistan, Indonesia, China and parts of central Asia.

The armed forces of ancient India had distinct organisational structures, groupings of various components, hierarchies, weapon systems, compensation policy, anticipated capabilities of military leaders and policies on rewarding performance in war. The military was composed of chariots, elephants, horsemen and the foot soldiers (infantry). Even at the most basic level that was known as *patti,* all these components were included. Thus *a patti* comprised of one charioteer, one elephant, three horsemen and three foot soldiers. It is interesting to note that the smallest brick of ground force was prepared to meet all the threats and operate in all terrains (plains, forests and undulating ground).

Generally, flat terrain at the outskirts of habitats was chosen as the battle field. This was done to avoid damage to the civilian population. Also, forests were spared to avoid damage to the eco system. The force level increased from *patti* to *gulma*, *gana*, *vahini*, *pratna*, *camu*, *anikini*. Each ascending level was three times its predecessor. Thus a *gulma* was equivalent of three *pattis* and so on. The largest organisation was called an *akshauni* comprising of ten *anikenis*. An *akshauni* consisted of 7,290 charioteers and accompanying numbers of elephants, horses and foot soldiers.

In the *Mahabharat* these scales were bigger, a sena comprised of 500 charioteers, equal number of elephants, 1,500 horsemen and an equal number of infantrymen.

The ascending levels in the *Mahabharat* had *pranta*, *vahini* and *akshauni* each ten times bigger than its predecessor. This gives us an idea of the challenges that military leaders faced in synergising the efforts of four different types at each entity. Even a *patti* leader had to be proficient in optimising the impact of the charioteers, elephants, cavalry and the infantry. Compare this to the modern combined arms team concept. The German ground forces in WWII included enough anti-tank capability (guns) at the smallest army units to face enemy armour. This released the German Panzers to operate independently using their inherent speed to emerge at places where the enemy did not expect them. In the Yom Kippur War in 1973, the Egyptians equipped their infantry sections with handheld anti-tank and anti-air missiles that made sure that they did not have to look over their shoulders when faced by enemy armour and air. The ancient Indian military formations applied this concept many millennia back.

The rank structure and their expected responsibilities were also well laid out. It will be interesting to note how close these structures were to the modern militaries. At the head of the armed forces was a commander-in-chief, the highest paid military appointment (48,000 *panas* equivalent to 2,400 sterling pounds). His role appeared to be strategising, helping the council of ministers and the king with his expert advice on whether to go to war or opt for other means, when to go to war, the exact timing and other operational details.

The commanders (who commanded a composite force consisting of all components, including the spies) below him were responsible for the actual conduct of operations as per the strategic goal. The special components of charioteers, elephants, horses and the foot soldiers were commanded by their respective chiefs who presumably were responsible for raising, training and maintaining their respective components. This looks similar to director generals or heads of armour, artillery, engineers, signals, and so on. These heads in modern armies are responsible for their service specific activities as well as ensuring that their service specific components deliver as per the operational objectives of their respective operational commanders. The chiefs of charioteers etc, had their respective superintendents.

At the lowest rung were the soldiers trained to operate from chariots, elephants, horses or on foot. The foot soldiers were equipped with a variety of weapons like bows and arrows, javelins, and swords of different kinds. The arrows shot by these bows had very high kinetic energies and were tipped with metal heads. These were capable of piercing through the body armour of the opponents. It will be fair to assume that operational employment of these ancient armies required tremendous cognitive and physical abilities besides strength of character.

The *senapati* was expected to be from the *kshatriya* (warrior) class or a *brahman,* though in several cases, men proficient in arms were also appointed in these top positions. He was required to be proficient in the Vedas (ancient scriptures), and in the practice of arms. He was also expected to be fully acquainted with actions in all forms of war, with a large-hearted, generous disposition, a student of *shastras,* with many friends and very few or no enemies and, last but not least, to have a towering personality. He was also expected to possess diplomatic qualities, and be someone who had travelled abroad, someone who evoked confidence among his forces and people and capable of seeing through deception practiced by the enemy. The *senapati* was invested with high status by the council of ministers even though he was not a part of the council.

Generally, more than 50 per cent of expenditure from the state treasury was on the military. It was considered an essential investment in the security and well-being of the people and not a wasteful use of treasury resources. For a big empire the total military force was divided into a number of small militias commanded by smaller kingdoms under the empire. The armed forces of these kingdoms were financed by the revenues earned by the respective kingdoms. In times of war, the forces of these kingdoms fought under one banner. This could be considered similar to the armed forces of alliance partners fighting together against a common enemy.

The troops for the military were recruited from racial denominations. There was a concept of martial races. However, men from other races too were recruited based on their loyalty to the crown and their physical condition, as well as their courage.

The Indian concept of national security, relevance of armed forces and character/selection of military post-1947, have been widely different from her own inherent deep-rooted beliefs and behaviours. The ancient Indians (Indus civilisation) had a well-defined concept of nation state, state-citizen dynamics, civilisation values, rationale and ethics of warfare and hierarchy of various organs of the nation state. The state was defined as much by geography as by the civilisation values and well-being of the citizens. The king who ruled the state was held responsible for the well-being of the citizens as also the territorial and value-based security of the region.

The civilisation values were summed up in the idea of *Dharma* which was considered universal. It had nothing to do with religion. Citizens could choose their own way of worshipping whomsoever they wished to worship. Even atheists could be the citizens and were entitled to be protected by the king so long as they abided by the universal *dharma.* With this as a brief background we can focus on the subject of warfare in ancient and pre-colonial India.

There are two Indian texts that have the strongest emotive appeal for the overwhelming majority of Indians: the *Ramayana* and the *Mahabharat,* the latter including the *Bhagavad Gita.* We will analyse some of the most basic and widely known aspects of these epics that resonate with the psyche of an average Indian soldier.

Ram is considered an ideal in almost all human endeavours as a son, a brother, a friend, a king, a husband, a leader and a military commander in war. His conduct and character act as beacons for millions of Indians. A large number of Muslims consider Ram as Imam of Hindustan. For our study, we will dwell on the aspects of war between Ram and Ravana. *Ramayana* brings out the concepts of nation-state, civilisational values, military leadership and the dynamics to organise, train, and motivate ordinary people to fight for a just cause no matter what the odds so that they can prevail against evil.

During Ram's exile, his journey from the North to the extreme South in India as an ordinary citizen with the steady process of awakening people, organising them into socially productive and strong units, inculcating a sense of equality, justice, fearlessness and peaceful coexistence is highlighted in the great epic of *Ramayana.* In the final battle against Ravana, the King of Lanka (present day Sri Lanka) displays the vision, strategic approach, conduct of operations and conflict termination which provide very important lessons that are timeless and more importantly, something that every Indian soldier would instantly understand.

- Ram initiated peace moves with Ravana on righteous terms to avoid bloodshed and destruction.
- When attempts to establish peace on rational terms failed, war became a justifiable, indeed the only option. Thus a righteous narrative was created.
- The strategic intent of war with Ravana was to destroy the evil power, while keeping the citizens unharmed.
- The operational plans were audacious, carried out with precision with utmost boldness. The offensive involved crossing a formidable water obstacle and penetrating through the heavily guarded fortress of Lanka.
- Ram led from the front, transformed ordinary citizens into invincible warriors and displayed an offensive and innovative approach in subjugating the opponent. Ram and the younger prince Laxman, were the only warriors who had the skills and knowledge of using superior weapons that were highly precise and destructive. The rest of the force used improvised means to fight.
- Ravana's forces were well-equipped, trained warriors accustomed to luxurious living, and were cruel to the ordinary citizens of Lanka. They remained on the defensive. Ram's forces lived on mere necessities.
- Having defeated the adversary in battle, the victorious side did not grab the kingdom of the defeated king. Instead Ravana's brother Vibhishana was enthroned in his place.

In the epic battle of *Mahabharat,* many of the principles we saw in *Ramayana's* time were adhered to. First, all efforts were made to avert the war before the two armies came to the battlefield. Second, the winning side had a smaller force (seven *akshaunis*) compared to (eleven *akshaunis*) in the losing side.

We have seen the strength and composition of this unit force earlier. To get an idea, a comparative strength of the two forces is given below:

The Two Forces in Mahabharat

	Kauravas	Pandavas	Remarks
Chariots & Elephants	240770	153090	Each chariot/ elephants with three/ four persons, a driver/ mahout
Horses	721710	459270	
Infantry	1102850	765450	Equipped with bows and arrows, javelins
Total number of soldiers	About three million, equivalent to about 46 corps sized force of modern armies	About two million, equivalent to about 30 corps sized force of modern armies	

The above comparison highlights a few major factors. First, the challenges involved in command and control of these massive armies was equivalent to more than a thirty corps-sized force with Pandavas and a forty-six corps-sized force with the Kauravas. Second, the Pandavas won this war inspite of this huge asymmetry in numbers. This shortcoming in numbers was mitigated by superior operational art, appropriate formation for war that suited a smaller force and steadfast conduct. Third, the winning side relied on wisdom, knowledge and skills. Fourth, they followed rules and ethics for the way this war was to be fought.

Most of the time these rules and ethics were followed. However, whenever a side faulted on these, the other side paid them back in the same coin. No war crime was forgiven. Fifth, there were ample examples of deception, strategic formations, optimisation of resources and speed in conducting manoeuvres. Sixth, the war was fought in a ground and in a manner that civilian population and their properties were safeguarded. The weapon systems used by the rival forces had precision targeting capability.

During the period 305-301 BC, the war between Chandragupta Maurya and Seleucus Nicator one of Alexander's generals, was fought in Sindh and Punjab (Magadh and Greek Forces) and has many lessons for modern day strategists. First, after Alexander stopped his campaign against India, Kautilya rebuilt the state of Magadh grooming an ordinary person (Chandragupta Maurya) to be an able king. When Seleucus crossed the Indus, he found that Punjab and Sindh were no longer small states fighting with each other. Unity among the states under Chandragupta Maurya's empire and Chandragupta's individual leadership, and proficiency in war fighting defeated Seleucus. Chandragupta had raised an army of 6,90,000 (6,00,000 infantry, 9,000 elephants with each elephant carrying three persons including the mahout, 8,000 chariots–each chariot carrying three including the charioteer, 30,000 horsemen). Against this Seleucus had an army of 60,000. However, even when Seleucus was defeated, Chandragupta signed a treaty of peace with him giving him 500 war elephants. Seleucus gave Chandragupta Kandahar, Herat, Kabul, Baluchistan, and Markan. The Maurya kingdom extended up to the Hindukush (included entire Afghanistan and Pakistan).

Kautilya's strategy of including diplomacy as part of military conquest paid rich dividends. Secondly, the people living in the territories assimilated into Chandragupta's empire flourished in times to come. Peace prevailed for several centuries after this treaty. Chandragupta incidentally married Seleucus's daughter.

After the advent of the Moghul period, wars between Maharana Pratap's forces and that of Akbar, Shivaji's exploits against Adil Shah's kingdom and Aurangzeb bring out some important lessons. In the case of Maharana Pratap, the famous battle of Haldighati fought on 21 June 1576, wherein Pratap made excellent use of the terrain, fought with a numerically superior enemy (8,000 troops of Mansingh with light artillery against 4,100 troops of Pratap with 3,000 horsemen, 1,000 foot soldiers, 100 elephants). Haldighati became the turning point for Akbar's forces. Pratap managed to keep Mewar independent from the Moghuls.

Shivaji emerged as one of the greatest Indian kings during the period of Aurangzeb. He displayed rare qualities in creating and sustaining a vision of nation building based on universal civilisational values, developed strategies and tactics ranging from guerrilla warfare to sustained campaigns on land and in sea. He had a sizable navy. One of his stellar performances was the Battle of Pratapgarh on 10 November 1659 against Afzal Khan. With 6,000 infantry, and 2,000 cavalry, he took on 35,000 troops of Afzal Khan that included 12,000 cavalry, 80 to 90 large canons and 300-400 small canons. Shivaji displayed his calibre, using surprise and deception, speed of operations, audacity and synergising a battle against a far superior enemy (in numbers).

There are two more battles during the Moghul period that help us in learning some important lessons relevant even today. The first battle of Panipat in 1526 and the third Battle of Panipat on 14 January 1761 highlighted some of the most relevant causes of defeat of a bigger but sluggish force. These include:

- **Leadership:** In both the battles, it was mainly a question of leadership. Ibrahim Lodhi was not of Babur's calibre in leadership. Similarly post Shivaji, Maratha leadership was poor compared to that of Abdali.

- **Lack of overall unity in the state:** Ibrahim Lodhi was not a popular king. The state was disintegrating.
- **Lack of synergy in application of force:** In both the cases the winning side synergised their smaller forces much better.
- **Reluctance to adapt to new technologies:** Though the local troops (Lodhi and Marathas) knew about the use of gun powder they did not bother to exploit its use in war.
- **Disruption of communication and logistics:** In the third battle of Panipat Abdali disrupted the lines of communication.
- **Quality of troops:** Lodhi and the Marathas had a large number of mercenaries. Hence the performance of their respective armies was poor. In both these cases, numerically smaller forces defeated much larger forces. So much for 'numbers'.
- **Lack of local support:** This is especially true for the third battle of Panipat.

The only Indian king who turned the tables on foreign aggressors and the British in the North West—Afghanistan and Khyber pass was Maharaja Ranjit Singh. He did not wait for the Pashtuns to attack. Instead Ranjit Singh launched a pre-emptive offensive on the Pashtuns and defeated them in their own land. Ranjit Singh started as a small chieftain in Punjab after his father's death. He quickly graduated from guerrilla tactics to sustained military campaigns. He displayed a rare capability of organising and expanding his forces with a very farsighted vision. His approach was disruptive, focused on long-term goals, transcending traditional thinking and parochial approaches. He was quick to realise the importance of infantry in an era of fascination with the cavalry. He raised and trained infantry units (900 soldiers per unit).

He also understood the importance of artillery and

transformed a primitive artillery into a formidable force integrated into his army. He was the first Indian king to initiate his battle strategy with an artillery barrage. His forces comprised of Sikhs, Hindus, Muslims and even included British, French and American officers. He placed immense emphasis on training and discipline. His leadership was extremely effective. During his regime the Pashtuns could never come across the Khyber pass neither could the British venture to cross the Sutlej and the Indus. The British found that a treaty of friendship was the best method to deal with Ranjit Singh. Unfortunately after his death in 1839, the edifice crumbled due to internecine fights within—a trademark of Indian weakness during those times.

***

War in India
Post-Independence

'We stopped a victorious army. We could have settled conclusions.'
Jawahar Lal Nehru to *Hindustan Times* 01 January 1949.

THE FIRST INDO-PAK war commenced on 27 October 1947 barely two months after the end of direct colonial rule over India. On 22 October, Pakistan organised an offensive into the princely state of Jammu and Kashmir using irregular armed forces (*kabayalis*). King Hari Singh of the princely state found his forces very inadequate and acceded to the Union of India on 26 October 1947. On 27 October leading elements of the 1st Battalion of 11 Sikh Regiment under Lt Col Ranjit Rai of the Indian Army commenced landing at the Srinagar airfield. The irregular raiders at this time were in close proximity.

It is interesting to note that just a month before, the Indian Army came to the rescue of the beleaguered princely state and were ordered to fight a war by their political leadership as the army was considered to be unnecessary. Some time in September 1947 when the Commander-in-Chief of the Indian Army Gen Sir Robert Lockhart presented a proposal on the size and structure of the Indian, Army for defence of India, he was unceremoniously dismissed by Mr Nehru, the PM, who told him that India believes in *Ahimsa* and does not need an army. 'Scrap the army' he almost shouted at the bewildered C-in-C. Thanks to the Pakistani offensive, the Indian Army was saved from being completely consigned to the scrap yard. For our study, this aspect is important as it indicates the mindset of the political leadership towards military matters. We will see subsequently that the realisation of this misconception did not dawn on the political leadership for the following several decades.

As we look at the relevant aspects of this war, four questions become germane to theatre commands. First, capability of the Indian political leadership to grasp the contemporary geo-political environment and formulate an apt national security policy. Second, employment of available military resources to meet the real external threat. Third, the strange culture of outsourcing critical strategic decision-making to foreign powers that proved to be inimical to India's security interests. Last, the price paid by the fledgling nation in terms of human/material cost and international standing.

Political vision of India's security that was formed in 1947 left its impression on India's politico-military and civil-military relations for several decades. Hence it will be pertinent to look at the genesis of this vision. The belief that India won her freedom through non-violent movement or *Satyagraha* is very widely accepted and assiduously nurtured in post-colonial India and the world around her. This belief is supported by selective sampling of data and information and hence is not even half the truth. Unfortunately, this assumption shaped India's politico-military relationship and decision-making.

More importantly, this narrative shaped India's perception about the prevalent geopolitical context. It is not our case to explore how and why the British did finally leave India, but some decisions that were taken post-Independence are bewildering.

First, the newly 'independent' nation requested the last British Viceroy, Lord Mountbatten to continue as the first governor general of a free nation. Second, when India and Pakistan were fighting a real war the chiefs of their respective armies were British Generals—Gracey for Pakistan and Boucher for India. It is impossible to believe that the two chiefs did not exchange notes and keep Mountbatten informed while the Indian PM for whose nation they were appointed remained oblivious to this critical information.

Maj Gen Kuldip Singh Bajwa in his book *Jammu and Kashmir War 1947-48*, suggests that the Indian leaders were fresh on the job and were not well-versed with the nuances of international geopolitics. But the fact is that the India of 1947 had some of the best military brains, with Lt Gen Nathu Singh being one of them. Besides, Sardar Patel who was India's Home Minister and Deputy PM had a very objective assessment of the threat faced by India in 1947. Most of the sane advice was ignored. Perhaps it was felt that by retaining Mountbatten and the top British Military officers India's cause would be served. The actual results were contrary to this expectation. The ill-fated declaration of ceasefire and lodging complaint to the UN was a decision influenced by Mountbatten. All this while, the UK was nurturing Pakistan to be a useful, small, pliable ally in the region to serve their USSR policy.

Our next key issue is employment of India's Armed Forces in 1947-48 war. On 27 October 1947, when the IAF was flying in the Sikh Bn to Srinagar, the comparative force levels of the two nations at war were as under:

Though Jammu and Kashmir formally became part of India on 26 October 1947, the Pakistani offensive commenced on 22 October 1947 itself. It is safe to assume that preparation for this offensive in Pakistan must have commenced much earlier—known to Pakistani Army Chief (of British origin) who in turn would have shared this information with the Indian Army Chief (again of British origin). However, the Indian, PM was unaware of all this till the King of the princely state approached him for help. When J&K formally acceded to India, the Pakistani offensive was deemed to be an attack on Indian territory. As a natural corollary, Indian decision makers were free to retaliate at the time and ground of their own choosing.

	India	**Pakistan**	**Remarks**
Army	400,000 men, 7,000 officers Armoured Regiments:12 Artillery Regiments: 19 Infantry Battalions: 88 Field Formations: • Armoured Division: 1 • Independent Armoured Brigade: 1 • Infantry Divisions: 9 • Parachute Brigade: 2	200,000 men, 4,000 officers Infantry Divisions: 2 Armoured Divisions: 6 Artillery Regiments: 5 Engineers Regiments: 34 Field Formations: • Armoured Division: 0 • Independent Armoured Brigade: 1 • Infantry Divisions: 7 • Parachute Brigade: 1	For Pakistan, out of three regiments only one was fully functional. Five of the seven Infantry Divisions were raised after 14 August 1947
Navy	Ships all types: 7	Ships all types: 3	
Air Force	Fighter Squadrons: 6 Transport Squadron: 11	Fighter Squadrons: 1 Transport Squadron:1	

Source: Bajwa, Kuldip Singh, 2021. pp. 102.

The Indian PM was reported to have made a statement to this effect that if Pakistan attacks J&K, then in retaliation, the Indian forces would be free to launch an offensive anywhere in Pakistan. This was also suggested by Lt Gen Nathu Singh that India should launch an all-out offensive on Lahore since Pakistan was not prepared and was also not anticipating any fight there. Loss of Lahore and part of Pakistani Punjab would have been unacceptable to them. This would create a situation where India could force Pakistan to vacate J&K in lieu of territory of West Punjab.

The force structures of India and Pakistan in 1947 were in favour of India by a wide margin for any offensive in the plains and deserts with preponderance of armoured units and combat aircraft squadrons. Whereas in the mountainous terrain of J&K the superiority in armour and even infantry formations did not matter much since the mountains favour the defenders. Thus, pushing the Pakistani forces back was much more difficult as compared to making them recoil by creating an unacceptable situation in Pakistani Punjab.

However, though the Indian premier talked of counter-offensive anywhere he stuck to fighting in J&K only under pressure from Mountbatten and fearing international backlash. In 1965, the Indian forces were to do exactly the same (attack across the International Border)—but under a different PM and a different Defence Minister.

As regards application of force level for this prestigious war there were undue restrictions laid on the field commanders to employ their own forces. India had 6:1 superiority in air power over Pakistan. Close Air Support (CAS) to the formations from 27 October 1947 itself would have been fully justified and most advantageous. This advantage was frittered away because the

British officers and Mountbatten would not have allowed use of air power. In fact, Indian Combat Aircraft did engage Pakistani replenishment flights for the battle of Gilgit and Skardu. Mountbatten objected to this on the plea that this will escalate the conflict. India not only stopped further air operations but had to declare that strike on the Pakistani Dakota carrying replenishments to Gilgit, Skardu was done by mistake and will not be repeated. For the ground battle, initially Gen Russel was the Army Commander for operations in J&K. However once the Indian leadership realised the British bias towards Pakistan, he was replaced by Lt Gen K M Cariappa (later Field Marshal). During a critical phase of operations Cariappa wanted additional formations to be inducted into the valley. This was denied by the Indian PM.

During this war, the Indian officers and men exhibited an overwhelming commitment to the national cause. Their performance was of the highest standards in terms of tactical planning, synergistic application of ground and air forces, innovative employment of armour and engineer resources, field manoeuvres, field craft and raw courage. Within the constraints imposed by the political bungling and naivety, procrastination and trend of ad hoc decision-making, and outright treachery by the British commanders, the results achieved were outstanding. Lt Col Ranjit Rai who led 1 Sikh into battle from Srinagar airfield itself displayed tactical boldness in seeking and contacting the raiders well beyond the outskirts of Srinagar. Once overwhelmed by their numbers, he fell back to a sound defensive position in a very planned and orderly manner and thus engineered the first major battle at Shalateng.

This battle proved to be the turning point of this war. Employment of a couple of armoured cars (under Major Rikhye) in conjunction with well coordinated defences across Shalateng, together destroyed the raiders' offensive. The initial bold advance by the raiders turned into a rout. They were followed in hot pursuit by 161 Infantry Brigade from Shalateng right upto Uri—a distance of 64 kms in just seven days (7 to 13 November 1947). Unfortunately, the 161 Infantry Brigade stopped their advance at Uri and wasted too much time in recuperation instead of continuing their advance to Muzzafarabad-Domel. Pakistani forces were not prepared to contest this advance.

Six months later when 161 Infantry Brigade as part of Srinagar Division attempted this advance, the Pakistani forces were fully prepared. Alarmed and scared by the Indian onslaught, they had moved three divisions to J&K. However, even at this juncture, 163 Infantry Brigade under Brig Harbakhsh Singh cleared the Kupwara, Chowkibal-Nastachun-Tithwal Axis. This was a spectacular achievement in a very difficult terrain (Nastachun is at a height of 11,000 ft) and the Indian Army faced stiff enemy resistance. Gen Harbakhsh in his book *In the Line of Duty: A Soldier Remembers* brings out some important issues that need to be considered for operational efficiency of theatre command especially in the context of battlefield leadership.

During the most difficult phase of the operation—after martyrdom of Lt Col Ranjit Rai, Commanding Officer 1 Sikh it was Lt Col Harbakhsh Singh (also from 1 Sikh) who was conducting operations of 1 Sikh and later of Kumaon Regiment and other units that landed for operations. He had planned and executed the pivotal battle of Shalateng. Though Brig L P Sen had joined the force, he remained confined to his office without taking any part in the planning and conduct of crucial operations. Sen was shaken by the martyrdom of Maj Somnath Sharma, PVC, of the Kumaon Regiment. When the Indian Home Minister Sardar

Patel and Defence Minister Baldev Singh visited their HQ, Brig L P Sen painted a very gloomy picture. It was Lt Col Harbakhsh Singh who met the Defence Minister separately and assured him that the situation was under control.

When the famous chase from Shalateng to Uri commenced on 7 November 1947, Harbakhsh wanted to lead the chase (for obvious reasons). However, the GOC of the newly formed J&K Force (Maj Gen Kalwant Singh) kept Harbakhsh for garrison duties at Srinagar and allowed a shaky Brig L P Sen to lead the unopposed chase to Uri. A golden opportunity was lost.

Southern sector operation 'Kipper' planned by Lt Gen (Later Field Marshal) Cariappa broke through the Naushera, Punch, Kotli and Jhangar defences. Brig Usman Ali conducted these operations with outstanding courage. Another big reason for the success of these operations was the fact that Cariappa did not share the plan with the Indian Army HQ (staffed by the British). In the North, Maj Gen (Later COAS) Thimayya played a master stroke in breaking through the defences of Zoji La by innovative employment of armour (one squadron of 7 CAV).

By December 1948, the Indian Armed Forces were poised for complete victory in the valley including recapture of Skardu, Gilgit, Baltistan. It is at this juncture (1 January 1949), that Nehru stopped the victorious armed forces in their tracks and accepted a UN sponsored ceasefire. Thus at the operational and tactical levels Brig (Later Lt Gen) Harbakhsh, Brig (Later Lt Gen) L P Sen, Maj Gen (Later COAS) Thimayya, Brig Osman Ali, Major Somnath Sharma, to name a few, planned, conducted and fought the battles with outstanding courage and innovative skills. For the brave men who fought the war, the task was accomplished with resounding success. But the score card of the political leadership that 'managed' this war was dismal. A war that could have been won within less than 14 days (remember Bangladesh operations) with negligible casualties was extended to 14 months with a total casualty of 4,255 (1,103 martyred, 3,152 wounded). In the plains of Punjab and in Southern Jammu, Pakistan had no answer to India's military superiority (Infantry 9:2, five of Pakistani divisions were not available in October 1947, Armour 4:1, Air Force 6:1). Pakistan had no ammunition factory, no ordnance stores and no capability to make these. This was accepted by Gen Gracey in command of the Pakistani Army in 1947. What were the preconditions for achieving this victory in less than a fortnight?

- Send the British packing to UK on 15 August 1947. India did not need Lord Mountbatten, and his cohort. They served British interests favouring Pakistan and harmed India for decades to come.
- Stop consulting the British PM (Atlee) or the American President (China did not consult any one after 1 October 1949 on how to run their affairs).
- Understand the geopolitical situation as it was explained to the political brass by Indian military officers like Nathu Singh, Cariappa, Thimayya and Harbakhsh. There was no dearth of talented patriotic military officers in India on 15 August 1947.
- Prepare a strategic plan to counter the inimical neighbours.
- Commence offensive in ground of own choosing (Punjab, South Jammu, Punch, Mender, Samba) to threaten Pakistani vitals.

Why did the leadership of the day not take these decisions? This is a critical question that would need in-depth analysis of a number of factors. Did we learn from the war? Not really. Once again the crippling inertia.

India China War 1962

This was the most relevant war in the context of this book. It exposed India's glaring shortcomings at all the levels that need to be addressed in a theatre command. To start with, the importance of Tibet to India's security was ignored. When the British left, Tibet was an independent nation with substantial Indian presence for protecting, 'India-Tibet trade'. Before China occupied Tibet in 1950-51, India had sent military expeditions to Tibet to assess their military capability to defend themselves from a possible Chinese offensive. The military commanders who undertook the expedition (Major later Lt General Z C Bakshi) found the Tibetan Army highly indisciplined, unprofessional and ill-prepared. Lt Gen Nathu Singh (who was General Officer Commanding-in-Chief of Eastern Army responsible for India-China border) was convinced that India must send a brigade-sized force to defend Tibet and train the Tibetan Armed Forces. However, the then Commander-in-Chief General Cariappa, thought that not even a battalion could be spared. Incidentally the post WWII India had more than 1.6 million WWII veterans who had just been demobilised. Mustering a brigade (about 3,000 troops) from this force would have been very easy.

However, this opportunity was not exploited due to two reasons. First, when the military expeditions were sent to Tibet, the establishment of a communist regime in China had become certain. Within months of this expedition, the Chiang Kai-shek regime fell and India, then considered friendly relations with the People's Republic of China to be of utmost importance. The Indian Government knew of the Chinese interest in Tibet and did not wish to antagonise the Chinese leadership by contesting their claim over Tibet—though the international opinion at that time was in favour of keeping Tibet free. It was India that pleaded the Chinese case of suzerainty over Tibet. Indian leadership also felt that once China occupied Tibet they would be too busy managing the turbulent affairs in Tibet to bother India. Advice from military and political leaders for the need of a buffer state between two big nations was completely ignored. When Nehru was reminded of the need for a buffer state by his political rivals in Parliament, he chided them with a counter question, 'Buffer between whom?' This mindset did not change in the face of very clear external indicators and advice from seasoned statesmen (Sardar Patel), top military professionals (Thakur Nathu Singh, Gen Cariappa, Gen Thimayya, and many others).

In 1954, the Chinese refused to accept the McMahon line as the international border between India and China. Incidentally, this was the period when *'Hindi Chini bhai bhai'* (Indians and Chinese are like brothers) was being popularised in India. China, on the other hand, had already made plans to build a road through the Indian territory of Aksai Chin. In 1957 they announced completion of the road linking their Xinjiang province to Aksai Chin through the Karakoram Pass. Same year they claimed the Barahoti grazing grounds in erstwhile Uttar Pradesh (now Uttarakhand).

On 25 August 1959, the Chinese killed two police personnel at Longju in the Eastern sector. Later, on 21 October 1959, a police patrol was ambushed in the same area killing 10 personnel. Finally when it dawned on the Indian political leadership that China did pose a military threat to India's territorial integrity, the Indian Army was employed as a police force for patrolling the border. Besides, the Prime Minister slashed the defence budget in 1959 by Rs 25 crores though he was warned of the Chinese threat by the top military officers. So much for India's vision for national security and reading the indicators of impending threats.

In a theatre command, planning and conduct of military operations including grand strategy and operational/functional details are in the domain of the military. How did the military commanders at the strategic and operational levels perform? First, the acceptance of a 'forward policy' (peddled by the politico bureaucratic combine) by the top military leadership highlighted a weak link in higher military command. There were a number of military commanders who could see the likely catastrophe this policy would cause. They either kept quiet or their suggestions were completely ignored. Those who seconded the forward policy for their own personal gains did a great dis-service to the nation and their respective commands. The IAF did not press for a more proactive role in the war. The political assumption (fed by the Intelligence Bureau) that involving the Air Force would tilt the war against India as the Chinese Air Force was (considered to be) much stronger, should have been contested by the IAF. The professionals in the game must have known better. As it emerged later, the IAF was in fact far superior to any air power and air defence the PLA had in 1962.

At the operational level too, the performance of the military was woefully poor. While the troops fought most gallantly in the Western Sector (Ladakh), commanders at brigade and even battalion levels were less than average in planning, conduct and control of battles in all subsectors. In the epic Battle of Rezang La it was Major Shaitan Singh's company of 13 Kumaon that fought with extreme courage and fortitude. They repulsed several multidirectional attacks by the Chinese. Major Shaitan Singh even launched a counter attack with a platoon to recapture a dominating feature (Pt 5300) but failed. This battle lasted for more than 15 hours. Out of 141 troops under Major Shaitan Singh, 136 were martyred. What was the battalion (13 Kumaon) doing at this time? It was the Battalion Commander's moral obligation to join battle. He had two more companies deployed at a nearby feature and one company with him at the battalion headquarters in Track Junction not very far from Rezang La.

Incidentally, close to the location where Shaitan Singh was fighting tooth and nail, the brigade had AMX 13 tanks at Chushul. A similar situation was repeated at the Battle of Gurung Hill which was defended by two platoons and company HQ of 1/8 Gorkha Rifles.The Chinese commenced the attack in the morning at around nine and after almost ten hours of bitter fighting, the position was captured. The Indian company lost 56 men. This company was supported by AMX 13 tanks in direct firing role. But again the rest of the battalion and the brigade did not join the battle. 114 Infantry Brigade with HQ located at Chushul, responsible for both Rezang La and Gurung Hill, had six infantry battalions, two batteries (12 guns) with a regimental HQ and three troops of tanks.

The Chinese against this brigade had almost similar strength but they were more determined to win. They coordinated their moves, and innovated new techniques. Besides, while the Indian troops were fresh in the battle, the Chinese had fought more than two to three battles in phase one of the war. The Chinese troops had traversed huge distances from the North to fight in this most inhospitable terrain (heights ranging from 16,400 to 20,300 feet), devoid of enough oxygen to breathe, rock hard terrain, deep ravines and vast, arid plains. The Indians, on the other hand, were fresh, in good numbers, had tanks (AMX 13) and adequate artillery support. However, the army here was used as a police force to patrol the border and not to deny ground by coordinated offensive defence. Apparently the cognitive abilities of Indian commanders were numbed and they were more concerned in protecting Leh in the rear than to deny every inch to the last man to the last round.

The Chinese had no intentions to advance to Leh. They had a much limited objective which was to push the Indian troops away in Aksai Chin and Karakoram areas for safeguarding the road they had built to link Xinjiang to Aksai Chin. They also had very limited force levels in this sector compared to what they had concentrated in the Eastern sector (Kameng Division). While most of the Indian top political and military brass felt that the Chinese would advance to capture Leh, Lt Gen Daulat Singh, responsible for the Northern Command, disagreed. He read the Chinese intentions correctly. But his sane advice was ignored.

In the Eastern Sector (Kameng Division) the rot was much deeper. It was an ideal case for proving that political blunders coupled with poor military leadership can turn brave and hardened soldiers into greenhorns with no cohesiveness and will to fight. The battles of Namka Chu, Dirang Dzong, Bomdi La, Sela were lost without any fight. Namka Chu is a river below the Thagla Ridge. The Chinese had occupied Thagla Ridge. The 7 Infantry Brigade of India's newly raised 4 Corps (commanded by Lt Gen B M Kaul, who was handpicked by India's top political leadership to command this newly raised corps because he supported their tactically unsound plan) was ordered to evict the Chinese from Thagla Ridge. Brig A J S Behl who participated in the battle of Namka Chu describes the morale of troops as low.

The orders to evict the Chinese from the Ridge were cancelled. For some unknown reason, the entire 7 Infantry Brigade continued to occupy linear defences stretching about 35 kms along the river dominated from the heights by the Chinese at Thagla Ridge. On 20 October 1962, the Chinese commenced their attack from features behind Namka Chu.

The attack commenced at five in the morning and by 8 am the brigade ceased to exist as a cohesive fighting unit. The rout that commenced on 20 October 1962 continued till the very end of the month-long war. Even at well-fortified positions in the depth such as Bomdi La, Dirang and Sela where the Chinese reached during the second phase of their operations, the Indian units and formation failed to exploit the excellent dominating defensive positions, the availability of fresh troops in adequate numbers, good artillery fire support and the fact that the Chinese lines of communications and logistics were stretched.

The mood at Bomdi La was casual with leisurely breakfasts and beer at lunch. There was complete lack of the urgency that is expected of units that are involved in fighting a war. Lt Gen Harbakhsh who commanded 4 Corps for a short duration during this war when Lt Gen B M Kaul fell sick describes two important incidents relevant to our study. First, the role played by GOC 4 Infantry Division at Dirang Dzong and the way the operational leadership was changed in the most clumsy manner. Harbakhsh found the GOC 4 Division at the Corp HQ (Dirang Dzong) while his formations were fighting 100 miles to the front. He was replaced. Gen Harbakhsh had reoriented the deployment and the plan for taking on the advancing Chinese and was conducting the defensive battle very successfully. He used to be constantly on the move during the day, and briefing his staff during the evening conferences.

On the sixth or seventh day of his command as he returned from his visit to the front he found Lt Gen B M Kaul in his chair in the conference room. Harbakhsh thought that Kaul had come in the capacity of Chief of General Staff to the Chief. But when he was told that Kaul had replaced him and even his residential accommodation had been shifted, he left for Delhi to meet the

Chief. This was a most unceremonious manner to change a corps commander in war especially when he was doing so well.

An American pilot who flew in war materials from the US to Bagdogra (air base near Siliguri) was surprised that there was nobody to offload the stores since it happened to be a Sunday.

Total casualties in this war: 3,708 (martyred 1,521; wounded 548; missing 1,729).

Indo-Pak War 1965

Sir you are taking charge of the highest decorated air force in the world that did nothing to help the ground battle.

(A 1965 Indo Pak War veteran to Air Chief Marshal PC Lal when he took over the command of IAF. Quoted by Major General Sukhwant Singh in *Defence of the Western Border*)

The humiliating defeat in 1962 operations shook the nation. Meanwhile there was a change at the top political leadership due to the demise of Prime Minister Nehru in 1964. The Defence budget was increased considerably. Several defence production public sector units were raised. The strength of the armed forces was raised. An analysis of the 1965 war on the same matrix of national vision, reading the war indicators, strategic-decision making in the three services (army, navy and air force) and operational dynamics in the combat zone will indicate incremental changes for the better.

To start with Shri Lal Bahadur Shastri the new Prime Minister and Shri Y B Chavan the Defence Minister were poles apart from their predecessors. Both were very clear-headed. Pakistan's ambition to settle scores with India (over Kashmir) had taken wings in the wake of India's military humiliation in 1962. The US and the British leadership found Pakistan a useful ally in the region. They had armed Pakistan with some of the latest fighter aircrafts (F 86, F 104) and tanks (Patton). India had WW II vintage aircrafts and tanks. Besides the Pakistanis had better guns with shells heavier than 200 to 300 pounds.

The Indian guns were 25 pounders. The Pakistani Sherman tanks were up-gunned to 90mm. The Indian Shermans still had 75mm. The US Secretary of State Robert McNamara even chided the Indian Defence Minister (Shri Y B Chavan) on India's military capabilities to take on Pakistan with weapon systems (that India had in 1965) that were more suitable as 'museum pieces'. But the way India responded to Pakistan's offensive in 1965 displayed firm resolve and clear intentions of defeating Pakistan militarily. The military professionals were given a free hand to plan and conduct operations. The political leadership surprised Pakistan by launching offensives across the International Border in retaliation to the Pak offensive across the Line of Control (LoC) in Jammu and Kashmir.

However, in this war, the military was found wanting in exploiting an excellent opportunity. The services remained confined to closed segments of various component parts that were considered to be working for national security. The army, navy and air force were as distanced from each other as ever. The Defence Public Sector Undertakings (DPSUs) were a different centre of power. Though the bureaucrats were not interfering in military affairs—both the army and the air force performed sub-optimally. The top commanders conducted the operations on tactics they had learnt from their erstwhile British masters. Tactics of a five-year long war were used for a short war between two nations that lacked the economic and military power of the WWII contenders.

At 1630 hours on 1 September 1965, Gen J N Chaudhury

the Chief of Army Staff rushed into the Defence Minister's office along with Air Chief (later Marshal of the Indian Air Force) Arjan Singh. The Chief explained the precarious situation in the Chhamb sector where a Pakistani Divisional attack supported by two regiments of armour had surprised the Indian Brigade in defensive deployment. The Pakistanis had reached the line of Munawar Tawi and were not very far from Akhnoor and the Jammu-Srinagar road. Within one and a half hours of the alarm being raised by the then Army Chief the first ground support mission consisting of 26 Combat Aircrafts (12 Vampires and 14 Mysteres) of the IAF was over the target. The mission accounted for ten enemy tanks, 30 to 40 vehicles and two automatic guns. Four Vampires of this mission were lost in air-to-air combat with the Pakistani Sabres.

The mission though successful taught them important lessons. In all future missions over this sector, Gnats escorted the ground-attack sorties. In the next mission, an IAF Gnat shot down the much touted Sabre in aerial combat. Subsequently, a Gnat could dodge a Sidewinder missile fired at it from an F-86 Sabre. During the next two days, the IAF not only blunted the Pakistani offensive but gained a favourable air situation. This was the most timely and effective offensive air support to the ground forces in the 1965 war. Unfortunately, this happened to be the only effective air support to the ground forces in the entire war that lasted for about three weeks. From here on, the IAF followed the strategies of WWII, for a conflict that was to last for 20 days.

The counter air operations in the form of air attacks on Pakistani air fields at Peshawar, Chaklala, Sargodha, Kohat, Chak Jhumra, Risawala and Badin in Sind did nothing to either deter the PAF in air-to-air operations (interception for air defence) or to blunt their close air support for Pak ground forces in Khem

Karan, Lahore and even Rajasthan sectors. In Rajasthan, though the PAF had made forward air fields from where their F 86 and F 104 Star Fighters could support the ground operations, the IAF had no such forward air bases in the desert sector.

Surprisingly, a third of the IAF assets were placed for operations in the East Pakistan region. No war took place in the East. Neither did the IAF switch these assets to the western theatre. One of the reasons being the vastly different maintenance support required for the combat aircraft reserved for impending operations in East Pakistan. The second and more worrisome reason was that before 1 September 1965, the IAF had no inkling of a possible war with Pakistan. In spite of this lopsided placing of resources, the IAF had numerical and operational superiority over PAF. The ratio was better than 2:1 in favour of IAF. The IAF had five bombers (Canberras) thirteen fighter ground attack (10 Hunters, 3 Gnat) squadrons besides Vampires, Mysteres, and Toofanis against seven Pakistani combat squadrons (two bombers Canberras, four Sabres and one Star Fighter).

In another account of this war the IAF was credited with 26 Fighter Squadrons against 17 Fighter Squadrons of the PAF. However, the PAF Star Fighter (Mach 2) and F 86 Sabre (high speed subsonic fighter) were superior to the IAF fighter aircrafts, except for MiG 21 which were still being assimilated into the IAF. No IAF combat aircraft could match the F 104 Star Fighter. Even then the Gnats and Hunters had shot down F 86 Sabres. The Gnat was popularly known as Sabre slayer. The attrition rate of the PAF was 17.4 per cent and that of the IAF 16 per cent. Both these attrition rates were much above the accepted norm of 5 per cent. Out of a total of 460 Combat Aircrafts the IAF lost 59 and the PAF lost 43 of its 186 Combat Aircrafts.

However, many of the IAF veterans commented on very poor

leadership and average professionalism in using the air power. Air Commodore PM Wilson has been quoted as saying, 'Nobody seemed to know what to do. The level of professionalism was extremely low. All the lessons learnt from this war were about what not to do. But these lessons were very valuable.'

As regards the Indian Navy, its aircraft carrier was under refurbishment (which could have been postponed). The Combat Aircraft on board this carrier was used piecemeal without any impact on the outcome of war. Admiral S N Kohli was quite disheartened by the fact that in 1965, the 'Indian Navy had gone to war with its hands tied at their back, and it was all but immobilised'.

As per General Harbakhsh Singh, General Officer Commander-in-Chief (GOC-in-C), Western Command (Khem Karan, Amritsar sectors) out of 99 immediate air support demands generated by 11 Corps, the Tactical Air Centre (TAC) accepted 32 and executed 21 missions. Even these missions were not very effective due to poor or non-existent ground to air communications. As per the IAF records, a total of 795 pre-planned and 212 immediate air support missions were flown by them in support of the Western Command.

Out of this number, 482 missions were planned and executed by the Joint Army Air Operation Centre (JAAOC). The ground forces for whom the JAAOC executed these missions had neither any pre-launch knowledge nor were they asked about the post-launch impact of these missions. The primary reason for this as per the Army Commander was lack of coordination, no communication and no concept of joint planning and execution!

General Harbakhsh quotes Air Vice Marshal Sondhi *(Tribune* 31 July 1968) '*....the IAF missed a rare opportunity to demonstrate more fully to the Army that it exists otherwise than as a fighting* *service for its good.'* Nevertheless, the young combat pilots and the technical crew performed exceedingly well to execute whatever tasks were assigned to them. The casualty of combat pilots was very high (the most precious asset an air force has). But it is heart breaking to admit that the efforts were wasted in the context of the outcome of the ground operations. The soldiers along the Ichhogil canal in the Lahore, Kasur or Khem Karan sectors were quite bitter to find their air force missing in action while the enemy air was pounding them relentlessly.

It is quite tempting to blame the IAF for lack of air support to the ground forces. This is what Air Vice Marshal Sondhi and Lt General Harbakhsh Singh did. But the above inferences may not be very objective. What is conveniently ignored while blaming the IAF is that there was no involvement of the IAF (even the Indian Navy) in the planning process of ground operations. It was only when the Chhamb defences were being overrun that ACM Arjan Singh entered the picture. Secondly, there were no radio or other communication links between the troops in the combat zone with the air fields or the Joint Operations Centre (JOC). Though the advancing brigades had signals detachments comprising of Air Controller Team (ACT) with tentacles, there was no communication with the supporting and supported elements. There was no ground to air communication with the fighter ground attack aircraft that came over the target. Due to the Doppler Effect, the normal Very High Frequency radio does not work with aircrafts that fly at near supersonic speeds. All these facts pertaining to lack of communication were accepted by the Army Commander. But what can be said in defence of the ground forces is that they had envisaged the requirements of pre-planned and immediate air support for the operations.

Keeping in view the conduct and seriousness of operations

in the Western theatre, the IAF still could have done wonders as it did in the Chhamb sector by blunting the offensive of the Pakistani armour. To illustrate this point we will discuss the 15 Infantry Division operation across the Ichhogil canal from 6 to 22 December 1965.

On 6 December 1965, the 3rd Battalion, The Jat Regiment of 54 Infantry Brigade (15 Infantry Division, XI Corps of Western Command) captured the damaged bridge over Ichhogil canal at 1130 hours and extended its hold up to Bata Shoe Factory on the outskirts of Lahore. At this time, 15 Dogra of the same brigade was holding a firm base at Gosal Dial. The third battalion of the brigade, 13 Punjab, was stuck at Attari (at the border). This was the most promising situation in the entire Western Theatre during the three weeks long Indo-Pak conflict. The 3 Jat battalion stationed at the bridgehead needed fire support and logistics. They also needed air cover against the PAF that had swung into action. None of these were provided to 3 Jat. The brigade commander could have sent the reorganisation stores (anti tank weapons, ammunition); squadron armour (an armoured regiment 4 Horse) was given to the brigade for this operation, but some elements of infantry could have been inducted into the bridgehead; the field company could have entered the bridgehead and commenced laying anti-tank mines. None of these actions were taken.

As regards the IAF, the Combat Aircraft from Amritsar, Halwara, Adampur could have undertaken close air support, air defence and short interdiction missions west of Ichhogil canal to disrupt the build-up (for counter attack) of Pakistani forces against 3 Jat. This also did not happen. If both the ground forces and the IAF had synergised to exploit this once-in-a-lifetime opportunity provided by 3 Jat, Lahore would have fallen by 8 or 9 September 1965, making it very difficult for Pakistan to continue the war leave aside their subsequent offensive in the Khem Karan sector led by their 1 Armoured Division. But the IAF did not seize the initiative since they had never planned it. The ground forces let go this great opportunity since except for 3 Jat no other unit or formation in 15 Infantry Division had the type of leadership that 3 Jat had (as per Lt Gen Harbakhsh Singh, the Army Commander).

Gen Harbakhsh narrates two more incidents pertaining to this battle that bring out issues regarding the divisional level leadership and inter service coordination. Gen Harbakhsh was driving along the axis of advance of 15 Infantry Division responsible for the bridgehead operation (3 Jat was part of this division) and recalls seeing massive destruction caused by the PAF strafing and bombing on the logistic and troops carrying vehicles of the division. He was passing through a trail of burning and mutilated vehicles looking for the GOC 15 Infantry Division. The PAF conducted raids over the Indian logistic columns without any opposition by the IAF since the IAF was conducting counter air operations deep inside Pakistan. Gen Harbakhsh explained the bitterness of the ground forces. He complained that his Chief of Staff had connived with the Chief of Staff Western Air Command in moving combat aircraft from the forward bases of Pathankot, Adampur and Halwara to the rear. This was done after paradropping of some Pakistani special forces near these bases. Even though these Pak SF elements had not approached anywhere near the airbases, a hasty action by the two senior officers of army and air force deprived the troops on ground of critical air support. These incidents are indicative of the fact that synergistic application of forces and jointness in operations need sound leadership and abundance of courage especially at the leadership levels.

Leadership as a vital ingredient of theatre command was again highlighted in 4 Infantry Division operations in the Khem Karan sector (1965). The division was moved from the mountainous terrain to the plains of Punjab (Khem Karan, Assal Uttar) in 1965. Pakistan had launched a major offensive led by their 1 Armoured Division in this sector. During the initial phases of defensive battle, the division was badly shaken that led the GOC 11 Corps to send a handwritten note to the Army Commander (Harbakhsh) that, 'all the infantry units have deserted and need to be disbanded. Another division needs to be made available for defensive battle in the sector'. When Harbakhsh visited the sector to assess the situation himself, he found that the situation was not as bad. He spoke to the divisional commanders, reorganised the defences, then grouped an independent armoured brigade for countering the Pak 1 Armoured Division offensive.

While he was busy doing all this, the Chief of the Army staff flew in and wanted Harbakhsh to withdraw to the line of Beas River (that would have handed over bulk of Indian Punjab to the Pakistanis without a fight). Harbakhsh refused and asked Gen J N Chaudhary to issue written orders (these were never issued). The reorganised and rejuvenated 4 Infantry Division and 2 Independent Armoured Brigades turned the tables on the Pakistanis. The Battle of Assal Uttar dug the graveyard for the Pakistani armour.

Major General Sukhwant Singh commented on the failure of the Chiefs of Staff Committee structure of conducting the affairs of war. According to him 'the appearance of fusion is not real. Each service chief is instinctively and emotionally committed to his service. Involved in winning own battle with attached credit and glory. Competition among the services takes over cooperation'.

Total Casualties: 11,886 (Martyred: 2,902 Wounded: 8,622 Missing: 362)

1967: Sino Indian Localised Limited Conflict

In September 1967, two small skirmishes were fought by the Indian troops of 17 Mountain Division at Nathu La and Cho La. The former, a local battle fought by 2 Grenadiers from 11 to 16 September 1967 and the latter by 7/11 Gorkha Rifles and Jammu and Kashmir Light Infantry from 28 September to first week October of 1967. But these two local short engagements bring out some important facts in the context of our study related to the hangover of the China fear among the apex political and military leadership.

Nathu La (height 14,140 feet) is a mountain pass located on the Sino-Indian border in Sikkim, about 54 kilometres East of Gangtok, along the Jawaharlal Nehru Road. The pass is overlooked by raised features (shoulders) to the North and South held by the Indian Army to prevent any ingress across this pass. The Chinese are located East of this pass. It is an almost eyeball-to-eyeball situation on both sides. A similar pass exists South-East of Nathu La known as Jelep La (height 13,999 feet) about 60 kilometres East of Gangtok and four kilometres South from Nathu La along the watershed. The watershed defines the Sino Indian border in East Sikkim. Nathu La was held by 17 Mountain Division and Jelep La by 27 Mountain Division in 1965. Both these divisions were under the 33 Corps based at (Sukhna) Siliguri. In 1965 the Chinese wanted to help Pakistan in their war with India. Hence they issued an ultimatum to India to vacate Nathu La and Jelep La.

As per 33 Corps operational plan in 1965, both these features were designated observation posts with main defences a few kilometers to the West of these passes. In August 1965, Lt Gen

G G Bewoor was the Corps Commander (33 Corps) responsible for Nathu La and Jelep La. Major General Sagat Singh had just joined in August 1965. The first operational briefing he got from the Corps Commander at Sukhna emphasised that in case the Chinese threat becomes imminent, 17 Mountain Division will vacate Nathu La and 27 Mountain Division (under Major General Harcharan Singh) will vacate Jelep La. The respective divisional defensive battles will be fought from the main defences around six to nine kilometres due West of these passes. Since Major General Sagat Singh was new to the situation, he did not raise any objections to this plan during the briefing. But he told the Corps Commander that he will first assess the situation himself. Hence when he assumed office, he moved around his divisional sector, met his brigade, battalion and company commanders, and gauged the morale of his troops.

Having seen the terrain, his own troops and the enemy across, he refused to vacate the pass. He maintained that since the border runs along the watershed, the area belongs to India. He said that holding Nathu La is important for the defences of 17 Mountain Division. Most importantly as a Divisional Commander he was responsible for the defences of 17 Mountain Division and hence he must have the freedom to fight the divisional battle as per his professional judgement. Meanwhile, 27 Mountain Division vacated Jelep La. The Chinese occupied this pass. All this happened in 1965. The Chinese opposite Nathu La were quite agitated that the Indian troops did not vacate Nathu La. In August 1967, Indians started laying barbed wire along the watershed at Nathu La, which was not liked by the Chinese.

This led to frequent physical scuffles. On the fateful morning of 11 September 1967, as the Engineers (field company) and Grenadiers were laying the barbed wire, the Chinese troops rushed to the spot along with their political commissar. Lt Col Rai Singh Commanding Officer (CO) 2 Grenadiers—was also at the watershed.

The political commissar asked Rai Singh to stop the work. Heated arguments commenced followed by routine pushing and jostling. In the melee, the political commissar got roughed up. The Chinese suddenly left. They got into their bunkers. The Indians were in clear sight at the watershed laying the barbed wire.

Unknown to them the Chinese took aim. At 7.30 am the Indians heard a whistle followed by accurate and devastating small arms and automatic fire on the Indians laying the barbed wire. Within minutes, hundreds of Indian troops were dead or wounded at the watershed. The CO was also among the wounded. When the Grenadiers saw their CO shot by the Chinese, they were enraged. The fire fight commenced. The Chinese opened artillery and mortar fire. The Indian side could not open up artillery since, as per the policy, the orders for opening the artillery fire were to come from the defence ministry. The divisional headquarters could not contact the right people up the chain. With each passing hour, the situation was becoming untenable for the Indians. At this juncture, Sagat Singh took a command decision to open Indian artillery fire (later when the Prime Minister was briefed she endorsed his decision). The artillery observation post officer was well positioned and had a clear view of the Chinese positions.

As the Indian medium and field artillery boomed, the Chinese positions were razed to the ground. On 13 and 14 September, more than 340 Chinese were killed and around 350 were injured. The Chinese defences lay in tatters. Sagat Singh wanted to launch an attack into the battered Chinese defences. He was not allowed to attack. Ceasefire came into effect on 16 September 1967. The Chinese could not stomach this defeat.

They made another attempt on 28 September 1967 to capture Cho La, located North of Nathu La. This time the 7th battalion of 11 Gorkha Rifles and troops of 11 Jammu and Kashmir Rifles foiled this attempt. This was the last time Chinese attacked the Indian defences in 17 Mountain Division Sector.

The Nathu La and Cho La incidents highlight four major issues. First, the political leadership of the time wanted to control organic battles in the combat zone at brigade and battalion levels. This handicaps the field commanders in doing what they are expected to do. Leaders like Sagat Singh are rare. Second, at the operational level, Bewoor's plan to fight the defensive battle after sacrificing the dominating features at the watershed betrays fear and lack of tactical acumen.

Incidentally, he was supported in this plan at the command and army HQ and obviously the political powers that be. Third, after achieving a spectacular victory in the local battle, opportunity for a counter stroke was denied. Such a behaviour encourages the adversary for future adventures. The Chinese do not respect the weak. Fourth, the media did not play it out the way it should have. On the contrary, Sagat Singh almost turned into a villain for defying the orders of the Corps and Army HQ. However victory over the Chinese saved him. He did not get any gallantry award for this achievement.

Eventually, we lost 88 of our men and had another 163 wounded. The Chinese lost 340 men and had 450 wounded.

Liberation of Bangladesh 1971

You made us touch the skies with glory and paint it with shades of red. The colours shall be fast for ever..... # 33 Squadron to Air Chief Marshall P C Lal at his farewell. (ACM PC Lal the Quiet Orchestrator, The 1971 Indo Pak Air War)

The most vehement and seemingly convincing argument against creating unified theatre commands comes from this belief among most of the senior officers and think tank organisations, 'we have done so well in 1971 without creating theatre commands, why disturb the status quo?'

There is no doubt that '1971' was a most resounding and historic victory. Very few armed forces have done so much, so fast and so comprehensively. Also the performance of the political leadership in stage managing the war, and in building international opinion was stellar. At the operational level Eastern Command excelled and surpassed all expectations that include tri-service synergy, overall planning and conduct of land and air battles. The Indian Navy (with able support by the IAF) stunned the Pakistani leadership.

But some very unique features of this war need to be recounted. First and foremost is the help India got from Pakistan. Second, availability of top military commanders like SHJF Manekshaw, and JFR Jacob, who persuaded the political leadership to postpone the commencement of this operation from March 1971 to November-December 1971. Third, the element of chance. Fourth, on the flip side we must also look at India's performance in the Shakargarh Bulge and in Rajasthan—failures teach us more.

Pakistan helped the Indian cause by monumental political bungling, by alienating the overwhelming majority of erstwhile East Pakistan, and thereafter by deciding on the ill-fated strategy of treating defence of East Pakistan with an offensive operation in the West. These offensive operations from West Pakistan were neither launched (Pakistan 1 Corps offensive in Shakargarh which never 'took off') nor the defensive operations conducted in an efficient manner (the PAF did not support the Pakistani 18

Infantry Division in Rajasthan). In East Pakistan, General Niazi's forces gave up the fight too early under tremendous psychological pressure. Major General Hakeem Arshad Qureshi of Pakistan who fought in the war observed, 'we lost the war without losing a single battle. At the time of surrender we had not lost even 5,000 soldiers out of a total of 50,000. Even the enemy was surprised at the speed of our disintegration. It was complete lack of foresight and failure to react to operational realities.'

Their air force abandoned functional fighter aircrafts (about ten F 86 Sabre Jets) and fled from the combat zone. Presence of Manekshaw as the Chief of Army Staff during the operation paved the way for appropriate selection of timing as also unity of command especially in the Eastern theatre. And the decision to capture Dhaka emerged from J F R Jacob's insistence. The political leadership and even Manekshaw would have been content with capture of 'sufficient territory' to push back the refugees.

The strategic planning and execution commenced as early as March 1971. During the preparatory stages of the 1971 operations, Lt Gen JFR Jacob, Chief of Staff Eastern Command, who was given the overall responsibility for conduct of operations in the theatre was a worried man on account of the complexity of coordinating air operations in support of ground forces. The Eastern Command Head Quarters were at Kolkata (Calcutta in 1971). The Eastern Air Command responsible to support the Kolkata command was at Shillong. Besides, the boundaries of air operations were so defined that the Eastern Army operations were to be supported partly by the Eastern Air Command at Shillong and partly by the Central Air Command located at Prayagraj (Allahabad in 1971).

General Jacob requested Gen Manekshaw to take up this matter with the Air Chief. Manekshaw refused since he did not have cordial relations with Air Chief Marshal P C Lal! Fortunately for General Jacob, the Air Chief visited Fort William (the Eastern Army Headquarters in Kolkata). Gen Jacob apprised the Air Chief of the problem he had with locations of supporting air headquarters and air operations boundaries. The Air Chief immediately agreed to place an Advance Eastern Air Headquarters at Kolkata alongside the Eastern Army Headquarters and to redefine the air operations boundaries so that single air headquarters could support the army operations. Gen Jacob describes another incident during this war that highlights joint decision-making at operational level in a fluid battle situation. Two bomber (Canberra) pilots came to him seeking detailed briefing on a target (old factory) that was selected by the Chiefs of Staff at Delhi. Gen Jacob realised that the target selected by the Chiefs of Staff had no strategic value during that phase of operation. He diverted the bombing mission to another target near Chittagong which was critical for the ongoing phase of operation. The strike was successful and contributed to the overall objective of ground forces.

But the staff at Chiefs of Staff committee was furious. They asked Gen Jacob under whose authority he had diverted a strategic bombing mission selected by the Chiefs of Staff. Gen Jacob explained the situation. The Air Chief was informed of Jacob's response; he understood the situation. What followed is remembered as the golden history of army and air cooperation in liberation of Bangladesh. The Eastern Air Command not only ensured maximum support to the ground operations but ensured that the Pakistan Air Force (PAF) was virtually incapable of supporting the ground operations of the Pakistani Army in Bangladesh. The IAF dominance was so complete that several F86 Sabre jets were captured at the Dhaka air field on 17 December

1971. However, we need to remember that the IAF enjoyed a superiority of 10 to 1 against PAF in the Eastern theatre. In case of ground forces, this ratio was 3 to 1 in favour of India.

The crossing of the mighty Meghna river, which is at least 4,000 yards wide at the point of the crossing by India's 4 Corps on 9 December 1971, under Lt Gen Sagat Singh provided an excellent case for not only jointness of army and air cooperation, but also for several other attributes as well. The main bridge over the river had been damaged by the retreating Pakistani soldiers. First, it points towards the bold and pro-active leadership of Gen Sagat Singh. Before undertaking the river crossing operations, Sagat Singh flew over the objective and inferred that the adversary is quite disorganised and will not contest the river crossing operation in any meaningful way. Hence, he took the risk of crossing the wide, fast-flowing Meghna River against weak opposition.

Second, the cooperation between Eastern Air Command and 4 Corps achieved spectacular results. 4 Corps was not only provided the most intimate close air support during its dash to Dhaka but was helped in helicopter-lift operations using IAF helicopters over Meghna. Each Mi4 helicopter could carry a fully armed section (11 soldiers). With this lift capability around 50 to 60 helicopter lifts were required to carry the battalion across the river.

The crossing of Meghna River by 4 Corps and heliborne operations around the same time in proximity of Dhaka are described by Gen Jacob who was actually directing and controlling the operations. These operations are also described by the IAF with legitimate pride. According to General Jacob, the heliborne lift commenced at 1530 hours on 9 December 1971 with seven to eight Mi4 helicopters out of a total of 14 helicopters available to the Corps. This was attributed to a maintenance problem. The heliborne lift of one battalion plus section of light regiment (artillery) was completed on the same day. On 11 December, another battalion plus two sections of mountain guns without gun towing vehicles were lifted across. Sagat Singh mustered even local resources such as boats, ferries, cycles and railway wagons for crossing the river and advancing closer to Dhaka (through Narsingdi and Tungi) so as to pose a serious threat. Meanwhile a Para Battalion (about 600 troops) was dropped in a heliborne operation at Madhepura on 11 December 1971.

The media reported a para drop of some 5,000 troops in the area. The Pakistani commander (Niazi) believed the media report and panicked. While all this was happening in 4 Corps zone, 101 Communication Zone (a division sized force) reached the outskirts of Dhaka.

Meanwhile, an intercept was picked up by India's signals intelligence unit that a high level meeting was planned at the Government House at Dhaka at 1200 hours on 14 December 1971. There were two Government houses in Dhaka. JFR Jacob inferred that it was the old Government House where the meeting was scheduled. He asked his counterpart in the IAF (Air Vice Marshal Devashar) to plan a strike at the old Government House on 14 December 1971 when the meeting was to be in progress. This attack was carried out very accurately by the IAF. The psychological impact on the highest leadership of Pakistan in Bangladesh (then East Pakistan) was devastating.

It may be interesting to know the description of these events by the IAF. In the book, *The 1971 Indo Pak Air War Reflections and Projections,* edited by Air Marshal Anil Chopra, Gp Captain Chandan Singh says that the Helicopter Task Force Commander assisted his Corps Commander Gen Sagat Singh in lifting more than 4,000 troops with most of their supporting equipment including ammunition and light artillery guns in three locations

(Narsingdi, Raipura and Narayanganj), flying 350 sorties including 100 sorties by night between December 6 and 12. The landing zones were barely 60 kilometres from Dhaka. Gp Capt Chandan Singh recalled that the heliborne operation was conducted amidst hostile enemy fire. Air Chief P C Lal had personally monitored the training of Forward Air Controllers (FACs) who were to be allotted for all close air support and heliborne operations. Second, the battalion was landed between 1600 hours and sun set (about 90 minutes of daylight available) in a landing zone that was under observation and domination by fire by the Pakistanis. Hence the first wave of troops (75 to 80 soldiers including the Battalion Commander) landed under hostile fire. The helicopter pilots were unaware of the enemy's presence in the landing zone. The troops jumped off the helicopter hovering about five feet above ground. After getting down the first wave fought through and cleared the enemy resistance for the second wave to arrive.

However, as successive waves continued to land the helicopters returning after the drop came under enemy fire. This did not deter the brave pilots to continue with the operations.

The IAF fought the 1971 wars with the same old combat aircraft that it had in 1965 except for one addition in the form of Su7. Besides the MiGs were fully assimilated into the service. They flew 500 sorties per day over Bangladesh adding up to 7,300 sorties in the fourteen-odd days of the liberation war. This is a good performance measured by an average scale. Compared to the Israeli Air Force (in 1967 and 1973) this may not be as good.

1971, Operations in Southern Theatre

In popular imagination and also for the military, the 1971 conflict is dominated by memories of war in the Eastern theatre.

Operations in the southern theatre under Lt General (later Chief of Army Staff) G G Bewoor and western theatre under Lt General Candeth are generally forgotten. India's performance in these two theatres could have been much better to say the least. In the southern theatre, the battle of Longewala is a famous event that is described in highly laudatory terms ignoring the major weaknesses, omissions and, at times, half truths especially in the context of jointness in planning and execution that could help in drawing some important lessons.

First, the IAF version as given in *1971 Indo Pak Air War*. The 12 Infantry Division of India's Southern Command was tasked to launch an offensive for capture of Rahim yar Khan that could have jeopardised Pakistani operations in Punjab as also in the Shakargarh Bulge. Major General Khambatta was tasked to launch the operation on 4 December 1971. He delayed the launch date by a day under the pretext that his forces were not ready. Meanwhile, Pakistan pre-empted India's 12 Infantry Division operation by attacking with two brigades plus two Armoured Regiments (equipped with T59 tanks) on 4 December 1971 itself.

According to V K 'Jimmy' Bhatia, the Divisional Commander 12 Infantry Division panicked and asked the Company Commander 23 Punjab at Longewala as also the Air Force Base Commander Wing Commander M S Bawa at the Jaisalmer air base to vacate the defended locality and the base respectively. Both these men refused and decided to fight.

The leading Pakistani armour reached Longewala just around midnight of 4 December and for some unfathomable reason stopped there. Early in the morning of 5 December, an Air Observation Post (AOP) aircraft flown by an army officer Major Atma Singh spotted them. Wing Commander (later Air Vice

Marshal) M S Bawa got this information and lost no time initiating one of the most daring and devastating ground support attack on the Pakistani forces. The Hunters from the base embarked upon a relentless 'seek and destroy' mission on the Pakistani forces. These sorties were conducted almost like an air bridge. Within minutes of a sortie finishing its attack, another sortie was over the target. There were times when the Base Commander took great risks in sending single fighter sorties since the other aircraft that was part of this sortie was under intense repairs after it sustained hits from the Pakistani Anti Aircraft Guns fitted in their tanks. On another occasion, a Pakistani T59 fired at a low flying attacking Hunter with its main gun (90 mm). The shell whizzed past the Hunter and momentarily disturbed the aircraft controls. The pilot could barely pull out from the dive scraping the top of a sand dune.

The devastation of Pakistani forces continued throughout the day and even on 6 December. Pakistani forces lost 37 tanks and several soft-skinned logistics vehicles. The offensive was decimated by a few brave pilots. The offensive force came to such a pitiable state that they were not even in a position to withdraw without air support from their own air force. The PAF never appeared for the fight. Even more surprisingly, the Indians never exploited this golden opportunity to launch hot pursuit and reach their allotted objective of Rahim yar Khan!

The description of this operation from the eyes of an officer (Brig later Major General Sukhwant Singh) of Directorate General Military Operations (DGMO) is similar in overall content but covers far more relevant details for the purpose of our study. Major General Sukhwant, a gunner, had served in 12 Infantry Division of Western Command as a Brigade Commander before moving to Military Operations (MO) Directorate at

New Delhi. It was during March 1971 when war with Pakistan was becoming more and more imminent that he was sent from the MO Directorate to Southern Command to check on their plans and preparations. For our study, the relevant aspects of his observations include the quality of leadership and military professionalism, jointness between the army and the supporting IAF in the theatre and overall impact of operations in this theatre. First, the quality of leadership. The Southern Army Commander Lt General Bewoor had decided to follow the operational plans that were prepared about three years back.

Meanwhile, before this operational plan could be launched, a brigade-sized force was taken away from his command considering India's overall goal for decisive victory in the East. Inspite of this depletion in his force level, he stuck to the same offensive plans of capturing Rahim Yar Khan and Sukkur Dam. He had based his offensive on two division sized forces along thrust lines that were separated by about 240 kms. Hence, there was no flexibility in the plan for switching forces from one thrust line to the other. According to General Sukhwant Singh who had served under Bewoor, the Army Commander was extremely defensive and a 'no risk' commander.

The 12 Infantry Division that was destined to advance to Rahim yar Khan and finally responsible for the Battle of Longewala was commanded by Major General Khambatta who happened to be Assistant Military Secretary to two chiefs before he was given the command of this division. To operationalise his offensive plan, he lacked the engineering resources (track material) and suitable tanks (he had AMX 13 tanks that were no match to the T 59 tanks that the Pakistani forces were expected to use in this sector). When told about the infirmities in his plan, he ignored the advice under the pretext that this was not his plan anyway and once the war starts, he would fight as per his plans.

General Sukhwant was not much enthused by the atmosphere in the 12 Infantry Division and Southern Command, the formation that was expected to fight a major war. Sukhwant also visited the IAF base at Jaisalmer commanded by Wing Commander M S Bawa and found the environment highly upbeat. The young pilots were raring for the fight.

The Army Air Force coordination was quite cumbersome in this theatre. The air effort required by Southern Command (located at Pune) was planned and allotted by Headquarters Western Air Command located at Delhi. The senior air force officer with whom the Army Commander was to deal was the Air Officer Commanding at Jodhpur. Control of air effort allotted to Southern Command was under Tactical Air Command (TAC) located at command advance HQ. Since the Southern Command formations and units located in Gujarat and Nal (near Bikaner) were not under AOC Jodhpur, their air support was coordinated directly with Western Air Command at Delhi. It is surprising that Bewoor or someone in HQ Southern Command did not find it appropriate to rationalise this with the Air HQ on the lines Gen JFR Jacob had done with Air Chief Marshal Lal before commencement of hostilities in the Eastern Theatre.

When Longewala came under attack on the night of 4 December, Wing Commander M S Bawa had four functional Hunters. These were the Hunters that decimated the Pakistani offensive on 5 and 6 December. Once Bawa completed his job, the Army Chief (Manekshaw) wanted immediate pursuit, destruction of the remainder of Pakistani forces and capture of the divisional objective at Rahim yar Khan. Bewoor instead took up a defensive position in 12 Infantry Division Sector! At this time, 12 Infantry Division was intact in its assembly area ready for the planned offensive. The IAF had complete air superiority in tactical battle area right up to the divisional objectives. The 11 Infantry Division in the same theatre was making good progress though a few 100 kms away from the 12 Infantry Division planned thrust. It is not difficult to imagine the dividends that could have been derived from the bold leadership, joint planning and operations and relentless offensive action. But this did not happen.

The spectacular performance of Wing Commander M S Bawa, Major K S Chandpuri and their men did not achieve the type of results they could have had due to sluggish decision-making and lack of synergy. It will be interesting to look at the air effort available for this offensive. Overall India had a total of 45 Combat and Transport Squadrons in 1971 compared to around 13 squadrons that the PAF had for this war. Besides, the PAF got around three squadrons of fighters from friendly Islamic countries. One squadron of Sabre F 86 was allotted for East Pakistan that left around 15 odd squadrons for West Pakistan. India had allotted 10 combat squadrons for the East and remainder 25 combat squadrons for the Western and the Southern Commands.

Thus, for operations against West Pakistan, the ratio was 2:1 in favour of India. In the East, India enjoyed a numerical superiority of 10:1. Keeping in view the operational radius of supporting Combat Aircraft, Air Chief Lal had activated new airbases at Jaisalmer, Uttarlai and Nal in the desert sector. The Southern Command tactical battle area was within range from the Jaisalmer air base. On the Pakistani side, the 18 Infantry Division located at Rahim yar Khan, and the Jacobabad airfield was the only base from where their Combat Aircraft could support the 18 Infantry Division planned offensive towards Longewala, Ramgarh, Jaisalmer and beyond. However, the Pakistani ground forces' request for air support from this airfield was rejected by the PAF on the plea that the Pakistan Army had not given them two weeks notice to activate this forward airbase. Hence, right from the beginning, the Pakistan ground offensive was denied of any kind of air support.

1971, Operations in the Western Theatre: Shakargarh Bulge

For India, the importance of this bulge emanated from its proximity to the Pathankot-Jammu road, connecting Jammu and Kashmir to the rest of the country. For this Pakistan had concentrated its strike corps in Pasrur. East of Pasrur Pakistan defended the Shakargarh bulge with two Infantry Divisions (one of the divisions had four brigades instead of the normal strength of three brigades). These two divisions were supported by an Armoured Brigade. Besides, close to the International border, Pakistan had deployed paramilitary forces strengthened by a recce and support battalion and an armoured regiment. Against this, India's strike corps (1 Corps) consisted of three divisions and two armoured brigades in the initial stages. Once the Pakistani strike element was drawn out for battle, 15 Corps in the North and 11 Corps in the South were expected to join the battle in the bulge. The approximate time plan for reaching Line Zafarwal-Narowal was five days after start of operations. Three days after reaching this line the Indian strike corps was to capture Shakargarh and then develop operations towards Pasrur in conjunction with 15 and 11 Corps from the North and South respectively.

Thus, the offensive was to cover about 15 to 20 kms for capture of Shakargarh, 60 to 80 kms to reach the general line of Narowal and another 20 to 30 kms to reach Pasrur. The Narowal line was to be breached within five to six days of the commencement of operations and another week or so to complete operations at Pasrur. The operations commenced on 5 December. By 15 December the strike corps was expected to be more than 80 kms inside Pakistan. Instead, by 17 December when the ceasefire came into effect the Indian strike corps was just 8 kms inside Pakistan and had engaged with the covering troops and some elements of Pakistani holding formation. What went wrong?

Two events, though very small when compared to the entire operation, define the characteristics of the entire campaign in this sector in the context of our study. These events pertain to an operation that Poona Horse was not allowed to undertake just in the beginning of hostilities and a linkup that did not take place with a company operation under a brave and dashing company commander of Grenadiers. On 5 December 1971, Lt Col (later Lt General) Hanut Singh, Commanding Officer of the famous Poona Horse, was deployed at the International Border in the Shakargarh Bulge. Hanut was told that he was facing Pakistani defensive minefield and a deliberate bridgehead operation would be launched by two Infantry Divisions of the Corps (India's 1 Corps) so that his own armour could be inducted for the offensive. A day earlier, Pakistan had declared war. The PAF strike aircraft were conducting a search and destroy mission in the area, though they could not see Poona Horse tanks due to some excellent camouflage.

Hanut saw a 30 feet high Pakistani observation post close to his position and felt that the enemy will be able to direct accurate fire on his troops from the observation post. He asked one of his tanks to get the tower down. As the Indian tank fired, three Pakistani tanks hidden in the elephant grass closeby panicked and moved back towards their rear location.

Hanut was quick to realise that the minefield that he was waiting to be breached for his advance did not exist. He wanted to cross through this gap in the minefield. His Brigade Commander Brigadier (later General) A S Vaidya Commander 16 Independent Armoured Brigade) did not allow this operation and asked him to wait for deliberate mine breaching operations. The 'deliberate' operations proceeded as 'planned'. Consequently, two Infantry Divisions of 1 Corps breached the 'minefield', which either did not exist or was insignificant. They also attacked in thin air capturing enemy positions where no enemy was present. The divisions then spent time regrouping. Thus, when Poona Horse and leading elements of Indian Strike Corps actually, contacted Pakistani troops after more than a week of this deliberate and cautious advance the Pakistanis were well prepared and ready to meet the offensive.

It took some exceptionally brave fighting by the men of Poona Horse under Hanut and 3 Grenadiers to beat back the brave counter-attacks by the Pakistani local formation. By the time the war ended, Indian Strike Corps had captured an area which did not have any strategic importance.

The second event pertains to an abortive attempt to invest Shakargarh by 4 Grenadiers and some armour on the night of 13/14 December. A company under Major Choudhary of 4 Grenadiers was tasked to conduct reconnaissance in force before his unit could attack the town. Major Choudhary commenced his move on 13 December in the evening. He encountered the minefield, found some gaps in it, crossed the minefield and occupied some houses in the outskirts of Shakargarh with his company. He left a few guides at the minefield gaps to help the armour and remainder of 4 Grenadiers to catch up. This message was sent to the Battalion Commander. The battalion commenced its advance on the night of 14 December. There was some firing at them by Pakistani artillery, a tank (perhaps a trawl) got bogged down in the river bed (Bein River). The armoured group refused to continue the advance. The battalion wilted under imagined threat and returned back to firm base. The company that had secured the outskirts of Shakargarh was left in the lurch. The Pakistanis surrounded the company on 15 December. About 72 men of the 4 Grenadiers were taken prisoners. Another attempt was made to attack Shakargarh on 14 December by 36 Infantry Division. This was the time when the air observation post flights informed the commanders that the Pakistanis were evacuating Shakargarh. Even this attack did not proceed beyond the start line.

During the entire description of these operations there is no mention by General Sukhwant Singh in his book, whether air support was asked for or air operations were launched to help the offensive formations. A brief but very comprehensive description of air operations in support of ground operations comes from a talk delivered by Air Officer Commanding-in-Chief and Deputy Chief of Air Staff, Air Marshal C V Gole on 23 August 1989 at USI (published in the USI Journal in October 2021). The Strike Corps was supported by 8 TAC for operations in the Shakargarh Bulge. Further 8 TAC had full control of air effort allotted to it. The air bases from where the supporting missions were to take off included Amritsar, Halwara and Adampur. Out of a total of 23 squadrons that were available to the Western and Central air commands during these operations, it is safe to assume that the bulk of the air effort was for 1 Corps offensive because the Southern Command operations were limited to 11 Infantry Division thrust line and for the Battle of Longewala along the 12 Infantry Division thrust line that too for just two days on 5 and 6 December.

Thus, approximately 15 Squadrons were in support of 1 Corps offensive opposed by around half this number of the PAF. Air Marshal Gole's observations on the close air support in this sector are not very encouraging. Since Indian forces were not allowed to initiate the war, pre-hostility support was not possible. Once Pakistan started the war on 3 December, the IAF did not take long to gain air superiority in this sector in air-to-air combat. Thereafter, the squadrons were fully primed to meet the demands of the ground forces. The photo recce missions that were undertaken did not prove very effective due to the quality of the air photos and cumbersome measures to send these air photos to the ground forces that demanded Photo Recce missions.

The immediate close air support was either not demanded in adequate numbers by the ground forces or demanded very late once the operations commenced. At this juncture, it was almost impossible for the combat sorties to have any meaningful impact on the outcome of the battle. At times, the targets for the missions asked by the ground forces were beyond the capability of the attacking sorties.

Such targets included 'bombing to explode minefields!' There was enough semblance of cooperation but no signs of coordination. The supporting air bases or even the HQ 8 TAC had no inkling of the operational plans of the supported ground forces and neither did they know the progress of their air operations. There was little understanding of each other's capabilities (and perhaps limitations). The ground forces never asked for pre-emptive strikes or offensive air support for softening the objective. The quantum of resources the IAF had for this operation and the air superiority they enjoyed provided an ideal opportunity for exploiting pre planned and immediate air support before launching ground operations. Thus, when

Hanut's regiment had identified the gaps in the minefield and were ready to exploit it, air efforts could have been utilised for softening the impending objective or short interdiction just ahead of the objective. Similarly, when Major Choudhary had occupied houses on the outskirts of Shakargarh, the town of Shakargarh itself could have been bombed or the Pakistani forces moving in to surround Choudhary company could have been targeted.

However, none of the descriptions of the operation by General Sukhwant or Air Marshal Gole bring out such air support demands by the ground forces. Instead, Air Marshal Gole observed that the air effort allotted for the operations was not utilised at all after four days of battle. Thus from 7 December itself most of the Combat Aircrafts were idling in their hangars at the three bases!

Total Casualties: 13,699 (Martyred: 3,630; Wounded: 9,856 Mising: 213)

Kargil War 1999

'The Army Asked for IAF Support on 7 May 1999. It took the IAF 19 Days to Launch the Air strike on 26 May 1999 (Role played by the IAF in the Kargil Conflict-Lt Gen Y M Bammi)

The relevance of Kargil war to our study is in the context of India's propensity for committing the same mistakes or learning the same lessons over and over again. First, the top political leadership appeared to have forgotten the lessons of accurate and timely threat assessment from a notorious neighbour. Pakistan succeeded in fooling the top leadership with friendly gestures while intruding the Kargil heights. It is not that the external intelligence agencies did not pick up the indicators. But the military leadership saw what they wanted to see. Secondly, having discovered Pakistan's treachery, the retaliation was on the ground of Pakistan's choosing. The army and the air force cooperation was not as prompt as the situation demanded. All these factors flag the urgency of deep reforms in India's national security apparatus and creating theatre commands is a part of these reforms.

During the summer of 1999, the 15 Corps troops of India's Northern Command learnt of the Pakistani intrusion into Kargil heights. After some initial confusion on the magnitude and criticality of this intrusion, it emerged that deliberate and large scale military operations would have to be launched to clear these strategic heights. On 7 May 1999, the ground forces asked for close air support from the IAF. Meanwhile 8 Sikh, 18 Grenadiers, 1 Bihar and 10 Para Commando commenced operations. Attack helicopters of the Army Aviation were supporting the ground operations. The close air support demand by the army was denied by the IAF. The army was asked to employ their own artillery and other support weapons. It was also felt that close air support will not be possible in the high altitude mountainous terrain. After a few days, the air support demand was renewed since the enemy concentration was too big for the aviation corps attack helicopters to tackle. This time the IAF wanted detailed target information. The IAF also flew MiG 25 and Canberra air reconnaissance sorties. The air photos from these sorties lacked adequate resolution and hence could not be used for launching fighter ground attack missions. On 17 May 1999, reconnaissance mission of the Aviation Research Centre (ARC, under Research and Analysis Wing-RAW) were launched. The air photos from these missions had good resolution.

On 20 May, General V P Malik, the then Chief of Army Staff returned from his trip abroad. The three chiefs met in his office. It was decided that in view of the grave situation, close air support from the IAF is most urgent. First set of air sorties in support of ground forces commenced on 26 May 1999. The delay of 19 days by the IAF allowed the Pakistanis to get their anti-air guns and missiles in the area. This cost precious lives of pilots and troops. Initially, the air attacks were not effective. Later, the IAF started using Mirage 2000 multirole aircraft that had the capability of firing precision-guided ammunitions. Two Mirage 2000 paired up for the attack. While one of them lit up the target with a laser beam, the other launched the laser guided bomb at the target. With this technique, 50 per cent of the bombs scored direct hits. These were heavy bombs and hence played havoc with the Pakistani defences. The tide turned in favour of ground operations. Towards the end of these operations, the IAF knocked out the Pakistani Army Advance Logistic Base in the area killing ten officers and 100 men. This had a major impact on the outcome of the Kargil operations.

The Kargil Review Committee (KRC) that was tasked to study the Kargil operations and forward their assessment and action plan for the future commented on National Security Management and Apex Decision Making. According to the report, the entire gamut of national security management, apex decision making and structure as also the interface between the Ministry of Defence (MoD) and the Armed Forces Headquarters was to be comprehensively studied and reorganised. They recommended more constructive and much closer interaction between the civil government and the three services. Many military observers feel that the KRC did not recommend the institution of CDS.

The KRC made it amply clear that 15 Corps as also the entire nation was completely taken by surprise. The committee also felt that no actionable intelligence was available with the commanders and everyone in the chain firmly believed that such a large-scale operation by Pakistan was not feasible in that terrain. The committee also admits that some inputs of large scale movement of artillery guns and logistics elements in the region were available as early as 1998. There were also reports of intensified shelling by Pakistan.

The 121 Infantry Brigade that was deployed in the region submitted a paper of heightened threat perception in the area. If all the resources required for the defence of the Kargil heights were available with one commander, then perhaps he would have ordered aerial reconnaissance of the area by MiG 25 as also by ARC of R&AW. The intrusions would have been detected much in advance, maybe in late 1998 or early 1999. The Mirage 2000s that launched the laser guided bombs would have been used right in the beginning without having to wait for the Pakistani build up with anti-air resources. It is also possible that the cabinet committee on security or duly empowered National Security Agency (NSA) had made up contingency plans to strike at Pakistan on the ground at a time of their own choosing to ensure that the intruders would be forced to pull back with minimum damage to their own forces. It is also possible that if Indian military and diplomatic responses to such transgression was clearly known to Pakistan they would not have taken such an enormous risk.

Total Casualties: 1,642 (Martyred: 481, Wounded: 1,159, Missing: 2)

Deductions from National Experience

We go back to the main question of appraisal of Indian Armed Forces in the context of jointness. There is no doubt that the Indian military did achieve astounding victories in the face of crippling deficiencies and against strong headwinds from other quarters. Then what is the need for an appraisal or change? To get to the right perspective, we will look at a very important but generally overlooked event in the famous battle of Dograi (1965). The incident is taken from the book, *The Battle of Dograi* authored by none other than the Commanding Officer (CO) of 3 Jat who led the battalion in this battle, Lt Col (later Brigadier) Desmond E Hayde, MVC.

On the fateful night of 6 September 1965, 3 Jat did the impossible. They crossed the Ichhogil canal over a damaged and burning bridge and entered Batapore, West of the canal. Two of the four companies were on the West of the canal and the remaining two were on the home side. The CO himself was across the canal and in Batapore. In doing this, the unit lost one officer, one Junior Commissioned Officer and 23 soldiers, with 78 wounded (3 officers, 3 JCOs and 72 other ranks). The victory was so astounding that even the Indian commanders could not believe this since most of the other units (of 15 Infantry Division) were still floundering. But then the biggest blunder of the war was committed in asking the unit to fall back from the lodgement. It was in this confusion that men with gaping wounds, collecting their dead comrades started to fall back. Most of these were withdrawing under orders of their CO, but there were a few who did not care to wait for orders and abandoned their positions on their own.

When the war ended, 3 Jat was the most decorated battalion in the entire army in 1965 (three MVCs, four VCs, seven Sena Medals, twelve mention in despatches and eleven commendation cards). The unit accounted for 900 enemy soldiers killed. The ratio between Pakistanis to the Jats in fatal casualties was 8:1. On the flip side, 3 Jat was also the battalion that saw maximum number of dismissals from service after the war—all those who abandoned their positions without orders were dismissed by Hayde. Why? This is Hayde's answer:

> A soldier of whatever rank when in a position of responsibility must know that dismissal or worse will be the cost of failure unwitting or otherwise because to perform his duty correctly in war is the sole reason for his being.
>
> Brig Desmond Hayde, MVC—Commanding Officer, 3 JAT in *Battle of Dograi*

We look at the performance matrix for theatre command derived from experience in WWII and extend the measurement scale enunciated by the victor of Dograi to all those involved in national security. The reader will agree that Brig Hayde's parameters of normal duties would be something like six sigma standard—less than four errors in a million. It is under this lens that we will revisit the brief details of our performance in all the wars discussed above. The unflattering inferences would be:

- Political leadership: Started with some of the most notorious blunders, took enormous time to reach a level where the top national leadership tuned to the right wavelength in proactive offensive defence of the nation.
- Military commanders did mature by 1971 in translating national objectives to military strategies but with two caveats. First, in 1971, it was the Eastern Command that performed to achieve an outstanding victory. In the West, the same errors were repeated and it was business as usual. By 1999, everything learnt in 1971 was forgotten!
- The force itself is courageous, committed and performs well under good junior leaders. Except in very limited cases the senior leadership has not been able to make any worthwhile impact on the men in battle. Sagat Singh, Harbakhsh Singh, Thimayya, Usman

Ali and a few more have been the exceptions. Overall, there have been major improvements after 1965. In 1967, 1971 and even in 1999 the tactical leadership and performance of troops on ground was extraordinary.

- Till as late as 2017, the technostructure has been less than average. As of now there are major improvements in the context of two front wars. The technostructure for the forces is in the process of being developed especially to cater for large-scale joint operations. As of now, it is a long way off. However, given the speed with which infrastructure projects are being implemented in India for the last few years, there is hope. But it is work in progress albeit with due alacrity. Another factor that somewhat weakens the 'inadequacy of resources or financial support' argument is that the performance of Indian forces was never affected by inadequacy of resources. On the other hand, the military was found wanting in using its resources to their full potential. Even the intra-service resources were not utilised fully. India has yet to employ its armoured or mechanised formation in war though there were ample opportunities to do so. Employment of the IAF was abysmally below its full strength. The Indian Navy was used to its full potential thanks to the initiative taken by Admiral Nanda.
- As regards staff we are still in the WWII era. Indian Armed Forces, especially the ground forces, are accustomed to large contingents of Staff Officers. Deficiencies of manpower in the units is common but not in the staff. The staff so far has not been developed to assist commanders in joint operations.

How can we learn from the past and use those lessons for building the future of our armed forces? The next chapters will attempt to answer this question.

★★★

Theatre Commands

The Chinese and the US Examples

Chinese military reforms are relevant for us because they are our adversaries. The US reforms become relevant because most of our think tanks and military scholars are deeply influenced by what the US Department of Defence does.

IT MAY BE appropriate to examine the relevant details of theatre commands formulated by nations that affect us the most. These include China and the US. China affects us directly. The US happens to be the trend setter in all 'new' concepts in military thinking. However, it would be prudent to guard against the urge to copy somebody else's concepts and systems without objective analysis. What may be good for the Chinese and the Americans may not be appropriate for India. It is with this caution that we may look at the reforms, organisational structure and operational dynamics of their current theatre commands.

There are five questions that we need to address while analysing their military reforms. First, what was the need or the vision that drives these reforms? Second, what role are their militaries expected to undertake as per their respective national ethos or ideologies? What external threats are they facing or imagining? What are the implications for India? The last question is especially relevant for China.

China's Theatre Commands

The Chinese national belief and self-view emanates from the philosophy of the middle kingdom where the Chinese emperor has a divine sanction from the heavens to rule Planet Earth. As per this doctrine, only the Chinese are cultured and refined. Those outside China are referred to as barbarians. Other countries of the world are either tributaries to the Chinese nation or vassals. There is no concept of dealing with other countries as equals. Post 1 October 1949, Mao added muscular militarism to the Chinese strategic approach. Expansionism comes naturally to the Chinese leadership. Any piece of land or sea where Chinese had ruled or had connections with any time in the past belongs to China and forms part of their one China policy.

This explains why the Chinese have running conflicts with almost all the countries with whom they share their borders. However, China has seen ups and downs. They have followed the policy of wait and watch many a time without giving up on their strategic goals.

When the Chinese Communist Party (CCP) took over on 1 October 1949 they broke free of whatever did not fall in line with the CCP philosophy and way of life. China considered India (especially the then Prime Minister) a stooge of the West (imperialist). Even when India was trying its best to 'prove' that they are not influenced by the imperialist West, the Chinese continued their propaganda to paint India as camp followers of the West, especially the US.

China regards threats in the light of its own self-view and core ideology. No nation with whom the Chinese claim to have border disputes has attacked them militarily. However, the Chinese have waged military campaigns against India and Vietnam. They fought a small battle with the Russians in 1969 and in 1954, they fought the US forces across the Yalu River in Korea. After the US, China appears to be the next most threatened nation going by the way their defence expenditure has been constantly on the rise.

The relevance of Chinese military for their political leadership is most critical. In fact, the PLA has an existential relationship with the CCP. The PLA exists to protect and propagate the influence of CCP within and beyond the Chinese borders. Hence, it may not be a national force. PLA is CCP's armed wing. It is based on this belief that Mao had made that famous statement way back in 1949 'power flows from the barrel of the gun'.

Economically, China is at the top in terms of purchasing power parity and the second largest economy in nominal terms. The CCP is known for using its economic muscle to pursue its expansionist agenda. In the context of theatre commands, China possesses huge assets to develop technologies and war assets to fuel its military might. Besides building up its military hardware, China spends on Research and Development for military systems. China is net exporter of arms (USD 759 million in 2020 compared to India's USD 151 million arms export in the same year). To that extent, Chinese military has some 'economic endurance' in war.

Chinese military leadership especially at the top is untested after 1979. Even in the 1979 war against Vietnam, the top military leadership did not display any brilliance. In the 1962 war against India, the PLA was primarily a peasant army directed and controlled by the top levels of the CCP and a few veterans of the Korean campaign who fought just eight years before. In recent times, the WTC top commanders have changed several times.

The Chinese join their military voluntarily, though a law for conscription exists but has never been enforced since enough volunteers are available. The quality of Chinese military intervention in modern wars is less than average. Since the bulk of the Chinese military consists of ground forces deployed in military regions charged with the responsibility of managing the local population (so that they remain loyal to the CCP), the military system has revealed the existence of fiefdoms. There were reports of large scale corruption by military leaders in the Military Regions (MRs). Creating theatre commands out of these MRs was necessary to arrest this trend. However, the theatre commanders now have larger areas to administer and protect over and above the administration roles that the MRs were doing earlier. This is unique to China and dilutes the fighting abilities of soldiers especially in a modern war. Incidents in Nathu La (1967), Galwan (2020) and Yangtze (2023) did reveal the lack of fighting capability and battle discipline of the Chinese soldiers.

China has been spending close to half (41 per cent) of what all the Asian countries put together spend on their respective militaries. China has traversed an enormous distance from the time of people's (or peasants) army. It is ranked third in global rankings of military powers after the US and the Russians as per global fire power. It has the world's biggest missile force with 39 Missile Services Brigades. It has made massive strides in cyber, space and electronics warfare coupled with computer attack systems. All these multifaceted modern military systems cannot be commanded through the rustic PLA organisation structure. In China's own words, 'Theatre commands are required to fight high intensity joint military operations on the lines of Unified Theatre Command Headquarters of the US'. Besides, the Chinese leadership has realised that in modern warfare, the predominance of ground forces (PLA) needs to be replaced by tri-service cooperation that includes the air power, maritime power and more importantly space, cyber and electronic warfare, elements. The last three form a part of its Strategic Support Force (SSF). Thus, theatre commands are allotted elements of the Missiles Services Force, SSF, Navy, and air elements as per the role and threat-driven requirements.

The theatre commanders in the new arrangements are responsible for undertaking operations in non-military as also military parts of the conflict spectrum. In the case of China, the organisation is characterised by extreme centralisation and well defined hierarchies. In the current situation, the Chairman of the CCP (Xi Jinping) is the commander of the Chinese military, the party and president of the state. It is likely that the police as also the reserve forces will be placed under him. Though the Central Military Commission (CMC) that controls the Chinese military power has 15 specific departments that have control over different components, the overall decision-making power rests with the president. Even the Vice Chairman's post that could have given some semblance of collective leadership, has been abolished (quite unceremoniously).

As regards the external threats to China, most of these are imaginary or at best can be termed more appropriately, military ambitions. In specific terms, China has earmarked one theatre command for India (Western Theatre Command—WTC), two theatre commands for Russia and one Theatre Command is for Vietnam. The fifth theatre command is at Beijing perhaps as a reserve. Thus seven military regions have been reduced to five theatre commands. Against India the military regions of Chengdu and Guangzhou have been merged into one WTC that happens to be the biggest theatre command in China.

The question is: what are the implications/relevance for India? The first and foremost impact of WTC on India would be in terms of focus and continuity. Earlier, the MR with its HQ at Chengdu was responsible for this region. That too the peace time and active hostility phases were separated. While the peace time conflict was addressed by one commander, the war time commander of the MR (at Chengdu) was to be appointed later. Now there is one theatre commander with both the MRs under his command who is responsible for the entire conflict spectrum.

This is most suitable in modern conflicts where the boundaries between peace and war are extremely blurred. Thus, the entire focus of WTC will be on India and it will be in continuity. This is reflected in the exponential increase of hostilities in the form of pushing and unarmed combats along the Indo China Line of Actual Control which functions as the border for the two countries. From an average of 300 transgressions per year, the incidents have increased to 416 ingresses during the Doklam period (2017). In 2020, 2022 and 2023 there were major (unarmed) clashes between the two armies across the Ladakh and Arunachal borders. Besides the border scuffles that are being reported by the media, the WTC is constantly conducting cyber intrusions, electronic mapping and surveillance. The troops are likely to be practising different contingencies as is normal in military organisations that are preparing for a war.

In addition to the preparations of PLA, there are joint patrols and perhaps exercises with the Pakistani forces in the Shaksgam valley and Kunjerab pass area in Pakistan occupied Kashmir that has been ceded to China by Pakistan. The WTC troops are present in this region. There are three takeaways from this. First, we need to have force structure and deployment against China that is capable of focusing on a continuous conflict from non-military to military as also from non-kinetic to kinetic (kinetic and non-kinetic are new terms for old concepts that would mean indirect application of force/leverage direct military application). Second, the Chinese threat can only be addressed by a Theatre Command. No amount of grouping, regrouping will help. There must be unity of command, clear political mandate and military goals. The ideal way to neutralise the Chinese threat is from a position of strength. The revised PLA structure is given below:

Revised PLA Structure After Implementation of Defence Reforms

It is very difficult to visualise how these reforms are likely to be operationalised. In 1962, even unit level movements and tactics were controlled by the Chairman C C P. Given the current centralisation of power with Chairman Xi, the WTC is likely to be directly controlled by him. This has its own limitations. It will be akin to Adolf Hitler controlling the German Armed Forces in WWII.

US Theatre Command

The US evolved into the present form in the third wave of its historical journey. The first wave comprised of the original inhabitants of the huge land mass that the world recognises as the US. The second wave was completely dominated by the European settlers (predominantly from Great Britain). It is this wave that commenced systematic destruction of the original inhabitants. The third wave surged on 4 July 1776 when the British dominance was done away with. There are marked discontinuities in these three periods. There are no noticeable traces of the original inhabitants in the way the nation functions today. After showing the door to the British, the Americans evolved their own systems, ethos and world view without carrying any baggage of British rule.

No American citizen tried to be more British than the British and there was no question of aping their former rulers. The US

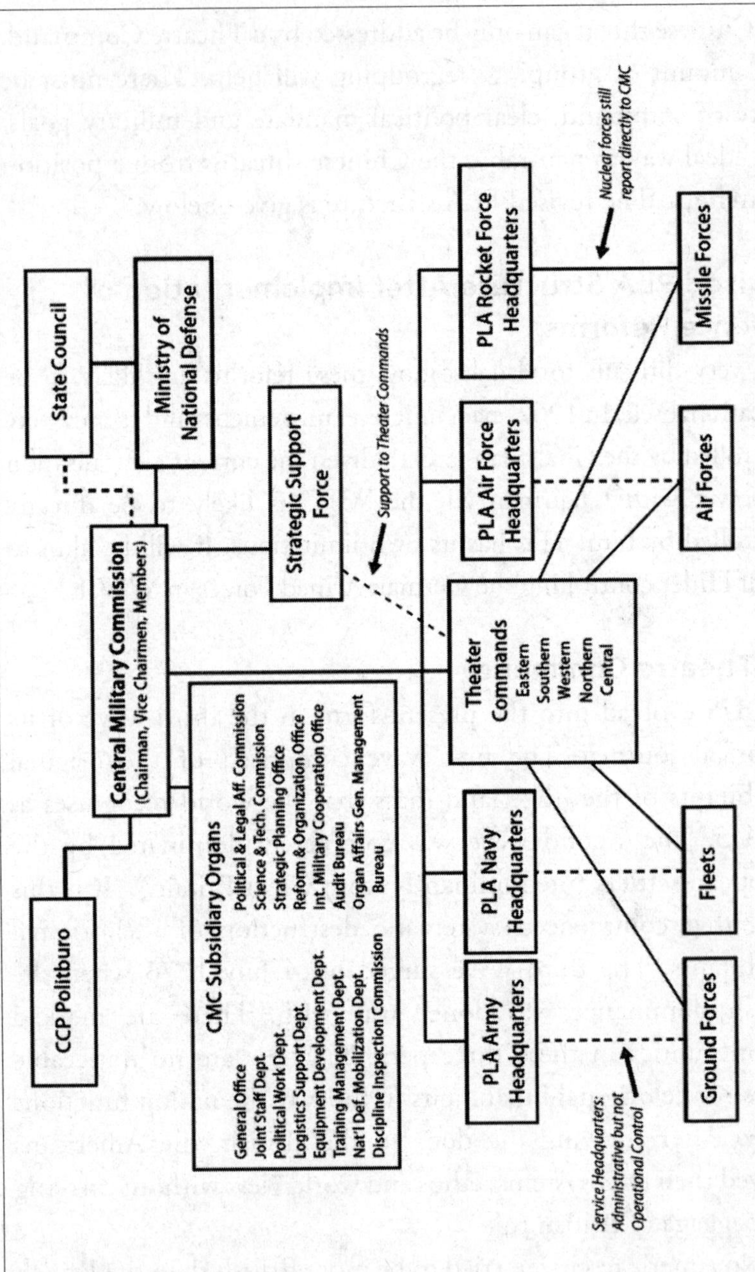

Source: Defence Reforms A National Perspective: IDSA

charted its own course to emerge as the only super power. It is also a self-appointed global policeman to safeguard democracy and free trade on the planet according to American interests. Their former rulers, the British, are satisfied to be committed camp followers of the Americans in most of the US global interventions. The defining feature of the apex political leadership in the US is absolute clarity in what they perceive as national interests, and they pursue their national interests in whatever way they consider is combined with the best strategic approach. There is remarkable continuity in pursuing their set goals.

Change of governments at the apex level does not change the goal nor does it dilute the effort. It has an unmatched capability to veer the international opinion in their favour. Their dictum has been that America is the best. What the US does or desires the world must follow or comply with.

Threats to the US are perceived by the establishment to suit their action plan, and determines the deployment and even use of military force with no provocation. The Americans have been deploying forces outside continental US to neutralise even the internal threats to their homeland.

Though they do not say 'power flows from the barrel of the gun' they exhibit this belief by their actions. The US military has been active across the globe after WWII. They have lost more than one hundred thousand soldiers post WWII in various wars—Vietnam, Korea, War on terror.

The US economic growth and strength have been phenomenal since the last global conflict. They have been at the top of global rankings among the comity of nations for decades, though all the ranking agencies and institutions are either funded or influenced by the Americans. Some of the lesser known facts of the US economic strength are their military exports USD 9.26 billion in

2020). They control the global currency. A very large percentage of global trade happens in US dollars. To achieve this, the US very carefully and meticulously executed their plans post WWII under the garb of rebuilding the global economy.

The international reserves of foreign currency is in US dollars controlled by banks under the tight leash of the US. In essence, the US controls the global economy by a mix of their productivity, technological edge and partly through carefully crafted politico-military policies. The US tops military spending in global terms (USD 2.1 trillion in 2023). The next ten nations on this list put together fall short of this mark. A very large part of this expenditure is recovered through military exports and international currency control.

In terms of military leadership, the US performance is impressive if it is viewed through the US media or media influenced by the US. The truth emerges after the dust has settled down on the event. Thus it was much after the First Iraq War of 1991 that the world came to know that the US had dropped a very large number of dumb bombs on hospitals and residential areas in Iraq. But by that time, most of the world had moved on and accepted the US-sponsored vision that precision bombing only destroyed Iraqi military targets. The US HQ are known for its huge staff. A substantial number of this staff is composed of war correspondents who tell the 'US' story from the warfront. Eisenhower had 3,000 war correspondents in WWII to tell the stories of Patton, MacArthur and other US military commanders. The more serious military historians (US origin) found the American generals depending more on preponderance of fire power enabled by modern weapon systems and failed to perform against a tough and determined adversary such as the Vietnamese, the Chinese forces across the Yalu River in the Korean campaign and Taliban forces in Afghanistan. Afghanistan 2021 exposed the American military leadership just as Vietnam did.

The bulk of American soldiers are from comparatively less affluent segments of their population and hence are hardy, battle tested and disciplined so long as the war goes as per plan. However, under adverse conditions, their staying power is limited. During WWII the Americans never faced the onslaught of the Germans from 1939 to mid 1942 when the German Armed Forces were rampaging through Europe with their blitzkriegs. The bulk of the fighting by the Americans was against the Japanese, which involved naval warfare and bombing of mainland Japan by US Army Air Force. The US troops are not known for doing more with less.

'The department of defence provides the military forces needed to deter war and ensure our nation's security'. US theatre commands by definition cover areas outside the continental US. They have a total of nine theatre commands. Five of these are based on geographical regions. The US African Command is to strengthen defence capabilities of African nations. The Central Command is responsible for cooperation among the nations in the Middle East to increase regional stability. The European Command works in tandem with the NATO nations for security and defence of Europe, some nations of the Middle East and Eurasia.

The Indo Pacific Command enhances development and regional security in conjunction with partner nations. The Northern Command is the only US Theatre Command that is responsible for security of the US, primarily homeland security. The Southern Command is responsible for South American nations. Besides these geographical commands, the US has cyber, space, transport, strategic and Special Operations Commands that are in real sense designed and based on specific functions and

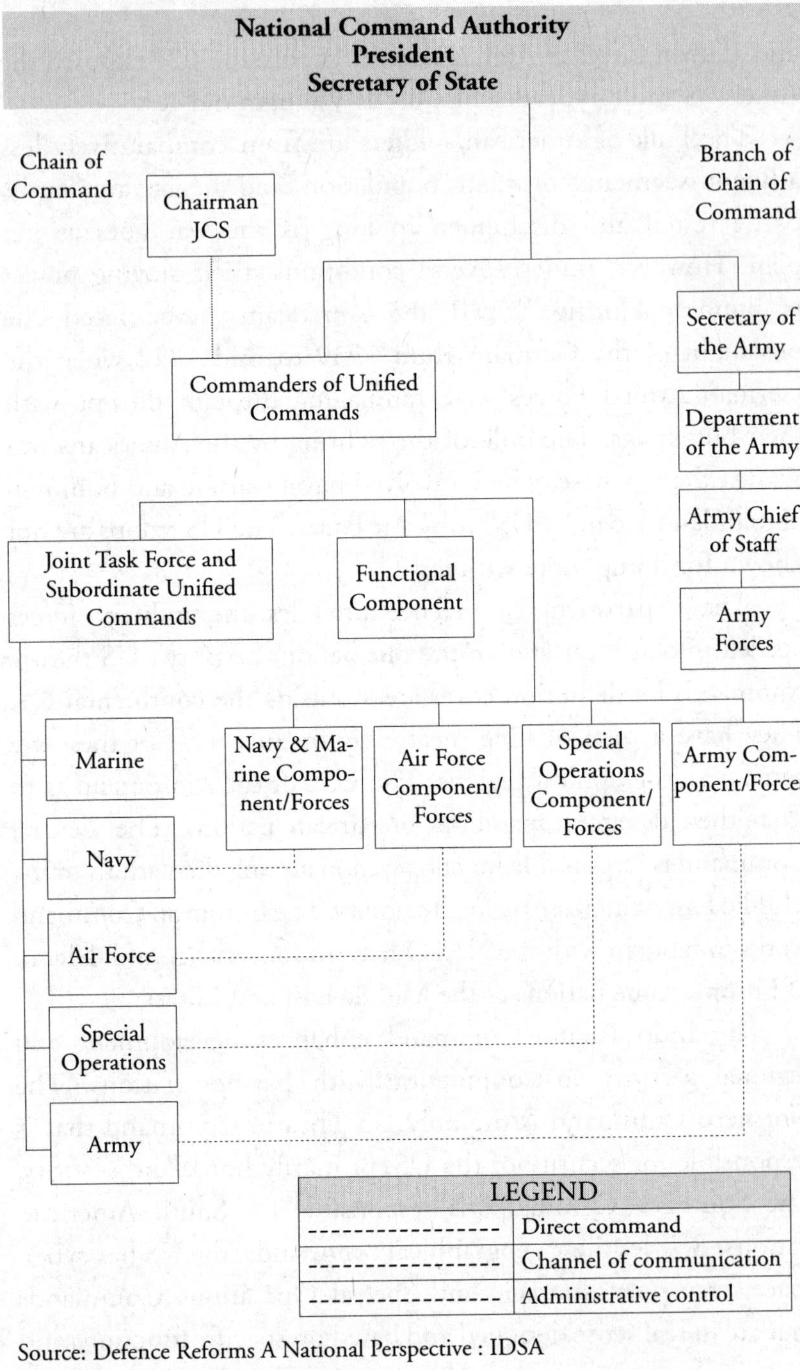

Source: Defence Reforms A National Perspective : IDSA

parts of these can be allotted for specific regions or tasks. With this in the backdrop, the US theatre commands are designed under the self-assumed role of global ombudsman. They undertake the role of global policing, ensuring a world order and international behaviour in line with American interests.

In operationalising the Goldwater Nichols Reorganisation (of Department of Defence - DOD) Act of 1986, the US DOD has formulated detailed policies, rules and processes. The relevant documents are in the public domain (the US lets the world know). While it is relevant for us to study the organisational structure, hierarchies, communication channels, modus operandi of the US theatre commands, prudence demands that we are constantly aware of the underlying vision of their national security and their strategic intent in employing military power. We also need to remember that the US heads the NATO. Their sense of European and global security does impact the NATO as also other countries (that are not in direct confrontation with the US). This at times creates friction within their alliances and may lead to a conflict situation for a nation that has not actually threatened US security. The broad defining features of their reorganisation are as under:

- **Global presence:** Except for their Northern Theatre Command all their geographical and maritime commands have Areas of Responsibility (AOR) outside continental US.
- **Multinationalism as Part of Organisational Culture and Structure:** The Commanders-in-Chiefs (C-in-C) and even the combatant commanders are expected to coordinate with military and non-military professionals/leaders of other nations.
- **Firm Political Control:** The Unified Theatre Commanders and the Combatant Commanders get their military goals/objectives from the National Controlling Authority (NCA)—the President of the US, through secretary defence or respective secretaries

placed with the military departments. These instructions may also be conveyed through the Joint Chiefs of Staff (JCS). Even the regional allocation of forces, force structuring in the theatre or combat zone is approved by relevant secretaries/JCS. They can also organise a Joint Task Force (JTF) for specific tasks.

- **Inherent Flexibility:** Force structuring, region for operations, for the Unified Theatre Command (UTC), combatant commands, JTF are dynamic in nature and can be changed as per the requirement/situation.
- **Well Defined Span of Control:** Commanders at each level have well defined authority, accountability and resources. The C-in-C of a UTC develops national security and military strategies, organises forces for combatant commands under him, allocates operational objectives for respective combatant commands and caters for logistics support and special allocations of central resources (signal intelligence, cyber force, engineer resources and special forces) as per the envisaged requirements. The combatant commanders have similar authorities over their resources within the overall plan of operations.
- **Maintaining Organic Command and Control Integrity of Individual Service:** When specific resources are allotted to a theatre or combatant commander—say from the US Air Force (USAF) or the US Navy etc.—the theatre or the combatant commander allocates specific tasks to these supporting elements. The actual execution or operationalisation of these tasks are done by the respective service commanders. Thus, an air force commander will actually operationalise the task allotted to his force in the theatre.
- **Modularity of Logistics and Supporting Force Allocation:** Bulk of the logistics and combat support for the US theatre commands originates from continental US. It is provided on modular basis for pre-assigned scales. Even the force allocation is modular in nature derived from a set of tasks that are pre-determined or war-gamed.

An insight into how the US Forces intend to fight in the context of joint operations (or integrated battles) is given in the *Airland Battle 2000*. Work on the concept of airland battle commenced in the wake of humiliating defeat in the Vietnam war. Initially the US DoD thought of a war of attrition against the USSR during the initial Soviet mass onslaught. This was not liked by their NATO allies especially Germany since conceding ground to initial Soviet onslaught meant loss of territory in Germany. Then came the concept of airland battle formalised in 1982 and operationalised with the entire range of systems for implementation in 2000. The idea of airland battle was initiated by Dr James Schlesinger Secretary of Defense (acting independently). Even the American President at that time was not willing to undertake defence expenditure for operationalising the doctrine of airland battle.

The American law makers as also most of the top ranking generals were averse to large scale offensive operations (envisaged by the doctrine). However, Schlesinger won the political war within. Thereafter, General Donn Starry of the US forces studied the battle at Golan Heights fought between Syrian and Israeli forces. By 1982, the concepts were formalised. It took another 18 years to get the systems and structure in place to launch it. The salient issues in our context are the level at which the operations are fought and the critical takeaways. The airland battle as per the US doctrine (FM 100-5) is fought at the corps level. It is here that the information (national and tactical levels) is integrated. The operational efforts are diverted to only those areas that provide the shortest route to the goal. For the US Air Force (placed under the command of the Corps Commander) it is more of a support role for land operations. In fact, Donn Starry's maximum effort and energy was spent in convincing the

US Air Force commanders to agree to this tenet. For the Army, the reserves were to be maintained at the corps level sacrificing divisional autonomy. Manoeuvre, synchronisation and fire power must all be integrated.

Which model should India follow? As per the Manohar Parrikar Institute of Strategic Analyses (MP-IDSA) India's theatre commands must follow the US model. Two reasons are forwarded in the book for this option. First, both India and the US are democracies. Second, the US has gone through similar debates on these reforms which India is undertaking, though 27 years after the US.

However, there are inherent drawbacks to following the US model (or that of any other country democratic or not). In case of India and the US, the similarities end at 'both countries being democracies'. They are democracies of very different types.

The current organisational structures of the Chinese and the American theatre commands are yet to be tested fully in an equal war. Hence it is difficult to comment on their efficiency or impact in situations for which these are organised. As opposed to this, the Israeli Defence Forces (IDF) operationalised the concepts of jointness in all the wars they fought with their much bigger adversaries. It may be interesting to analyse jointness in the IDF.

★★★

Jointness in Israeli Defence Forces

A Case Study for Creating UTP

IDF first published their doctrine in 2015. After putting all their strategies into practice in the wars they fought, the Israelis are speaking from experience—they're talking about things they've already done, not just making future predictions.

IN ANY MILITARY doctrine, it is almost impossible to find reference to IDF in the context of theatre commands, jointness, integration of services or synergy in operations. In the case of Indian think tanks and military professionals, the famous Goldwater Nichols DOD Reorganization Act of 1986 billion provides the benchmark.

Surprisingly, the Israelis themselves do not use much of these phrases and doctrines pertaining to jointness. Perhaps they do not have to. Jointness, synergy, integration come very naturally to them hence there is no need to talk about such obvious concepts in war.

The famous American military historian Brigadier General SLA Marshall writing in the book, *Israel's Hundred Hour Conquest of Egypt East of Suez...* describes the IDF as 'consistency in all forces, extraordinary boldness in planning at all levels, sustained momentum of offensive power and extreme rigour among ranks when under fire'. According to him the Israeli generals are incapable of double talk; they have tidy, organised minds and mistrust generalities. Marshall found the Israeli forces completely 'unprofessional' by Western standards 'no outward form of discipline, no concern for smartness and dressing sense, not particular about saluting and calling every one including the top ranking officers by first names and more often by nicknames. With this as the backdrop it may be interesting to analyse the way Israel as a nation fights a war. We will use the framework deduced earlier consisting of political leadership, top military leadership, the force including operational commanders, technostructure and the staff.

The War of Independence: 1948-49

Towards the end of WWII, it was becoming clear that the British occupation of Palestine would come to an end and the Jews persecuted and expelled from Germany and other places would be settled in Palestine and around Jerusalem. It was also clear that the Muslim nations around this new Jewish settlement would oppose this move tooth and nail.

The war between the Arabs and the Israeli Forces erupted in January 1948. In May 1948, Britain prepared to withdraw its forces from this area. For the next 13 months till the armistice on 24 February 1949, the Arab Legion and other Arab forces greatly superior in numbers, with regional advantage and better equipped than the hurriedly raised Israeli civilian army tried their best to annihilate the Jewish settlements and the newly raised IDF (28 May 1948). However, this unequal war ended in favour of the new nation. Israel was born to live and prosper. It may be educative to look at the prominent learnings from this war that are essential for joint operations.

First the political leadership: David Ben-Gurion, the

unquestioned leader of the new state had envisaged the possibility of a full-scale war when the British decided to leave. Israel had opted to fight in WWII alongside the Allies. This gave them two brigade-sized forces that later formed the core of the IDF. He also decided and worked for complete unity of efforts.

Hence, when the Irgun and the Lehi militias decided to fight their own battles for Israel against the Arabs, Ben-Gurion quickly disarmed them. He had to launch military operations against these fellow Jews who wanted to form their own militia. Thus, after 28 May 1948, it was just the IDF and no one else conducting military operations against the common foes—'The Arab Legion', Keku's Forces and some other loose Arab groups against the state of Israel. Third, Ben-Gurion realised right from the beginning that given the disadvantage in numbers (Arabs vs Jewish people in the region) the IDF had to be a civilian army with very few regulars and very large reserve forces. Hence, during the war of independence every able-bodied man and woman fought for the state.

As regards the top military commanders who translated Ben-Gurion's vision into military strategy and allocated forces for various sectors during the year-long war, Israel was fortunate to have some of the most outstanding leaders of men and women. Yitzhak Rabin, Haim Bar-Lev, Moshe Dayan, Yigal Allon and many more were the top military leaders during this war who later rose to be the prime ministers, defence ministers, chiefs of staff. This legacy continued and helped Israel to wade through the uneasy truce that prevailed after this war ended.

The Force and operational commanders: Battalion, company and platoon commanders in case of Israel were outstanding. Military leaders at these levels followed a very simple tactical approach. First, they acquainted themselves with the combat factors—terrain, enemy, own capabilities and plan of action. Having done so, they entered combat with a completely open mind since battles never go as per plan. These leaders were completely at ease in changing the plan as per the combat situation. Second, when their operations were stalled for some reason they never waited to be informed by the forward echelons. Instead, they reached the trouble spot themselves and took corrective actions.

Thirdly, they took extreme risks when the situation so demanded. Thus, the Israeli armoured troop leader never withdrew because the opposition was very heavy or his own infantry had not arrived in time. They always led the attack. The total Israeli Force comprised of two regular brigades, some four to five brigades raised from the citizens, an air force platoon with eleven aircrafts, a very nascent navy with half a dozen combat vessels, but all these together, gave their all during this war.

About one per cent of the Israeli population in 1948 made the supreme sacrifice to create the new nation. The Israeli Armour with WWII vintage tanks and the Israeli Air Force (IAF) made the maximum impact. The armour attacked fortified defences with great courage and impact. Many times the armour units suffered setbacks because of poor infantry-tank cooperation. However, the Israeli armour never waited for the infantry to fetch up. It was the infantry that learnt to keep pace with their armoured units in later wars (1956, 1967). The IAF never fought their own wars. It was always in support of the ground forces. In essence the armour, infantry, air and the naval forces along with the civilian population fought in unison. The road to connect Tel Aviv and Israeli positions in Jerusalem (called the Burma Road) was constructed by the civilian earth movers under hostile fire.

The Israeli commanders had minimal to no staff to assist them in this war.

The 100-Hours War

The setting for this war was also in the form of 'do or die' for Israel except that this time there were two other players who promised Israel to help, though in the final conduct Israel did it alone without waiting or asking for any help.

Smarting under the humiliating defeat in the 1948-49 war, the Arab nations were preparing to destroy Israel through economic stranglehold, Fedayeen attacks and large-scale military offensives from Jordan, Syria and Egypt. The Suez Canal was blocked for Israel (contrary to the 1948-49 armistice agreements). The opening to the sea from other routes was blocked by deploying coastal artillery. Fedayeen attacks increased in number. Four to one superiority in armour, infantry and artillery, air power was achieved against Israel.

David Ben-Gurion, the Israeli PM acted against these odds. On 29 October 1956, Israel commenced the 100-hours war by dropping a Parachute Battalion 156 kms deep in the Sinai Desert at Mitla Pass (just 45 kms from Suez Canal). On the subsequent day supplies, anti-tank guns and some artillery were dropped for this battalion. Then the linkup force of the remainder of the Parachute Brigade under Ariel Sharon commenced ground operations clearing Egyptian defences enroute. Once the linkup was established, the Israeli Forces had cut off Southern Sinai from the tactically important Northern part. By 5 November 1956, Israel was in full control of the Sinai desert (200x500 kms of desert). The Suez Canal was now with them.

The entire force level Israel used for this operations comprised of eight brigades and only three of these brigades were regular. The IAF was in unison with the paratroopers for the remainder of the ground operation. As per Chaim Herzog, the Israeli aircraft flew as low as 12-feet to cut down the overhead communication wires of the Egyptian command and control with the wings and propellors of their combat aircraft.

On the jointness matrix discussed earlier, the political leadership, the top military commanders, the operational commanders and the troops in combat acted with complete synergy and consistency to achieve this unimaginable feat. The movement was conducted in hired buses, armoured troop carrying vehicles, AMX tanks and so on. The Egyptians were completely surprised and bewildered by this offensive.

Six-Day War: 6-11 June 1967

This war tested the entire security matrix of Israel in one of the most difficult positions the new nation found itself. To avenge the 1956 defeat, Syria, Jordan, Lebanon and Palestine (Palestine Liberation Organization-PLO) were preparing to attack Israel. The French who were with Israel in 1956 withdrew their support—since the war in Algeria was over and the French had no commonality of interest with Israel. The British and the US were neutral since the Suez Canal was open to commercial shipping. The Russians were deeply involved in arming the Egyptian and Syrian Armed Forces. Thus, when the Arab forces encircled Israel with some 250,000 troops, 2,000 tanks and some 700 combat aircraft, the Jewish state was internationally isolated.

President Nasser of Egypt went back on the 1956 treaty with impunity. He closed the Suez canal for Israeli vessels, and blocked the Gulf of Tiran (Israel's opening into the Red Sea). On his behest, work started for diverting water from River Jordan (border of Syria and Lebanon). All this was meant to strangulate Israel and deprive them of water required for irrigation as the River Jordan flows from Syria to the northern plain of Israel. The political leadership tried their best to persuade international institutions to intervene. No one was interested. Premier Eshkol of Israel also knew for sure that Nasser's aim was to destroy Israel. Given the political and geopolitical odds and the huge disparity in military strength the Israeli top brass needed nerves of steel to decide on a pre-emptive offensive.

First, they blasted off the workforce that was working on River Jordan. Within days of intense Israeli air attacks the diversion work stopped permanently. Thereafter, came the most difficult task of striking at the Egyptian forces concentrated in Sinai for imminent attack on Israel.

Translating the National Goal into Military Strategy

This is where the military top brass pitched in. The Chief of Staff Lt Gen Yitzhak Rabin with his top commanders namely, Major General Yeshayahu Gavish, Major General Abraham Yoffe, 'Talik' Isarael Tal and Major General Ariel Sharon had to launch an offensive using three divisional groups on the Egyptian forces of five infantry divisions, two armoured divisions, hundreds of artillery pieces and around 340 serviceable Combat and Transport aircrafts. The Israeli offensive commenced with the biggest air operation after WWII. The Israeli Air Force in the course of a day (6 June 1967 from dawn to dusk) destroyed 309 of the 340 Egyptian aircrafts. In the evening of 6 June 1967 the ground attack commenced on two axes with two divisions (Northern and Central Axes). As these attacks were making headway, the third division was launched on 7 June 1967. Within nine hours, the third division covered 35 miles (56 kms) to isolate the Egyptian divisions from the West (of Suez) and the South and deprived them of mutual support as the third Israeli division was in between the Egyptian divisions to the North and South. The IAF was in complete control of the skies and devastated the

Egyptian armour. By 9 June 1967, the Egyptians were completely demoralised and were in full flight. The Israelis commenced moving some forces towards the Syrian border (Golan Heights) on 9 June.

On 10 June 1967, the offensive on the Golan Heights commenced. This was an offensive against well prepared defences comprising of three infantry divisional groups and two armoured brigades. The Israelis could muster three armoured brigades and five infantry brigades for these operations. It took two days to decimate the Syrian defences. By 11 June 1967 the Golan Heights including Mount Hermon was under Israeli occupation. The war ended on 11 June 1967.

Operational Commanders and the Force

Troops in combat displayed rare courage and fighting spirit. On a pitch dark night one of the Israeli armoured companies (comprising of 14 odd tanks) got mixed up with an Egyptian Armoured Battalion during the Sinai operation. The entire tank column was moving along a road towards Suez. The Egyptians were withdrawing from their positions and the Israelis had lost their way. It was the Israeli Company Commander who realised that they were in a tank column consisting of 45-odd Egyptian tanks. He asked his company to continue moving as if they were moving with their own convoy. On a given signal, all the Israeli tanks were to turn right, move away from the road and after moving about 50 meters turn left, focus their searchlights and aim their guns towards the road and shoot down any tank or vehicle that was moving along the road.

Within minutes, a complete tank battalion of the Egyptian division was destroyed. At the Golan Heights the Israeli forces used bulldozers along with tanks for the attack. Most of the crew members of the bulldozers who were firing from their weapons were hit by the Syrian defenders. The attack persisted. The last two tanks that survived the initial attack were commanded by a lieutenant bleeding profusely from his wounds. It was this commitment, courage and innovative spirit that made the difference for the IDF. The IDF never learnt the 'art of set piece battle' from the British with whom they got the war experience while fighting the Germans in WWII. The Egyptians on the other hand, gave their entire commitment to set piece battles. Unfortunately for the Egyptians, the Israelis never gave them the chance to arrange a 'set piece battle'!

The Yom Kippur War: 6 October 1973

Israeli's political leadership was aware of what was happening in Egypt, Jordan and Syria. Chaim Herzog in his book mentions the information that the Israeli intelligence head was able to gather. There was hardly any information deficiency. The intelligence chief knew (and briefed all the operational heads and also the political leadership) about the acquisitions made by Egypt, Syria and Jordan. They knew that the three countries were preparing for war against Israel. They also knew the exact region in which the Egyptians would start the war. However, the intelligence head and the Israeli Minister of Defence General Dayan made one critical error. They thought that the Arabs are just faking and that, they would not be able to launch an offensive before 1975 when they were expected to obtain appropriate deep strike aircraft (MiG 23, Phantom, Jaguars). It is interesting to note that the operational head General Elazar (Chief of General Staff) was not convinced with the interpretation of the intelligence team. The political leadership listened to the intelligence chief and authorised only limited mobilisation to Elazar. Nevertheless, once the balloon went up the political, intelligence and the operational head came on board and retrieved a situation in a series of very timely and bold decisions. This period depicts the way the Israeli top establishment recovered from some serious mistakes.

Again, when the Egyptian offensive was stopped in the Sinai Desert, the timing of the counter offensive to the West of Suez was debated among the top military commanders and the political heads. There were some who wanted to launch a counter offensive immediately, while others (Bar-Lev) wanted to wait for the Egyptian armour formation to get committed East of the canal. The collective decision was to wait till Egypt launched the bulk of its armour East of the canal into Sinai. As soon as the Egyptian armour crossed and got embroiled with the Israeli forces, the counter offensive was launched. This paved the way for negotiations on an equal footing. What could be noticed during these two critical phases was the Israeli capability to take collective decisions, amend their mistakes during the conduct phase and come out with the best alternative. They committed mistakes, differed and then came around with the best decisions within hours with complete synergy between the political and military top brass. Incidentally, many of the former military top brass happened to be the political bosses in 1973 as has been the case with Israel during all the wars after 1949.

The military top leadership on the operational side was able to read the enemy intention better than the minister of defence and the intelligence fraternity. However, they never crossed the line and waited for proper authorisation. Once authorised, the top military leaders as usual went on the offensive right from the start. Even their defensive operations, were filled with extreme aggression. The army and air cooperation was at its best. Having neutralised the Egyptian Air Force on the first day of the operations, the IAF focussed on supporting the Israeli ground operations. It was because of the IAF support that the numerically disadvantaged Israeli forces could launch such a successful and swift operation.

The Structure of IDF in the Context of Joint Commands

Noor Dahri, founder and executive director of Islamic Theology of Counter Terrorism—a UK-based counter-terrorism think tank specialising in Islamist terror, published a book on the IDF in 2022. It will be interesting to note the level of jointness in the IDF organisational structure.

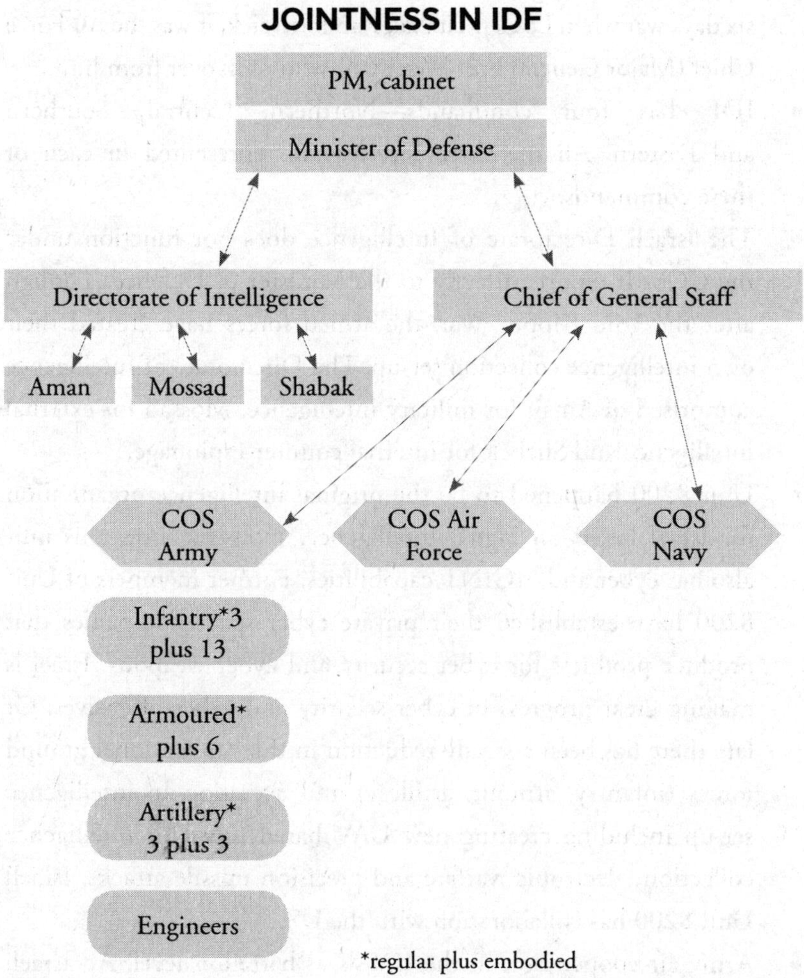

In the context of jointness, the IDF has some very unique features that allow this small nation to achieve big results:

- The three services, the army, the navy and the air force report to a single military commander, the Chief of General Staff (CGS) of the rank of Lt General. Incidentally the IDF has similar rank structures in the three services. The Chief of Air Force is a Major General so is the case with chiefs of army and navy.
- The CGS can be from the army, the air force or the navy. During the six days war when Lt Gen Yitzhak Rabin fell sick, it was the Air Force Chief (Major General Ezer Weizman) who took over from him.
- IDF has four commands—Northern, Central, Southern and Eastern. All the three services are represented in each of these commands.
- The Israeli Directorate of Intelligence does not function under the CGS. It reports directly to the Minister of Defence. Though after the Yom Kippur War, the armed forces have created their own intelligence collection set-up. The Directorate of Intelligence comprised of Aman for military intelligence, Mossad for external intelligence and Shabek for internal counter-espionage.
- Unit 8200 happened to be the original intelligence organisation for Israel based on Signal Intelligence. However, now this unit also has cyber and SIGINT capabilities. Former members of Unit 8200 have established their private cyber space companies that produce products for cyber security and cyber weapons. Israel is making great progress in cyber security and cyber offensives. Of late there has been a steady reduction in the conventional ground forces (infantry, armour, artillery) and accretion in intelligence set-up including creating new UAV based units for intelligence collection, electronic warfare and precision missile attacks. Israeli Unit 8200 has collaboration with the US.
- Army air cooperation in the IDF is at battalion level. An Israeli

battalion can communicate directly with the IAF for exfiltration or fire support.

At this juncture, it may be interesting to look at some of the major aspects of the IDF Defence Doctrine. To start with, the IDF came up with their first defence doctrine in August 2015, written in Hebrew, by Lt Gen Gadi Eisenkot the Chief of General Staff, IDF. The English translation was done by the Belfer Center Harvard Kennedy School on 12 August 2016 with permission from the IDF. The national objectives to be achieved include safeguarding the existence of Israel as a state, preserving the value system, social and economic strength and international and regional status. The IDF has a defensive security strategy (prevent war by deterrence) and an offensive military strategy (go all out and achieve military goals quickly). The GHQ headed by the Chief of General Staff (CGS) is to be the only and direct link with the political echelons. The CGS is also the 'Battle Commander'. The subordinate commanders have the authority to make decisions (in the course of fighting) that differ from the initial planning. Special forces are required to conduct unplanned operations deep behind enemy lines.

At this juncture, we have enough facts and analysis in support of reforms in the Indian Armed Forces for creating unified theatre commands. We may now visualise the scope and contours of reforms for creating theatre commands in India.

★★★

Joint Theatre Commands

A New Initiative

Inter-Services Organisations (Command, Control and Discipline) Bill, 2023.

(Political Push for Reforms for Unified Joint Theatre Commands in India)

THE BILL HAS been passed by the Indian Parliament. Some of the major constituents of this proposal in the context of our study include the Central Government's intention to constitute inter-service organisations by notifications, ushering in an era of theatre commands. Second, the CDS can be from any of the three services—Army, Navy or the Air Force. Third, the level of command for inter-service joint organisations will be with officers of the rank of major general in the army, flag officer (rear admiral) in the navy and group captain (equivalent to colonel in the army and captain in the navy). These are the ranks who can be entrusted with command of inter-service organisations. According to media reports, efforts will be made to arrive at a consensus across three services without diluting the essence of jointmanship. Also, the number of officers in the ranks of brigadiers (and equivalent) and above will not be reduced. There is some likelihood of increasing the number of four-star generals. Presently, there are three four-star generals and equivalent officers. The three service chiefs come in this category.

Besides the above Bill, there have been a number of other parallel activities undertaken by the government for smooth implementation of defence reforms. These include the Agnipath Scheme (Please see Appendix for details of this scheme in global perspective) directed to lower the average age profile of the Indian Armed Forces from 32 years to 24/25 years. Presently the scheme is for personnel below the officers rank. It is likely to be extended to the officers cadre.

An important decision to indigenise the defence industry has been taken by merging 41 Ordinance factories into seven Defence Production Public Sector Units (and thus corporatise defence production) doing away with a 246-year-old legacy, removing preferential treatment to public sector units over the private sector and increasing the indigenous production of weapon systems for own consumption as well as for exports, starting inter-service transfer of officers (Army, Navy and the Air Force). Even the tone and conduct of combined commanders' conferences have changed since the last few years. These conferences are being held across India and are not restricted to the traditional locations. Men in all three services are being included into the conference and the 'importance of enhancing indigenisation in the doctrines, procedures and customs practiced in the armed forces' is being stressed by the PM. The pace of these changes (by periodic nudges) is fast compared to what the ecosystem used to witness earlier. Hence the ripple effect among the 'older generations' used to the 'status quo' regime and the 'ours was the only way' syndrome has been sharp. Even those young officers in the services who are enthusiastic about the change will need to make an extra effort to adjust to the changed realities.

Looking at the rapidity and the caution with which the Indian establishment is moving to bring in the Indian way of doing things including dealing with India's security, the changes are going to be on a very broad spectrum and much deeper.

Besides addressing the structural and personnel-related issues, the reforms will be directed to break free of the inertia and the habit of aping the West. These reforms will encourage original thinking, boldness in planning and conduct, strategising on the model of stretching the resources and, above all, inculcating legitimate pride in being an Indian.

In the context of this approach, we made an attempt to scan five major factors that can help in visualising major reforms leading to creating modern inter-services organisations. We analysed the global experience of WWII, and India's own experience in the half a dozen wars it has fought so far, besides analysing our ancient military culture. Organisations, the US and Chinese theatre commands as these exist today, and benchmarked cases of the Israeli Defence Forces (IDF) were also studied.

The study brings out five levels at which the reforms need to be undertaken for a comprehensive restructuring of India's armed forces into joint theatre commands. At the first level will be the national vision related to India's security. This will have to be addressed by the political leadership, the Parliament as well as the politicians in general. In a democracy like India, it is the political discourse that sets the agenda. The second level will be the top military commanders and concerned staff. This would include the CDS and the theatre/component commanders.

At this level, national security-related vision is translated into military strategies. Also, dynamic force allocations are done by the apex level commanders. The third level would be the combatant command commanders who are the ones actually involved in executing military plans. These commanders exercise operational command over the inter service forces allotted to them. The fourth level will be the technostructure and facilities available to the military. The fifth level would be the staff that conveys command decisions and execute control functions on elements actually involved in combat at functional levels.

Evolving a Vision

The vision of a nation flows from the deep-rooted values and beliefs that people have about their identity, their goals, their positioning with respect to other nations and most importantly, what the people hold most dear to themselves for which they would be ready to make the ultimate sacrifice. In a representative democracy like India this vision is manifested by the thoughts and actions of their elected leaders. The greater the concurrence between what the people actually envision and what the elected leadership propagates, the more synergistic is the functioning of the nation and the more secure the nation becomes. If what the people envision and what the leadership portrays through their behaviour diverge, then there is lack of consonance and high intensity of internal conflicts, increasing friction in the growth trajectory and so on.

When the British transferred power to the political leadership that represents the Indian people, the new nation, a top economic power before the British colonised it, was completely ravaged and impoverished by the extremely exploitative policies and governance of their colonial masters. The British also presided over the partition of India into two nations on communal lines, an act that resulted in the worst bloodbath in the Indian subcontinent. India started the famous tryst with destiny as an independent nation on 15 August 1947 on the 'wrong foot'. We need to learn a lot from the West to stand on our own feet.

The West has dominated the general Indian psyche. Those

who practised and professed the traditional ways (*desi culture*) were considered regressive. Nevertheless, the timeless ancient culture and civilisation values survived and a steady return to our own values is quite evident today.

The learning process for this 'system' has been slow, erratic and at times, very traumatic. Seven and a half decades after Independence, the old narrative is being challenged. The India of 2024 is much more assertive, proud of her ancient past and is willing to think independently without any British/Western advice. However, a large section of the intelligentsia still thinks in the 'English idiom'. Unfortunately, the armed forces have a major chunk of 'professional experts and opinion leaders' who are accustomed to learn from the US, British and even China. There are rare instances when the Indian military professionals study the ancient Indian sages, warriors and great military commanders and try to adapt their attitude and warfare principles into modern day warfare.

To be representative of the Indian people and their deep beliefs, our vision must flow from our ancient scriptures that resonate with the people, where a nation is defined by her civilisational values and beliefs. The Indian constitution symbolically derives its essence from the scriptures of ancient India as evidenced by the pictures of Indian deities in the Constitution. How do the scriptures define the core of our nation? From time immemorial, the idea of a nation was based on two factors: first, the people (citizens) and second, the geography (territory). In the past, several Indian kingdoms expanded their respective kingdoms beyond the inherited or traditional geographical boundaries. The extended regions became part of the nation including their inhabitants.

The Indian material and cultural richness permeated in these regions without any sectarian concept. Thus, in essence, the citizens formed the most basic unit of the state according to the Indian ethos. Kautilya went to the extent of causing minimal damage to the people in the enemy nation during war because victory in war makes the successful king responsible for the well-being of the citizens of the captured kingdom. Thus for Kautilya, the citizen *(nagrik)* become the most vital and basic unit of the nation even more important than the territory. But who is a citizen?

According to the *Arthashastra,* every person living within the territorial boundaries of a nation does not become a citizen automatically even if they have been living there for some span of time. The citizen has to earn their 'citizenship' by performing their duties. Only then do they get their rights. People living in a nation are governed by *Dharma*, which enshrine universal expectations from every human being. *Matri Devo Bhava, Pitra Devo Bhava, Acharya Devo Bhava, Atithi Devo Bhava* (One's mother, father, teacher and the visiting guest are all worthy of being worshipped). These principles were considered universal and linked with rituals or faiths. In ancient India, people following different social practices and rituals coexisted without much conflict.

The concept of national security as envisaged by the Indian scriptures can be broadly represented as under:

Pictorial Representation of Concept of National Security

National security encompasses three broad factors as given above. Security across these factors is overlapping and not in tight silos. This brings in the ecosystem of cooperation, collaboration and common understanding among the agencies specifically involved for each one of these. Neutralising geographical threats is primarily the task of the armed forces. However, the foreign office (external affairs), external intelligence agencies and international allies form part of cooperating institutions. Threats to the citizens either through crime, terrorism, narrative pushing, etc. primarily fall in the domain of police, Central Armed Police Force, judiciary and cultural organisations.

All these organisations and institutions are expected to cooperate. Safeguarding the civilisational values of India is the most complex, difficult and critical task. This is where knowledge creation and educational institutions play a major role. Given the shaky past that we have had at the time of Independence, it is here that the most careful and subtle measures need to be undertaken. Nations with compromised and threatened civilisational values perish faster than those with weak militaries. We will discuss this in some more detail in the light of our ancient wisdom.

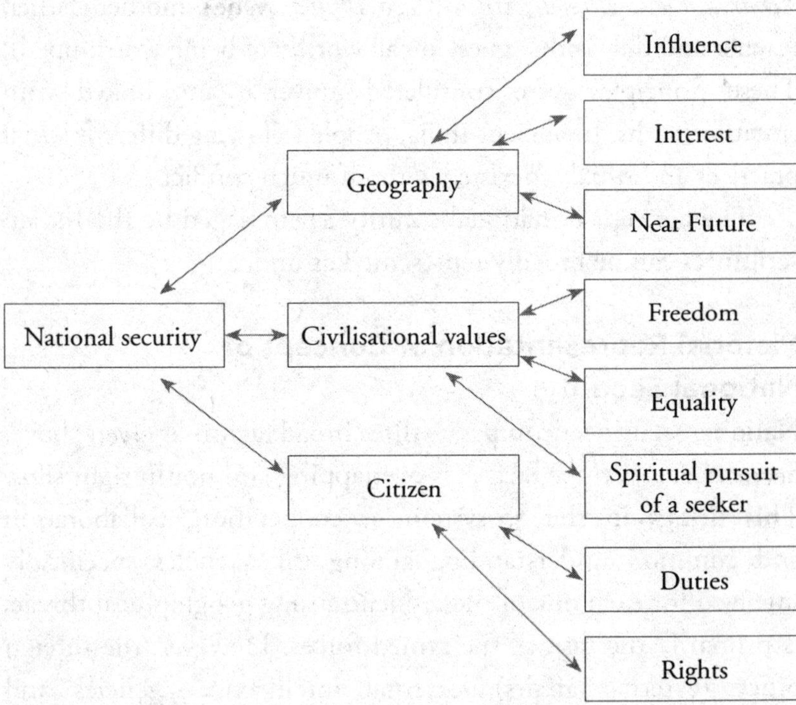

The *Arthashastra*, Kautilya's treatise derived from the *Atharvaveda,* also describes the duties *(Raj dharma)* of the King (the ruling class). The King's *dharma* is to protect territorial integrity, civilisational values and ensure the well-being of the citizen. In essence, the political vision helps in answering five basic questions that relate to national security that are relevant for our study. What needs to be protected in terms of territory, people and civilisational values? Second, the threat indicators and modus operandi to neutralise the threats.

Our ancient wisdom on national security suggests that the threats need to be neutralised as soon as they emerge. Based on the type of threats, Kautilya described four types of war—the war of counsel (diplomacy), open warfare (this is where military is used at the time and place of their own choosing), concealed warfare, and psychological warfare. According to the wisdom of the Vedas and Upanishads, open warfare must be the last resort, it must be fought for a brief period of time with minimal damage to property and human lives (on both sides).

The third and most critical question is about major components or organs of the nation-state including their relative positions. Kautilya believed that the armed forces of the nation are positioned sixth after the treasury (economy). The king (elected political leader) occupied the top place followed by the council of ministers, next being the land and the people (territorial integrity and the well-being of citizens). At fourth place were the fortified towns and cities (due to their defence potential), fifth place in order of priority was the wealth of the nation (economy) followed by the armed forces at the sixth place and allies (international relations) at the seventh place.

The armed forces of the king were commanded by the *Senapati* who was part of the council of ministers but did not attend routine meetings of the council. He was called upon for advice related to war and aspects of national security that involved participation by the armed forces. Hence, though the armed forces were placed sixth in the order of priority with regard to the seven organs of the state, the chief of the armed forces retained a prominent position under the king. We will come back to this aspect while discussing the position of the CDS in the national security apparatus in the modern knowledge-driven information war environment.

If we adapt Kautilya's theory to the modern knowledge era democratic ecosystem, then the seven layers can be, people and the leadership, knowledge and productivity, economy, internal security, armed forces, technostructure, and international relations. Consequently, the war forms will also be in accordance to these modern-day pillars of national security. The conflicts will occur at people (net war), political (political war), economic (economic warfare), internal threats (terrorism, proxy wars), conventional warfare involving physical destruction, electronic warfare, psychological warfare and so on.

While the CDS and theatre commanders will primarily be structured, equipped, sourced and tasked to meet external threats ranging from cyber to conventional and finally the nuclear, there will be organisations, infrastructure and policies to deal with and neutralise other threats. Since the threats will be overlapping with varying degrees in each domain, all the agencies involved in the business of national security will have to be inter-linked at some level through specific gateways for sharing information and synergising their respective actions with others. The military commanders at the highest level will be expected to visualise the military as well as non-military threats and prepare their forces accordingly/advise the cabinet according to their professional knowledge on the subject.

The higher direction of military affairs or war will always emanate from the political top. How is the political top organised and connected to the institutions that actually translate strategic intent into plans? According to the Indian representative democratic system, the Prime Minister is the Chief Executive who is advised by the cabinet committee on security. Since the cabinet committee on security in India comprises exclusively of civilians (generally devoid of military experience and without proper understanding of military affairs) they need to be informed and briefed on the situation at regular intervals. They may be advised, but theirs is the final call and rightly so. Small mistakes at these levels get magnified when these strategic decisions reach the operational levels.

In India, the office of the National Security Adviser (NSA) performs this task of advising the top political executives. The NSA is thus expected to grasp the entire gamut of security—geography, civilisational values and the citizens. Keeping this in mind, the NSA has been raised to the level of cabinet minister with ministers of defence, home and external affairs reporting to him for briefing and advice. Where does the CDS fit in here? Earlier the secretary of defence reporting to the Defence Minister was made responsible for the defence of India (under the factor of geography). This arrangement will deprive the Defence Minister and the NSA of critical military advice as interpreted by a military professional. Hence, the institution of CDS must replace the Defence Secretary as an adviser on external security (related to the factor of geography).

The National Apex for National Security

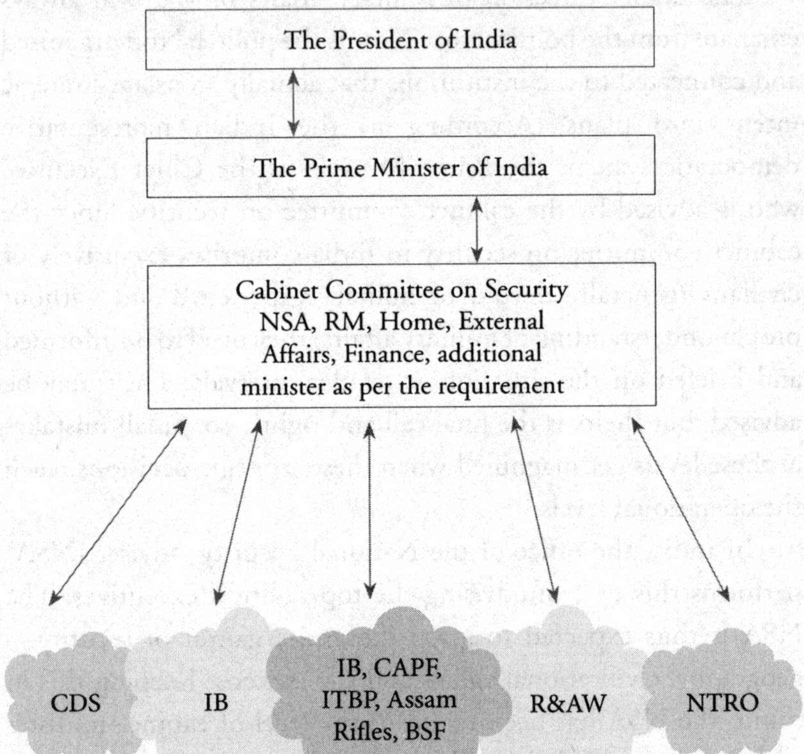

CDS	:	Chief of Defence Staff
IB	:	Intelligence Bureau
CAPF	:	Central Armed Police Force
ITBP	:	Indo Tibetan Border Police
BSF	:	Border Security Force
R&AW	:	Research and Analysis Wing
NTRO	:	National Technical Research Organisation

It is for the top political leadership to visualise and monitor the national security environment in terms of threats and initiate timely and appropriate measures to neutralise these threats before they manifest themselves in harmful proportions. Since the ministers in the Cabinet Committee for Security (CCS) are without proper understanding of national security, the NSA with the help of specialised agencies makes the political leaders aware of the implications of various events that can lead to national security threats. The CDS provides the inputs for the external threats that pertain to our geographical location—establishment of military bases by an adversary, military movements, upgradation, training, alliances and so on. He is also responsible for apprising the CCS directly or through the NSA of the capabilities required by our own forces to meet the challenges. This would include the personnel, equipment, knowledge, education and skilling requirements. Similarly, the heads of other national security institutions keep the CCS apprised. Recently, there have been cases where the CDS and even the three service chiefs have met the Prime Minister together in a group and individually. This gives an indication that the highest level of national leadership is inclined to obtain inputs directly from the service chiefs.

Since the national security threats in the knowledge era emanate from a very large spectrum of activities, the environment scan needs to be that much wider. Besides, even the capability building for neutralising the threat goes beyond the conventional military systems. Non-military domains of the nation need to be involved in national security. Thus, cyber security, psychological warfare, perception management, narrative war, civilisational conflicts within and outside are all subjects that traditionally belong to the non-military domain. However, threat vectors are often carefully packaged in these external covers. This leads us to 'all of the nation' approach for securing the nation at all times.

The knowledge sector, industry, infrastructure and even the

cultural sector needs to be watched to identify and neutralise any potential threats.

CDS: The Military Top Brass

The role of the military apex, headed by the CDS, is strategic in essence. It envisages the geographical aspects of external threats through land, maritime and air, identifies resources to meet these threats, and suggests modalities of raising, maintaining, training and allocation of resources. While the CDS consolidates the advice and knowledge for preparing the broad outlines for military force structure, broad distribution, periodic review and upgradations, distinct roles of operationalising and raising, maintaining and training are performed at two different levels. While the theatre commanders are responsible for operationalising the plans, the service heads (army, navy and air) are responsible for raising, maintaining and training their respective forces. Besides these discrete services (also known as component forces) there are other specialised forces that are headed by different specialist commanders that form part of the military force. These include the air defence, logistics and acquisition, cyber, defence intelligence, space, nuclear, special forces and rocket component commands. The specialised forces operate along all the three domains—ground, sea, air, of the geographical threat vectors. Thus, the Air Defence Command would be expected to defend the airspace of the entire nation from enemy air and missile attacks. Similarly, the cyber command would provide defensive and offensive cyber cover to the entire military force. The CDS will have three verticals under him, joint operational command, component forces command and specialised forces command. A schematic layout of the broad structure is outlined here:

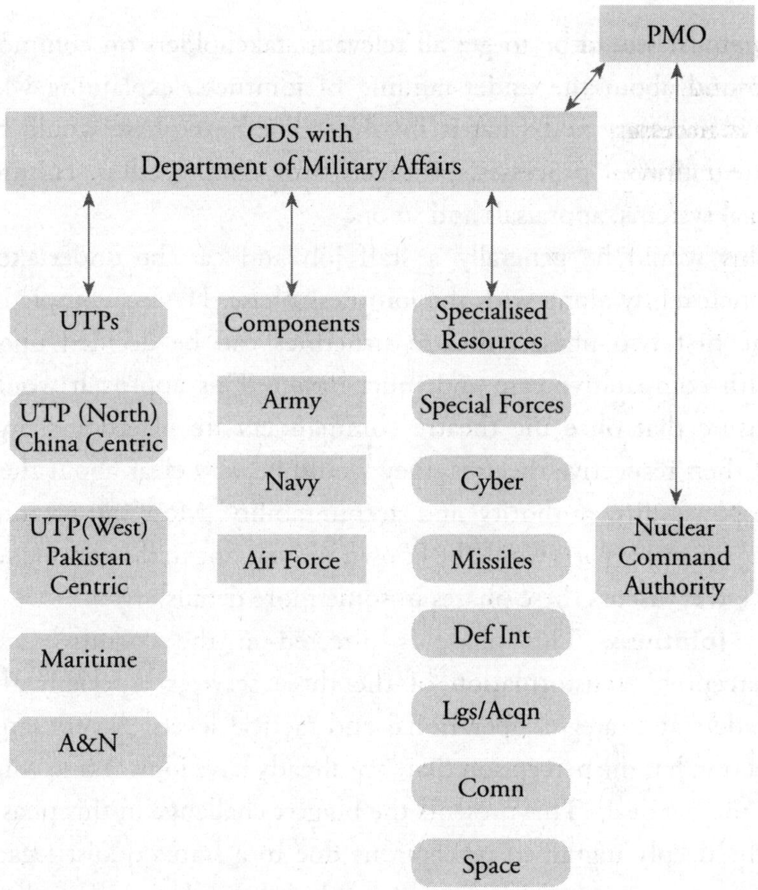

Note - UTP: Unified Theatre Command for synergistic joint operations, SF: Special forces, Def Int: Defence Intelligence, Lgs/Acqn: Logistics and Acquisition, Comn: Communications and networks management.

Three Phases of Implementation—Jointness, Integration and Theatre Structures

During the author's interaction with the prominent CDS (Gen Anil Chauhan) on 4 September 2023, he did not talk much about the structure because he found that to be the easiest of the tasks compared to other major 'work to be done' on jointness and integration. He was very clear about the sequence. First and foremost would be to get all relevant stakeholders on common ground about the understanding of jointness, explaining why it is necessary and what it involves. The next phase would be integration of processes, protocols, functioning ethos, culture, legal systems, appraisals and so on.

This would be generally a staff job and can be undertaken concurrently along with the jointness phase. Having completed the first two phases, theatre structures can be decided upon with comparative ease and much faster. This approach would ensure that once the theatre commanders are placed incharge of their respective theatres, they would be very clear about their responsibility, authority and accountability. Most importantly the operative parts would be known to everyone in the command. We will discuss these phases in some more details.

Jointness: This phase is directed at the cognitive and perceptive transformation of the three services especially the leaders at strategic, operational and tactical levels. A very large section has the perception that, 'we already have jointness so what is the big deal?' This presents the biggest challenge in this phase. The deeply ingrained perceptions due to a status quoist legacy need to be removed by very carefully planned activities where the participants begin to see for themselves the fallacy of their previous perceptions. In the slow deliberate implementation, the target environment is likely to go through the following:

- May come out of their respective silos and start appreciating the situation with a positive attitude.
- Realise the payoffs and importance of cooperation, collaboration, commitment to a joint goal and plan. The element of 'control' would slowly give way to self-driven synergy in a flatter hierarchy.
- Enhance the trust factor among the three services as also with all participants in the big team.

- Learn to visualise, envision and plan on a common canvas that makes sense to all the leaders involved in the joint planning for a mutually supporting set of strategic and operational intents.
- Learn to respect the unique strengths of each service and have faith in their capability to achieve the desired goals. Also, realise tasks that should not be given to a service or component command due to their inherent force structure.

Integration: This involves aligning procedures, protocols, syntax, documentation and interoperability of communications. In simple terms, integration deals with bringing all factors to a common denominator so that these create a cumulative impact. To illustrate this by a relevant example, we may consider the activities of appreciation and preparing the operational order that each service undertakes in their planning phase.

Each service visualises their respective operational aims, identifies contributing factors, does analysis of each factor to arrive at likely courses of action and then selects one of these courses to prepare their respective plans and operational orders. It is in the plans and operational orders that resources are allotted, contingencies are thought of, reserves are earmarked and timelines are laid down. In a single service situation, all the leaders have the same understanding of glossary of terms used, same connotation, and are capable of executing the orders in a uniform manner. The series of actions that are taken by different groups, units, formations for whom the plan or the operations order is written all add up (integrate) to create the desired impact (outcome).

In a tri-service environment, the situation changes drastically. In the appreciation phase itself, the ground, air and maritime forces have vastly different goals/aims/objectives to achieve. Further, the factors that affect the aim and their analysis are different for each service. So are the courses of action, selected course, the plan and the operational order. If a tri-service operational staff officer or a theatre commander has to go through the entire range of activities from appreciation to the operational order, the format needs to be such that each individual service agrees and understands the activities involved. Only then will the conduct of the three services add up to a cumulative or synergistic outcome.

Bringing these activities on a common platform (like the Operating Software or OS, of a computer) is a major and very tedious task. We have taken two very common and widely known activities in our illustrative example. There are hundreds of such activities undertaken by each service for which each service uses its own format, phrases, methods and objectives to be achieved. Where logistics are concerned, stocking, demand generation, movements and actual replenishments are based on messages and protocols. These are different for each service.

Modern forces use modular systems of replenishment supported by Electronic Data Exchange Interfaces. This would require considerable work in preparing common systems and logistics communication interoperability. In case of appraisals and promotion systems, as of now, each service has different punishments for the same offence. Even if the punishment is the same, the implication on the appraisal and promotion are different. This will have to be harmonised. The concerned officers will have to unlearn and relearn in a manner that they think, write, speak and act in a common idiom. This would involve massive overhaul and in some cases, transformation of training of leadership from the very top to the basic leaders. Needless to say that integration of a given range of activities will only be possible once there is broad understanding of the jointness at a cognitive level.

Theatre Structure

This is the final project that can be undertaken only after the first two phases are over. Establishing theatre commands involves the following:

- **Identifying the threat in the region:** The threat assessment in the theatre will have to be proactive. This would entail identifying the threat much before it is fully manifested. Some innocuous activities such as in international relations, internal environment of the hostile nation, global geopolitics, cyber space, and social media may be an indication for bigger threats to emerge or depict the beginning of any major threat. Hence, staffing and resource allocation to the theatre command will have to cater for this capability.
- **Stating the geographical contours of area of interest and area of influence in the region:** Theatre commanders will have to look at the area of interest besides guarding their respective areas of influence.
- **Appointing a unified theatre commander:** This will have to be based on the type of threat, cognitive ability of the commanders to be selected and most importantly, the inter-personal relations of the theatre commander with the component commanders. There have been cases when excessively charismatic, gifted public speakers, officers with an enviable record of service on paper have done more harm than good to the organisation. The theatre commanders should be enablers, motivators, humble in dealing with people and steadfast in pursuing the organisational vision. We did discuss the qualities of a *senapati* earlier. All those qualities are relevant for top military commanders in the theatre.
- **Allocating Resources under the Theatre Commander:** The theatre force capability needs to be in consonance with the threat and tasks allotted. There may be a requirement of placing components and specialised force elements under the theatre commander. Thus

elements of signals intelligence, electronic warfare, HUMINT, ie, human intelligence (which are generally under the Field Security units), terrestrial and satellite-based technical intelligence resources along with their personnel, air elements and so on will have to be placed under the theatre commander. It will be the discretion of the theatre commander to choose delegation or direct command of the resources based on the technical or functional complexity of the force. Ideally, giving a free hand to the respective force commander in an environment of trust and commitment achieves the best result. It is here that collaboration, cooperation and coordination need to temper the urge to directly control these forces. Thus, if the air component commander is made part of the team and allowed to use his own experience and talent to employ the air power in furtherance of theatre goals, the outcomes are likely to be much better compared to a situation where the air power commander is told 'what to do' and 'how to do it'.

- **Stating Clear Responsibilities, Accountability and Authority:** Though there have been cases where joint operations have been conducted with remarkable impact without fixing any clear authority—respective component force commanders are responsible for their own part and no single commander is responsible for the overall force objective—the probability of such an ideal situation generally remains very low. Hence, formal enunciation of authority along with accountability and responsibility is spelt out in very clear terms. This is what the Americans followed during WWII. The British on the other hand, followed a policy of collective accountability in an environment of consultation and consensus, where Prime Minister Churchill had the overarching authority to intervene even in operational details and deployment. The British model was not very effective.
- **Specifying the span of control:** This aspect will deal with theatre commanders' authority to take decisions without reference to higher

authorities. These decisions may include appointment/change of formation or component force commanders, interaction with other countries that are within the area of interest of the theatre. These interactions can only be through the Ministries of External Affairs. Generally allocation of tasks within the areas of responsibilities of the theatre, resource allocations and timelines are within the span of control of the theatre commander. There may also be restrictions on the technical aspects of component and specialised command elements placed under the command of the theatre.

- **Laying down chain of Command:** A theatre commander would normally have access to the CDS on most matters. There may be some areas where the theatre commander can access the superior or lateral organisation directly, say, training, logistics, procurements etc. Even within the theatre, the chains of commands of organic and allotted resources will have to be laid down.
- **Legal provisions:** Since this is a new organisation, all the aspects pertaining to authority, accountability and responsibilities will have to be covered under legal sanctions by the government. Besides the three services will have to come under the same legal provisions unlike the current situation where the ground forces are covered by the Army Act 1950, the IAF under IAF Act 1950 and the Navy under the Navy Act 1950.

Joint Operational Commands

It is here that jointness of planning and execution is sought to be achieved under one commander authorised for goal setting, tasking, resource distribution and dynamic monitoring of operations within a given geographical area for a given span of time or on a permanent basis. It is akin to the erstwhile command HQ with a major difference that this joint command now comprises of all the services (army, air force and the navy) that are required for achieving the operational goal and it may be allotted some additional resources from the specialised force components as well as other national resources (space assets, R&AW, IB, Cyber etc.)

Ideally, the service HQ in the joint commands must be colocated though some experts feel that given the modern communication systems, colocation is not necessary. However, the Indian experience on this issue suggests colocation of HQ. This was done for the Eastern Army Command HQ Kolkata and the Eastern Air HQ at Shillong (an advance air HQ from Shillong) were colocated at Kolkata (Fort William). The cooperation between the Army and the Air Force, in the Eastern theatre was splendid during the 1971 war since the senior IAF officers used to meet Lt Gen J F R Jacob who was orchestrating the ground operations. The IAF officers knew the details of ground operations before these were launched and hence were able to task air resources in the most effective manner. At the corps level, the 4 Corps operations were most intimately supported by the IAF since the supporting IAF HQ (Tactical Air Command—TAC) was with the Corps HQ.

It is important to note that the commander of this joint force must resist the temptation of getting involved in tactical planning and execution of operations in the combat zone. This task is best left to the troops on the ground (Corps and below, ideally down to the Brigades). The organic battles in the combat zone are too fluid and self-regulated that it is only the man on the ground who knows the correct picture and he can take correct decisions (if trained and supported properly). What happens if the commanders at lower levels are found wanting, as was seen in 1965 (calling back 3 Jat from the lodgement), or 1971 (Longewala, Shakargarh)? In such cases, the higher commanders can only limit the damage. They cannot turn the battle around even after providing all the resources and motivation.

There have been numerous cases where the commanders were changed during the conduct of the campaign/battle. Take the case of Lt Gen Harbakhsh Singh who replaced Lt Gen B M Kaul during the 1962 war when Kaul fell sick and had to leave the 4 Corps Zone. During the short period of a week, Lt Gen Harbakhsh had ensured stability in the 4 Corps defences. But in this case, the leadership potential and combat experience of the two generals were vastly different. Harbakhsh was far too superior as a leader and as a combat soldier. This brings out the importance of having quality leadership at the subunit, unit and formation levels.

Resource allocation to the joint operational command is done according to the operational role. This allocation is dynamic. Though once the role and the threats are evaluated properly, the integral tri-service resources available with the theatre commands remain (or should remain) the same. Additional resources can be allotted from the specialised commands (cyber, space, rockets, SF etc.). Even specially composed task forces can be allotted to the theatre commander. The command and control of the task force so allotted can either be with the theatre commander or with the task force commander.

The latter arrangement is generally found more useful. According to the latest information available in the media on the subject, the three services have arrived at a broad consensus to have four unified theatre commands of this nature. UTC (North) for China with HQ at Lucknow, UTC (West) for Pakistan, with HQ at Jaipur, Maritime Command with HQ at Karwar in Andhra Pradesh and Andaman and Nicobar Command HQ, at Port Blair which already exists. Eventually from 17 odd command HQs, the Armed Forces forces would settle for five theatre commands for the time being.

Theatre Command (West)

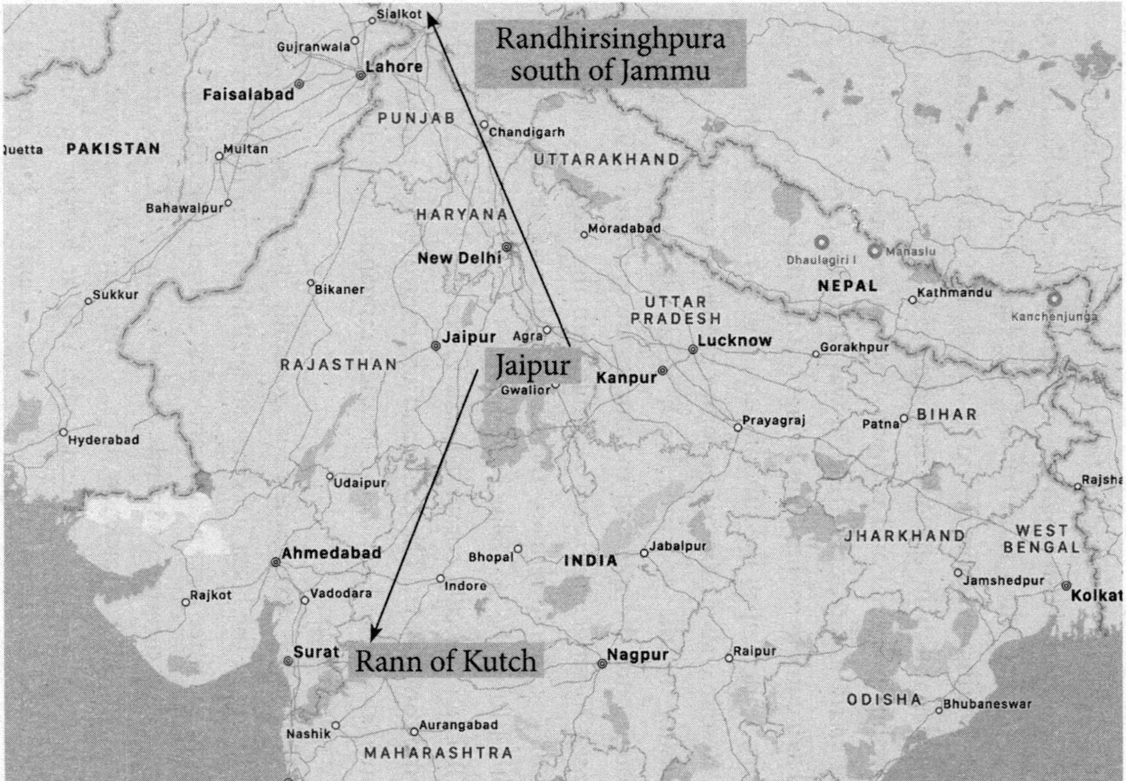

Source: Singh, Mayank, 'Indian armed forces likely to get their first Integrated Theatre Command in August,' *The New Indian Express*, 12 July 2023.

Proactive approach by this regional command will entail its role in three domains. First, international in conjunction with the MEA, second, offensive defence of the LoC and last, coordination with the Western Fleet of the Maritime Theatre Command (MTC). In the international domain, the theatre commander will have to watch Afghanistan, friendly countries in Central Asia and Iran. The offensive capabilities will have to be based on taking back Pak Occupied Kashmir and coordination with the MTC will be in the Pakistani, East African Coast line areas. Currently, four single service commands are responsible for this border part of Northern command, UT of Jammu and Kashmir, Western Command located at Chandimandir, IB Punjab to North of Rajasthan, and Southern and South-western command from North of Rajasthan to Rann of Kutch.

Theatre Command (North) HQ at Lucknow

This regional command will have to be proactive in its role. This will involve three layers of roles. First, in the international domain, second, offensive defence and last, coordination with Eastern Fleet of the MTC in the Bay of Bengal. In the international domain, the focus will be on liaison, intelligence gathering and intervention when necessary as part of national vision. The theatre commander will have to keep himself abreast of situations and activities in Nepal, Bhutan, Myanmar and Bangladesh ideally in collaboration with the Ministry of External Affairs. The offensive defence would entail a demonstrated and credible capability to take proactive action to maintain sanctity of the LAC. Mere reactive defensive policy against China would not be sufficient. Ideally, this offensive capability should be oriented towards taking back China Occupied Kashmir (Sakshgam Valley) and Ladakh (Aksai Chin). Coordination with the MTC will

Theatre Command (North)

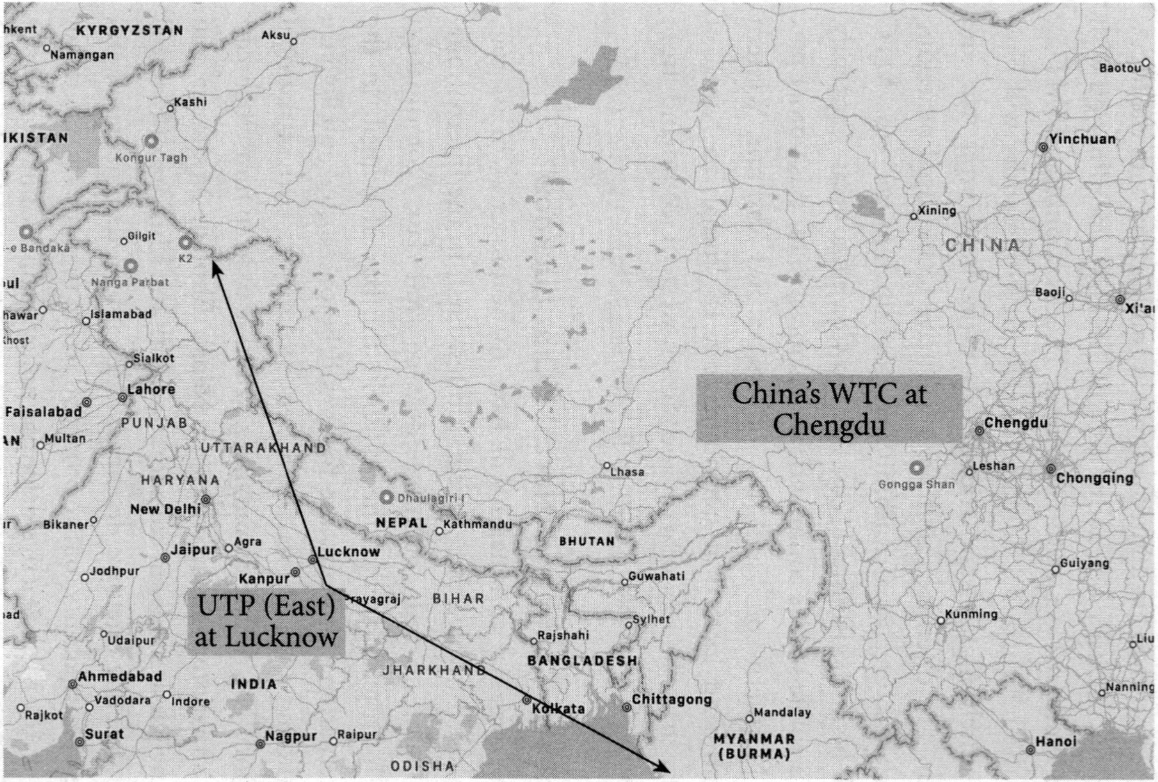

Source: Singh, Mayank, 'Indian armed forces likely to get their first Integrated Theatre Command in August, '*The New Indian Express,* 12 July 2023.

have to be based on beefing up both the defensive and offensive capabilities ex ANC in Andaman and Nicobar islands. Currently three theatre commands (Western, Northern and Eastern) are responsible for this region.

If the MTC is carrier-based, then one carrier group is likely to be in the West (Indian Ocean and the Arabian Sea), and the other carrier group would be in the East (Indian Ocean and Bay of Bengal). It is likely that India will raise one or two more carrier groups looking towards the Chinese Navy in the South China sea. As India's international and economical influence grows, the MTC will have to look forward to expanding its footprint in the Indo-Pacific in the East and the African continent in the West. Its dominance of the Malacca Strait would be part of immediate defence and presence in the Indo Pacific in conjunction with other friendly nations (Japan, South Korea, Australia, the US, South East Asian countries) as part of contesting the Chinese expansionism towards the Indian Ocean. According to media reports, the Indian Navy is likely to get 130 additional ships by 2030, and the air component of the Navy itself would be 500 carrier/ground-based fighter aircraft. This would be the most conservative estimate of accretions in the Indian Navy to support India's force projection in the new world order in which, the Indian Navy would be looking far beyond the traditional areas of the Indian Ocean, the Arabian Sea and the Bay of Bengal. They will have to extend to Indo Pacific, Red Sea, and the Persian Gulf. The MTC Commander will have to be staffed and beefed up accordingly.

At this level, joint operational planning for each phase of the operation is done. The plans are executed and subsequent phases of operations are undertaken according to the timelines laid down by the theatre commanders. This, in essence, will be the

Maritime Command, and A&C Tri Service Command

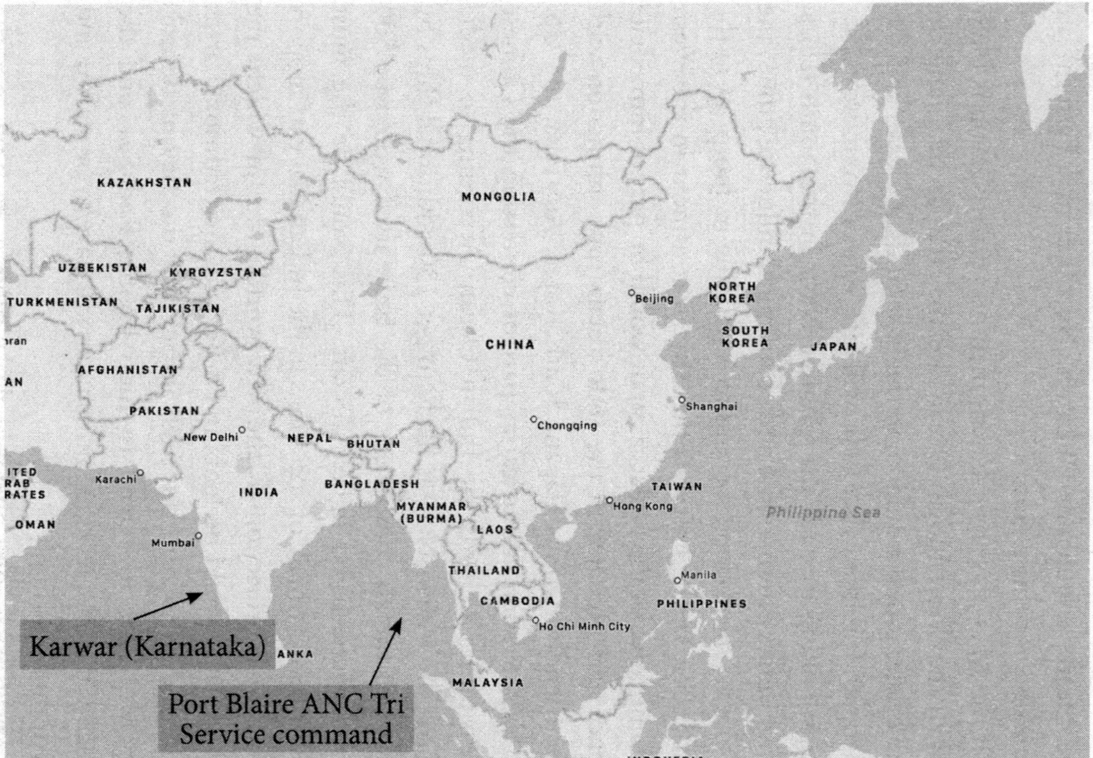

Source: Singh, Mayank, 'Indian armed forces likely to get their first Integrated Theatre Command in August' , *The New Indian Express*, 12 July 2023.

functional level where the respective fighting units of the three services—army units, air bases and naval ships will be actually cooperating and collaborating in joint operations to achieve the theatre goals. The combat events at this level are fast-paced, unpredictable (seldom go as per the plan), require very high level of innovative thinking and adapting to the battle field conditions and the moves by the adversary.

In the Indian context, combat at this level is characterised by reduced quantum of technological support especially for the ground forces. While the air and the naval components fight from their high-tech platforms (combat aircrafts and ships), the bulk of the ground forces who are fighting in close quarters use their instincts, and innovative skills in combat. Efforts are being made to enable and empower the ground forces at squadron, company and battery levels with the requisite technologies to reduce their sensor to shooter time cycles, enhance precision targeting, improve situational awareness and link them to higher echelons for fire support, intelligence and mobility.

The IDF caters for direct involvement of their air force down to battalion level for close support and exfiltration. The US provided data links from the Joint Surveillance Target Acquistion Radar System down to the level of combat teams (built around a company or squadron). India had enabled their Para SF strike teams with strategic means of intelligence, fire support and exfiltration during the surgical strike in the Uri sector (2016). In September 2023, India used the Heron Remotely Piloted Vehicle (Israeli origin) to conduct search and destroy missions against terrorists in Anantnag district.

The specialised component forces—like the air force, long range artillery, surveillance, command and control, fire support networks assist the ground forces at the level of combat teams to accomplish their missions. Operating as combined arms (intra service synergy) and joint operational (inter-service synergy) teams become most critical. The ground force commanders need to balance delegation with control. There have been instances where the company or combat team leaders get much better situational awareness and great windows of opportunities compared to ground force commanders at the brigade, division and corps levels. These junior leaders must be allocated resources and given authority to use these as per their judgement for the given phase of the operation. Centralised planning and decentralised execution needs to be practised. The battle at this level can never be controlled by the staff or the higher commanders who are not 'seeing the battle' themselves.

Component and Specialised Commands

Modern Armed Forces are composed of vastly diverse forces besides the traditional army, naval and air components. These range from cyber warriors who are proficient for defensive and offensive operations in cyber space, network creation and sustaining force who enable surveillance, decision support, command, control, and fire support. Besides, there are special forces, logistics forces and space-based systems that have highly specialised roles to play. Given the broad spectrum of technologies and knowledge that is required for each of these specialised forces, it is humanly impossible for the combat force commanders (theatre commanders) to raise, train, maintain and even make optimal use of these forces. Hence, the need for component commands comprising of naval and air services and highly specialised forces.

While the army, navy and air components are raised, trained and maintained by the respective Chiefs of Staff and provided to the UTC commanders for actual operations, the specialised forces by their very nature are operationalised by their respective heads based on the requirements of the UTC commanders. Allotment of these forces to the theatre commanders will be based on combat requirements. Generally, the command and control of these forces is delegated to the specialised force commanders. However, the theatre commanders can command these forces directly as well. This depends on the personality and leadership style of the combatant force commander.

Air Force Component

During WWII, the air force was integral to the ground forces in the US Army. It was only after WWII that the US Air Force (USAF) emerged as a separate service. Russia has a separate air arm and its primary role is to support ground operations. The Russian Air Force does not harbour any separate strategic role that is not in support or in consonance with ground operations. The Israeli Air Force performs a similar role.

The Royal Air Force (RAF) is the only force that propagates a separate strategic role for its air arm. During the Battle of Britain, Churchill acknowledged the role of RAF in saving Britain against the Luftwaffe bombing. Towards the closing years of WWII, the RAF did the same to the German cities and industrial installations what the Luftwaffe had done to the British cities and industrial bases during the famous Battle of Britain. The RAF failed to cripple the German industrial production and subjugate the German people's will to fight back just as the Luftwaffe had failed to do so to the UK in the beginning of the war.

The US Army Air Forces too, did extensive and most insensitive bombings (using high incendiary napalm on residential areas, schools including hospitals) in Japanese cities

Tri-service Command ANC

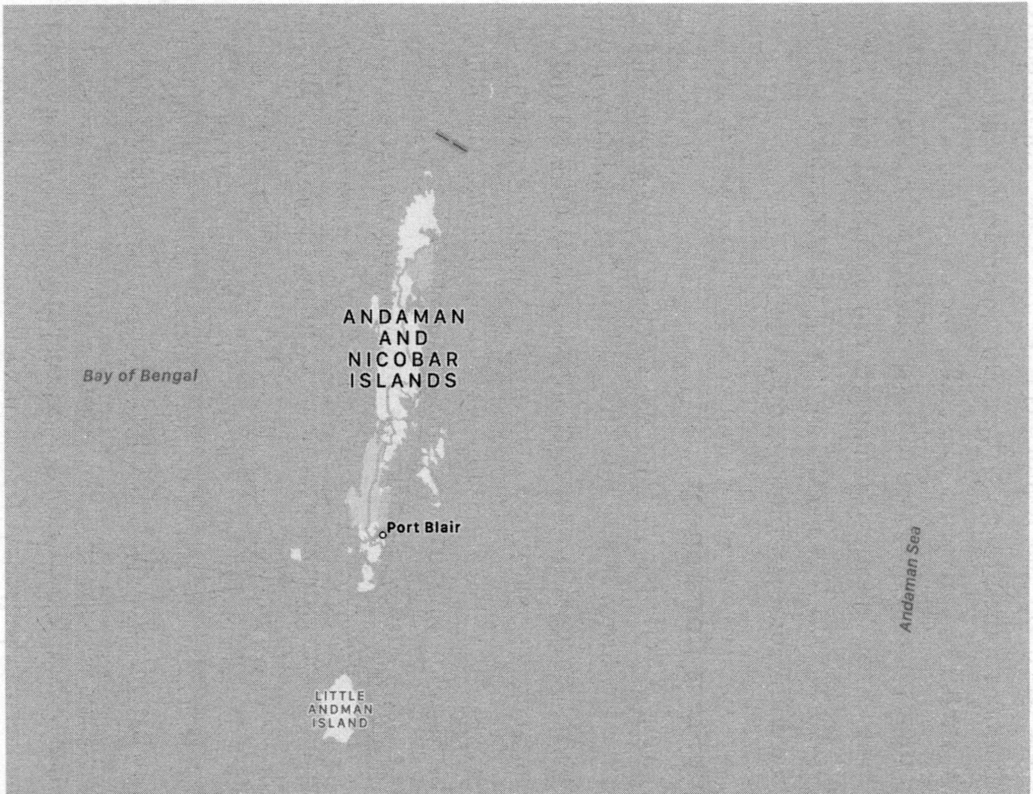

for months together. The Japanese continued to fight. The fate of the Japanese resistance was decided by the defeat of their ground forces. In Kosovo, more than three months of incessant bombings by the coalition forces failed to force Slobodan Milošević, Serbia's former President into submission. It was only when the NATO threatened him that Milosevic agreed to surrender and negotiate. So much for independent air operations and an independent air war doctrine! It has been proved time and again that there are no separate ground, air or naval wars. It is just one war.

Against such a historical backdrop, it is evident that air power is a highly potent arm characterised by its strategic reach, swiftness of deployment and operationalisation, precision, stand-off capability, lethality and psychological impact. It is also an extremely specialised force in terms of raising, maintaining, training and employment in war. The best employment of air power can be done by telling them the plan and overall objective. The air force would then evolve their own air plan to support the ground fighting. The worst way of using air power in war is to tell them what to do, how to do it and when to do it without sharing with them the plan and the objective. Unfortunately in India, the most potent component of the armed forces was kept away from the preliminary planning processes and were asked to attack targets or blunt the enemy offensive only after the battle had already begun. Even then the IAF delivered. In this (unfair) ecosystem, the air warriors surpassed all expectations and saved the day for the nation such as in Chhamb in 1965, Longewala in 1971, crossing of Meghna river in Bangladesh in 1971, in the attack on the Governor's House in Dacca in the same year, and in the capture of Tololing during the Kargil war of 1999.

Thus, irrespective of how much of air power is allotted to a theatre commander, the ideal manner of employing them for maximum impact is by delegation, involving them in planning and giving them the freedom to make their own air plan to synergise with the ground operations.

In the current reforms for creating joint commands, the entire responsibility of air defence has been given to the Air Defence Command to be commanded by an Air Marshal. The Indian Air Force did not appreciate this. It is quite likely that there will be changes through the creation of a separate Air Defence Command.

The Indian Navy

Compared to the air force, the naval forces were established much earlier. Indian scriptures and medieval history reveals that several Indian kings and monarchs had naval fleets much before the emergence of Western navies. Also maritime and ground forces have fought joint operations even before the two world wars.

India did inherit a sizeable naval force at the time of Independence in comparison to what Pakistan and China had in 1947 and 1949, respectively. However, the Indian Navy had generally been a forgotten force during all the major wars that India fought except for their operations to block Bangladesh ports and attack the Karachi harbour in 1971. In fact the daring attack on the Karachi harbour in 1971 was a joint Air-Navy attack and the then naval chief had urged the Indian Government to let the Indian Navy have a go at Pakistan. The navy performed well beyond expectations and proved to the national leadership that maritime forces can change the outcome of war if employed well and in conjunction with the other two services.

The existing Eastern and Western Naval commands are being merged to create a single Maritime Theatre Command which will have army, air and Coast Guard forces allotted to it.

The MTC will be based at Karwar with air bases at Jamnagar (Jaguars) and Thanjavur (Tejas and Sukhoi 30 MKI) supporting the command. The Coast Guard though grouped with this command will continue to report directly to the MoD. The Coast Guard have their own maritime and air assets.

The MTC will be responsible for Maritime Security and force projection. The Andaman and Nicobar Command (ANC) has already been given resources accordingly and expansion is on the way.

Besides the Navy may undertake amphibious operations comprising of the navy, army and air forces. The command and control of these operations are decided by the phases of the operation. During the movement and beach head operations, it is the navy that is in the lead. Once the beach head is established, the ground forces take over the command and control of subsequent operations. Amphibious operations can also be launched by specially constituted task forces for the purpose.

In a nutshell, the Indian Navy would be called upon to undertake three major roles. First, the maritime role of force projection and contesting the Chinese encirclement/expansion in the Indian Ocean and if required in the Indo Pacific. This role would need active participation of the IAF and other specialised commands such as Space and Missile Command as and when raised. Second, a strategic island security will have to be ensured by the Indian Navy. The Andaman and Nicobar Tri-Service Command that secured these islands is one such command. There may be similar commands or tri-service task forces in the future for other islands in India's areas of interest. The third role would be amphibious operations, again a classic tri-service operation.

Specialised Commands

Special Forces Command

India traditionally employed Special Forces (SF) in support of ground operations. These forces were characterised by mode of transportation (airborne or heliborne forces), self-containment for a period of 72 to 96 hours and at times living off the land for a brief period. Their tasks involved capturing or destroying some bridges, demolitions behind the enemy lines, destruction of enemy gun positions and so on, all in conjunction with the main conventional operations.

Major military powers have more enduring, high impact and continuous roles for their SF. The US has their SF deployed in several countries involved in tasks ranging from intelligence gathering, subversion, training of hostile/terrorists groups (it was the US SF that trained the Taliban against the Russians in 1979), engineering coups and perception management of the target nation. The Chinese have members of the CCP or PLA trained in special operations posted with their personnel involved in various projects in the target countries. Their roles are similar to that of the US Special Forces. Similarly, Israel, UK, France etc. too have SF that have roles quite different from those undertaken by their regular militaries. The SF in essence are active in target countries all the time.

India has embarked upon transforming the roles and outlook of the SF by taking two major steps. An Armed Forces Special Operations Division has been raised. The HQ of this division is at Bengaluru and not at Agra where the ground forces SF was originally based. Thus, the SF has been taken out of the ambit of 'paratroopers', where its role was defined by the mode of transportation. Second, the SF of the Navy (MARCOS), and the IAF (Garud) as also NSG are all clubbed together in the

Special Operations Division. Thus, right from the beginning, these forces were structured as a tri-service organisation and it is quite likely that a broader canvas will be available to them. As of now, they have been training in target designation tasks for the deep strike precision attack combat aircraft. Given the range of tactical missiles (Pralay150 to 500 kms, Brahmos 350 kms, Prithvi 150 to 250 kms, and even Multi Barrel Rocket Launchers with extended ranges of up to 70 kms) the SF may be required to penetrate deep inside enemy territory to create high impact from the precision long range missiles and artillery.

Discussing issues mentioned in *Employment of Special Forces: Challenges and Opportunities for the Future* at the Centre for Joint Warfare Studies (published by Vij Books), most senior military veterans flagged the need for raising the force for expeditionary, counter insurgency tasks below the threshold of conventional war. The veterans also raised concerns about the deteriorating relations between the Special Forces and the conventional military. These lukewarm relations emanate from three major reasons. First, the conventional military is 'all conventional' driven by (outdated) Standard Operating Procedures (SOPs), bulky logistics, emphasis on mass against substance, inferior weaponry and guidance systems, and lower levels of combat endurance. As against this, the SF excel as small teams, are highly agile, and make their own rules and processes as per the task and the situation. From their appearance and behaviour, they do not look like 'smart soldiers,' but when the action starts, they spring surprises and display their potential in making difficult tasks look easy. Hence, when the SF is allotted to a commander of the conventional military, the mismatch becomes obvious. Like the air force, the SF just need to be given the overall objective and should be left alone to make their own action plans.

Armed Forces Cyber Command

The Indian Armed Forces operate in the digitised world governed by opportunities and threats in cyber space. The cyber space extends from the most basic to the most advanced components of the armed forces at three levels—cognitive, software and physical. Given the nature of cyber space, defensive measures are more relevant in gaining a position of advantage compared to offensive measures, though offensive capability will have to be built to disrupt, disorganise, demoralise and incapacitate the adversary when felt necessary. The offensive capabilities will have to be centralised at the national level and are not recommended to be provided or delegated at the combatant theatre commands or the component commands. The defensive capabilities have to be built at the individual soldier, network and platform levels. This would need a very vast scale of continuous and dynamic training across the entire spectrum of the armed forces.

Besides military cyber space, the nation also has non-military cyber space where the citizens, non-military organisations, institutions and industries operate. It is extremely difficult to separate the military and the non-military cyber space in a 4G environment. However, all efforts need to be made to insulate the military from non-military cyber space; wherever this is not possible, extensive monitoring, de-radicalisation, and data monitoring need to be done.

Thus, when it comes to cyber command, the following aspects become legitimate requirements and also dictate its structure and relationship with the theatres:

- Centralised offensive capability: The NSA should have the authority to launch cyber offensives.
- Extensive defensive capabilities down to the individual soldier, airman and naval ratings.

- Continuous training, upgradation and monitoring.
- Domain knowledge needs to be prepared for four levels:
    - **User or cyber literate:** Each individual soldier who uses a mobile phone and a computer. The trainees would gain basic capabilities in observing digital security discipline while using their individual devices—mobiles, laptops and desk tops.
    - **Cyber Operator:** They would be proficient in vulnerability detection and resolution, cyber security audits etc.
    - **Cyber Warrior:** They would be trained on offensive operations and will act on specific sanction from the national level agency on the type, target and duration of attack.
    - **Cyber Leaders:** They need to have multidiscipline knowledge—psychology, sociology, cultural behaviours, linguistic skills, and in depth knowledge of the ICT. They would be involved in making policies, developing cyber weapons, authorising cyber offensives and monitoring their impact.

During the Combined Commanders Conference held at Air Force Station, Jodhpur on 28 September 2018, the raising of a Defence Cyber Agency was approved. It will have tasks related to cyber security as well as cyber offensives. The government also has plans to raise an Armed Forces Cyber Command in the hinterlands of Madhya Pradesh that will give a fighting edge to the theatre commands. Cyber Command will ensure security of military communications and systems especially in forward formations like the Siliguri Corps, Tezpur Corps and the Northern Command including the Ladakh Corps facing Tibet.

Defence Intelligence Command (DIC)

There are no substantive reports on Defence Intelligence Command in the media though the need exists for integration of national level intelligence (obtained from R&AW, IB, NTRO and relevant ministries such as Ministry of External Affairs, Ministry of Finance etc.) with defence intelligence. If raised, this command will get inputs from its own internal sources—signal intelligence, space-based systems, troops in contact through their respective HQ, special forces and specifically tasked agents. Besides they can seek specific inputs from other agencies at the national level (R&AW, IB, NTRO, Ministries). The primary function of a DIC would be to collect, collate and interpret the input. It is only after interpretation that the data/information becomes intelligence that is now capable of generating alternative courses of action for envisaged operations. At this stage, the operational commanders including the CDS come into the picture. In the Israeli Defence Forces, the intelligence agency is divorced from the military. They provide their assessments to the political leadership. However, the IDF has created their own intelligence set-up in the wake of the Yom Kippur experience.

Space Command

The US, China and France are major players in space war. China has militarised its space war capabilities by successfully testing Anti-Satellite capabilities in 2007. India has had a very advanced commercial space capability for a long time. However, since 2018, India has demonstrated military intention in space by testing its Anti-Satellite (ASAT) capabilities. The Defence Space Agency (DSA) with HQ at Bengaluru has the task of operating dual purpose space capabilities ranging from surveillance, navigation to monitoring space assets of adversaries, anti-ballistic missile defence, launch and guidance of own missiles, operating laser weapon platforms in space, offensive cyber operations from space and providing command control capabilities to our own military forces.

The space command in any form will be a strategic centralised national asset to be employed in a supporting role in most cases except in the case of an all-out space war where the space command (DSA) will conduct full-fledged defensive and offensive operations from space. It is likely to be placed under the overall command of the IAF. The outer space today is characterised by proliferation of military and non-military systems. Since the first half of 1960, the US and USSR (as it existed then) commenced active development of space weapons—kinetic, directed energy, conventionally launched from space orbits as well as from the ground, air and from maritime platforms. Today, several other nations including India and China have developed these capabilities. The outer space also provides non-military facilities to the world that include navigation, communication, weather forecast, disaster management and so on. Hence, this domain involves diplomacy as also national security.

Logistics Command

The decision to establish Joint Logistic Nodes (JLN) at Mumbai, Guwahati and Port Blair was taken at the end of 2020. These nodes will cater to the logistics needs of the Army, the Navy and the IAF for small arms ammunition, ration, fuel oil and lubricants (FOL), general stores, civil hired transport (CHT), aviation clothing, spares, engineers support. Similar nodes are expected to be established in other parts of the country to provide logistics support to the functional and geographical commands.

However, establishing JLNs is a baby step towards creating an organisational structure and operational model of Logistics Command in the context of UTC. The pay-offs and obstacles for creating a joint logistics command would become clearer by looking at the functional aspects or series of activities that are involved in military logistics. Generally, the logistics activities are grouped according to two distinct situations. First, during operations and second, during the maintenance for operational readiness state. During the operations phase, logistics involves stage management of forces in a secure and camouflaged manner to their respective concentration and assembly areas which are the launch pads for commencing operations. Once the operations commence, then replenishment of war stores that are expended during operations, repair and maintenance during operations (*in situ* or at the forward repair echelons), medical support by way of initial treatment of casualties and their evacuation to hospital for further treatment, all these activities are undertaken in an hostile combat environment.

In the operational readiness phase, routine activities require maintenance of logistics preparedness of the force that involves creating and maintaining infrastructure (roads, living accommodations, shelters, bunkers, water and electricity supply etc). This is done by the Engineer-in-Chief. Stocking, and replenishment of ordnance stores ranging from ammunition of all types, clothing etc, is done by the Directorate of Ordnance. Repair and maintenance of equipment, guns, platforms, vehicles etc, are undertaken by the Directorate General of Electrical and Mechanical Engineers; stocking and replenishment of rations, FOL and, last but not least, providing means for movement of forces is a task undertaken by the Director General of Army Services Corps.

Besides this, the Defence Acquisition Centre (DAC) coordinates procurements for the three services. The organisational structures, tasks, processes for all these were formalised during WWII. Most armed forces have transformed their logistics set-ups based on the modern transportation infrastructure, availability of technology, operational changes and modern means of supply chain management. Indian Armed Forces as usual have remained outliers in this field. More surprisingly, many among the top hierarchy wish to remain so. Creation of a logistics command on the lines of creating a UTC will involve the following strategic approach:

- Merge organisations that are involved in logistics tasks. Thus, the services, ordnance, engineering support, repair and maintenance, operational logistics organisations need to come under the umbrella of one unified logistics command.
- Outsource tasks to the organisations that are best suited for the job. Thus, repair and maintenance tasks need to be undertaken by the Original Equipment Manufacturers (OEMs.) The companies that are providing vehicles to the armed forces are best placed to repair and maintain these including training users for appropriate use to avoid unnecessary faults. This aspect can be inbuilt in the procurement agreements. Rations, general stores and other such stores can also be stocked and provided by the outsourced non-military organisations. The stocking based on the War Wastage Rates can be pre-decided.
- All the Joint Logistics Nodes need to come under the Logistics command.
- Movement of goods and services need to be done through latest SCM technologies and managerial practices such as coding of stores, AI assisted networked inventory management, movement tracking by GPS assisted systems, and order placements based on Electronic Data Interchange (EDI). Supply chain management technologies are the most widely used in the commercial world. These technologies can be conveniently used by the military with adequate security overlays.
- A separate logistics network needs to be created that uses smart agent-based communication systems and AI tools.
- A network of warehouses need to be created as per the operational requirements.

- All stores need to be coded for identification and robotic handling.
- Movement of stores and services need to be continuously monitored by indigenous NavIC system (The Indian Regional Navigation Satellite System that provides much more accurate positioning information).

Missiles and Rocket Forces

Post the Galwan incident (June 2020) against the Chinese, India has focused on creating a missile force that can counter the Chinese Rocket Force which they have deployed in Aksai Chin and in Tibet. The missile command that is being created will be another tri-service organisation to be commanded by the officers of the three services in rotation. India has missile systems that can be fired from ground, air and the sea. These missiles range from a strike distance of 40 km (Exocet) to 8,000 kms (Agni V). Several of these missiles are supersonic. The most potent missile system that India has is the Brahmos Missile System with a range extending to 350 kms (800-kms range Brahmos Missiles are also under development). These missiles are terrain mapping (cruise missiles, difficult to detect and neutralise) and extremely precise in hitting their targets. Their circular error of probability is as low as one meter at a range of 300 kms.

The missile systems require an elaborate surveillance, guidance and target acquisition system. This is where the fire support net, surveillance net and terminal guidance systems will have to be incorporated.

Nuclear Command Authority

It was some time in the 1980s, almost ten years after the first nuclear weapon test in 1974 that India's former PM late Shri Rajiv Gandhi on being urged by the then Chief of the Army Staff

General K Sunderji, ordered DRDO to start developing a rugged miniaturised and safer nuclear device along with reliable sub-systems and components to keep the country's nuclear deterrent capability at a minimum state of readiness.

Initially, the device was to be carried by the deep strike combat aircraft, Jaguar due to its excellent terrain mapping navigational capability. However, due to very low ground clearance from the pod carrying the device, Mirage 2000 was chosen for the purpose. As of now, Sukhoi 30Mk1, Rafale, MiG 29 and even indigenously built Tejas MkI have the capability to conduct nuclear strike.

Subsequently, a large number of short-range, medium-range and long-range missiles have been developed with adequate payload capacity to strike at distances ranging from a few hundred to few thousand kms with circular error of probability of a few meters at those distances. Along with this, according to information, major improvements have been made in the bomb design in terms of quantum of fissile/fusion material required for the same yield and total weight of the device for same result at the target end. A 200 to 300 kilogram device could provide 30 to 100 kiloton yield at the target end with remarkable accuracy.

Besides, the air delivered and terrestrial launch modes, India is close to developing submarine launched systems thus completing the nuclear triad. For obvious reasons, details about the number of devices and their actual yields should remain a closely guarded secret. There is general consensus among the Indian and the Western scientific communities that India has a potent nuclear deterrent from sub-kiloton to 100-300 kiloton devices that can be delivered at short notice if the need arises. Again, the scientific community believes that India has enough stock pile of weapon grade Plutonium-239 and highly enriched Uranium-235. Besides the fast breeder and conventional reactors have sufficient capability to produce more of these radioactive materials if required.

The Strategic Forces Command have their own most secure command, control and damage assessment system. Since India has no first use policy (unconfirmed reports suggest that India now has decided on first use if the situation so demands), location and activation procedures would have taken into account the survivability factor (after the initial nuclear attack by the adversary). This command comes directly under the PMO. Once the political decision is taken to activate the nuclear option, the concerned military component (mode of delivery) will be activated perhaps through the CDS. During normal course of operations, the theatre commanders will remain out of this loop.

Communications for Theatre Commands

In the literature review part of this study, a brief on the author's interaction with former Signals Officer-in-Chief Lt Gen Rajeev Sabherwal has been included. Gen Sabherwal was the Signals adviser to the first CDS, the late Gen Bipin Rawat. He was entrusted with interacting with the communication heads of the three services to formulate policies for creation of joint networks for the three services, protocols for interoperability, security overlays and perhaps identify applications.

Sometimes in the beginning of 2020, before the pandemic struck the world, issues related to jointness in tri-services communications were discussed on a public platform (at the Manekshaw Centre, New Delhi). Those discussions would have been compiled in some minutes for internal consumption. Besides these internal minutes and discussions, information on how communications aspects for joint organisations are addressed by several professionals, there are articles on Command

Control Communications Computers Intelligence Information Surveillance and Reconnaissance (C4I2SR) that describe the efforts being made for tri-service communications.

As per various discussions and papers on the subject published as late as 2023, the major achievements and gaps in this domain are as under:

- Strategic Communication: The Defence Communication Network (DCN) that caters to the strategic network comprises of 30,000 kms of OFC (Optic Fibre Cable) laid by the BSNL that would connect 238 military stations. These military stations will have interoperable tri-services nodes. This infrastructure has helped in connecting the three services with a media that has more than adequate bandwidth. The Air Force Net (AFNET) of the IAF and the Navy Enterprise Wide Network (NEWN) of the Navy get integrated with this communication infrastructure thus integrating the service specific networks of the Navy and the IAF with the strategic three services network. Since the maritime and air borne platforms are integrated with this infrastructure, the backbone of the tri-services communications to a great extent becomes that much more effective for the three services. However, optimising data communications in the three services is still in the nascent stage.
- The requirements of ground forces are vastly different from the maritime and air powers: Here high bandwidth data communication networks need to be extended to the battalion, regiment and company levels. Advanced phases of ASCON are reaching out to these echelons. However, as of now this is work in progress. Since there are no major hurdles in the execution of this phase of ASCON extension, the full integration of forward combat zone with the apex HQ is just a matter of time.
- The three services have their own command control, communications, decision support systems; the Army Command

Control and Communication Systems (ACCCS) for the Army, Indian Air Force Command Control Systems (IACCS) for the IAF, Navy Command Control Communication and Information (NC3I) for the Navy. Also, these systems are not interoperable at present.

- The Tac C3I network that comprises Command Information and Decision Support System (CIDSS), Artillery Command Control and Communication System (ACCCS), Air Defence Control and Reporting (ADC&R), Battlefield Surveillance System (BSS) and Electronic Warfare (EW) are still in the process of being fully developed and then integrated for the tri-services operations. The most critical aspect would be to integrate the ADC&R with the weapon platforms networks.
- The cellular communications to replace the existing Army Radio Engineered Network (AREN) in mobile operations across the LoC, LAC and IB are still being developed. However, the innovativeness of commanding officers and communication engineers have evolved their own methods of mobile secure grid-based communications that would keep pace with mobile operations across the LoC, LAC and IB. The bandwidth based (2 MB, 8 MB) Radio Relays (RR) are being connected with Commercial Off-the-Shelf (COTS) equipment to function as switches. In the near future, 100Mbps RR would be connecting these switches (Routers, Mobile Switching Centres). These rolling grids can be connected to the Public Switched Telephone Networks (backbone). Thus, an innovative way to field cellular like systems has been devised by the Army Communication Engineers.
- The Software Designed Radio (SDR) for the three services for the combat net radio is still under development. Army units are procuring COTS equipment (SDRs) under special financial powers at various formation headquarters to meet the emergent

requirements. It has been learned that the Navy has accepted the Defence Public Sector Production unit (DPSU) developed SDRs.

- The Navy and the IAF are reported to have developed their own logistics network whereas the Army logistics network is still work-in-progress.

One of the most critical gaps in the current communications systems is the lack of integration with the troops involved in contact battle. Apparently, the Non Contact Warfare (NCW) doctrines are being taken too seriously by the communications engineers in the armed forces. These are just doctrines with no real-life relevance as of now. The most developed militaries of the world gain and maintain contact with the adversary. Even in the current Russia-Ukraine war the infantry, armour and other ground forces do get in to battle. The missiles and other long distance weapons are in addition to these organic close range battles. The tri-services teams fighting the contact battles need to be enabled to see, engage, destroy and disengage. They need the best in the kitty. Right now, unit level actions are being taken as a stop gap arrangement. A more sustainable and integrated approach needs to be taken at the earliest.

Global trends on communication networks for the armed forces indicate very high priority in budgeting for the C3I systems, fielding modern communication systems expeditiously before the technologies become obsolete and upgrading the systems in time becomes a priority. Some specific global trends in the field of communication systems and jointness in planning and conduct of operations include:

- Increasing component of software, signals processing, AI, Big Data in communication systems, weapon platforms and discrete weapon systems.

- Expenditure on ordnance is on the decrease whereas expenditure in making the ordnance intelligent and smart is on the increase.
- Modern militaries have given much higher priority to data transmission.
- The US ensured that jointmanship runs through all their communication systems and platforms. They raised TRITAC, a full-fledged organisation to iron out inter service interoperability problems.

Training Command/Knowledge Organisations

Using Indigenous Indian Systems for Military Knowledge: We have seen that the ancient Indian system of warfare was advanced, complex and needed specialised knowledge and skills to plan and conduct military campaigns with their huge, multidisciplinary forces. Where was this skillset and knowledge generated and then imparted to the concerned people? During the *Ramayana* period there is enough evidence of Ram, the prince of Ayodhya in exile for 14 years, learning the art and science of warfare from the sages. There are two prominent names that emerge in the epic. Vishwamitra and Agastya. Both these sages not only specialised in knowledge related to creation of powerful weapons and war materials but were also proficient in imparting skills for use of these special weapons to the deserving recipient.

The *Mahabharat* period too has mention of these forest universities where the sages taught the art and science of warfare. Sahana Singh, a member of Indian History Awareness and Research, a Houston-based think tank, mentions military science as one of the subjects taught in Takshashila University. In her book, *The Educational Heritage of Ancient India*, she mentions that 104 princes studied archery in Takshashila University. It is safe to assume that military knowledge and skills flowed from these hundreds of universities spread all over India.

Military scholars as also soldiers must have been learning the desired aspects of warfare and joining the armies of the kings or the nobles. With the advent of the Mogul invaders, especially under the Khiljis, these great centres of knowledge were systematically destroyed. The British colonisers completed the job that was left half-done by the Muslim rulers. The British did a more enduring job of destruction by mixing half-truths and imposing their systems on the Indians. Fortunately for the British, the Indians who were fighting for self-rule adopted a method that suited the British design.

Military Training in the British Era and Post Independence: During WWII, Lord Claude Auchinleck was made responsible for 'Training Command India' for training Indian officers and soldiers for WWII. A large number of military training institutions in India today were established way back in early 1940s. In 2012, the military had 142 training institutions of different types including five for the Defence Research and Development Organization (DRDO). These training institutions are under the respective service except the five institutes that are under the DRDO. Once jointness becomes a reality these training establishments may come under one organisation and perhaps may be revamped. According to the IDSA document referred earlier (editors Gurmeet Kanwal, Neha Kohli) that has analysed the reform processes in the Indian Armed Forces, the 'military training' domain is depicted as adequate. However, if we correlate the existing training ecosystem in the three services with the organisational performance, the following gaps become quite obvious:

- Training institutions that were established to bring in jointness, eg the NDA, the National Defence College, the Defence Services Staff College etc. to name a few have failed to achieve any semblance of cooperation and collaboration in the services. The silos remain watertight. The literature review in the beginning of this study is a testimony to this silo-based thinking even at the highest levels of military leadership.

- Most of the training is based on the Western model. The information war doctrine of the Indian Armed Forces is almost a copy of what the Americans wrote in their Field Manual 100-6. All military operations still follow the WWII approach—counter air and air superiority operations in a short war at the cost of close air support (1965), large bridgehead with proper armour protection before the break-out starts (Shakargarh operation in 1971), Indian Army sending request to IAF for close air support and the latter asking for target description, considering a 'battle tank' as the best anti tank weapon, using armour in support of infantry, failing to use concentrated armour (combat command and above) in any of the wars India has fought, are some of the long shadows cast by the British way of fighting dating back to WWII.
- There appears to be a lack of academic rigour and scrutiny in creating and adapting new military knowledge. Even tacit knowledge gained during wars is not documented and used for improvements in the next war.

Military Science and Defence Studies in Indian Universities: There has been a proposal to establish a National Defence University (NDU) for some time. Nothing much has happened on this account. However, Indian universities have introduced courses in defence studies at the undergraduate and postgraduate levels. Besides, state level defence universities are being established. The Prime Minster Narendra Modi dedicated National Defence

University at Gandhinagar, Gujarat to the nation during their convocation in 2023. Apparently the approach now is to follow the ancient past where military knowledge (creation, adaptation and internalisation) flows from the institutions of education to the military.

Likely Amalgamation of Training Institutes of Individual Services: Given the complexities of modern warfare and the intense efforts required to prepare soldiers in various warfighting skills, the existing training institutes of the three services will remain indispensable. However, their curriculum, pedagogy and performance evaluation will have to be tailored to meet three critical factors. First, use of available technologies in increasing the learners' base. Second, alignment of training with organisational performance. Third, making the training institutions open to review by external evaluation bodies. Internal evaluation has its own limitations. Members of the armed forces are involved in a number of tasks while in service. A very large number of these tasks require skills and knowledge that are relevant in non-military productive activities. To that extent, two-way movement of skills and knowledge between the military and the civilian institutions will enhance the overall national outcomes in production and exploitation of knowledge. This will also ensure participation by the citizens in military as also non-military domains. Hence, educational and skills development activities for a purely military domain need to be restricted to those that are strictly for warfighting. For all other dual-use knowledge creation and exploitation activities, jointness between the military and non-military institutions will be an enriching factor.

How Americans have Approached the Subject: The Americans appear to have a seamless integration between the military and non-military training institutions. Most of their prestigious universities have specialised courses in military science and defence studies. Besides academic institutions, even their industrial infrastructure is coupled to military requirements. Hence, their weapon systems, managerial ecosystem, psychological and leadership training are addressed in an environment of mutual cooperation and collaboration. The military institutions address the pure military domain activities which their department of defence calls, 'just in case' activities that are required to be performed in the military only. The American investment in defence technology and knowledge creation (in the form of R&D) is the highest in the world.

The Chinese Approach: The Chinese military have established universities specialising in Information War and Cyber Security. They have universities that create knowledge in military science. The most noteworthy aspect of the Chinese military education system is the very short time cycle in identification of need, decision making in selecting the course of action for fulfilling the need and completion of the project. It is this speed that enabled them to undertake fifth generation reforms in the People's Liberation Army (PLA), which back in 1949, was established like a peasant army.

Integrating Finances, Defence Budgeting and Procurements with National Economy

We have seen in the literature review that there is a general consensus on inadequacy of the defence budget (most of the senior military officers suggest 3 per cent of GDP should be allotted for the defence budget as against the current 1.6 per cent). There is hardly any suggestion for reviewing the way we look at the defence budget. We need to consider some critical factors in this context:

- The process and quantum of budgeting for any activity are linked with the overall vision and goals. In the context of defence budgeting the planners need to focus on our vision on national security and achievable goals for defence capability in the context of realistic threat assessment. The current process of budget allocation and monitoring of expenditure ignores both these factors. The Long Term Perspective Plans that address the envisaged capability does not form part of the process.
- The requirements that are projected by the three services as part of budget process are isolated from each other, not connected with any central theme and seem to be inflated. These are scrutinised by organisations that lack the professional acumen for national security. There needs to be one agency that prepares and projects the budget for the defence sector to be analysed and approved by the top political executive.
- The time-bound method of expenditure and the excessive involvement of financial services professionals results in hurried and wasteful expenditure towards the close of the financial year. The emphasis is on following rules as against achieving the desired objectives.
- Budgeting is seen as an allocation and expenditure activity and not part of an economic model.

When we compare the structure, size and budgeting for theatre commands formed by the US, whom we wish to emulate, or China who are our principal adversary, our focus is on the allotment of funds for defence expenditure and the percentage of GDP they spend for the purpose. Two major issues skip our attention. These are the level at which the military budgeting is scrutinised in these countries and the process of identifying capabilities to be created and matching allotment of resources. Both these countries are not able to meet the long wish list of the requirements for defence budget as projected by their respective militaries. However, the cuts in the demands projected by their forces as against what is allotted is based on programmes and capabilities.

Many of their decisions are not very popular with their armed forces. For example, in one of its Quadrennial Defence Reviews (QDR), the US establishment decided that the country cannot afford 250 modern aircraft as recommended by the concerned Service, and upgrade of only 187 current aircraft with modern avionics was approved. Also, the Review recommended that F-22 aircrafts should not be procured and the department would not fund the F-35 program. Recently, the US Government has decided that F-16s suitably modified, will be used till 2050.

The Chinese top brass decided that they should accord highest priority to Information Technology (IT) in the defence forces. They created a Task Force for Information War and set up four Universities for this field of military knowledge. Hacker group supported exercises were held in China and Information Warfare (IW) units were raised in 2003.

In the UK, the demands for defence budget are placed by a single tri-service organisation that is responsible for the tri-service logistics also. Thus, 'Defence Equipment and Support Organisation' is responsible for logistics as also for acquisition.

Let us look at the aspect of linking budgeting for the defence sector as part of political economy in India. First, given the demonstrated and real threats to India, the Indian defence sector has huge internal demand. We have been among the top nations that have huge expenditure in the sector besides being the top importers of weapon systems from 2013 to 2017. Hence there is an attractive incentive in boosting indigenous production through efficient manufacturing processes. According to Laxman Behera (when he was with the (Manohar Parrikar-Institute of Defense Studies and Analysis), the modern MNCs involved in defence production are four times more productive than the Indian Defence Production Public Sector Units. India spends less than one per cent of GDP on R&D compared to two per cent by China and 3.6 per cent by South Korea. These are 2016-17 figures. During 2016-17, our export of defence systems was at Rs 1,521 crores.

However, things are changing for the better. In 2023, the defence systems exports by India jumped to Rs 15,920 crores, a ten-fold increase from what it was in 2016. In 2022, forty-one ordnance factories were merged into seven DPPSUs, thus doing away with a 246 years legacy (a case of breaking free of monumental inertia). Twenty-five per cent of the R&D funds will be allotted to the Defence Industries. Thirty-seven projects have been awarded to the MSMEs. The government decided to fund 250 startups in the defence sector. The Raksha Mantri announced 68 per cent of capital expenditure for indigenous procurement. The government has decided to reduce the import content of defence components to 36 per cent in next two years. In 2023, out of rupees one lac crore allotted for capital defence budgets, three-fourths will be spent for procurement from Indian companies. All these measures have linked the defence expenditure to the political economy of India.

Organisational Dynamics for Jointness

Lt Col (Dr) Noel Sproles and Alex Yates of Command and Control Division Information Science Laboratory, Department of Defence, Science and Technology Organisation, Australia, in their *A Historical Study of Operational Command: A Resource for Researchers* addressed the organisational aspects of theatre command based on Mintzberg's and Drucker's theories. Mintzberg suggested different levels, namely, the apex commanders, subordinate commanders, staff, technostructure and so on. We adapted this in our analysis earlier in this study. Drucker on the other hand, used the value chain concept for organisational dynamics, such as result producing activities, support activities, housekeeping and top management activities.

These theories explain the structural concepts. These structures are designed for organisations that operate with a certain level of certainty, involving no risk to life or property by any adversary, with attractive profit incentives and well-defined cognitive capabilities for various levels of functions or activities. Military institutions function in high risk combat zones. The organisational structures suggested by the management gurus can be applied for component or functional commands that are not in direct contact. In contact battles, military organisations are characterised by:

- Extreme risk to life.
- Diversity and complexity of resources at hand for achieving military objectives.
- Organisational differences within the ground forces, the air power and the maritime powers have vastly different structure, culture and operational processes.
- All activities are to be carried out under enemy action.
- There is no profit orientation though the penalties for failures can be devastating.
- Inherent incentive to play safe.
- Military environments bring out the best and the worst of human behaviour. A critical mass of desired courage, boldness and sense of

sacrifice is required for success.

- The environment and the outcomes are uncertain. Even probabilistic maths cannot predict the outcome. Though a number of wargames have been developed, their efficacy in predicting the causal relationship cannot be taken for granted. Unfortunately, with increased automation, casualties due to friendly fires have increased. Hence human intervention remains a necessity.

Like Mintzberg and Drucker, there are a large number of management professionals who have addressed the organisational dynamics for management of business enterprise. All these suffer from the same inadequacies. Nonetheless, organisational dynamics for military as an institution still remains extremely important. We can look at the issue in the reverse order. We start with the desired end-state first. Then identify how best these end-states in the context of military organisation can be achieved. For jointmanship where cooperation, collaboration and coordination are more important than individual efficiency and competence, the organisational dynamics depend on five key attributes.

Character: In the context of Indian values, desired human character–especially for the leaders, is based on selflessness, sacrifice, self-regulation, humility (absence of ego), friendliness, concern for those at the lowest rung of the hierarchical pyramid, simplicity, setting lofty goals and steadfastness in actions. Jointmanship emerges as a natural corollary of selflessness and humility. Commanders with intrinsically strong character do not consider their command as their personal asset. They are more concerned with high levels of performance by their respective commands in collaboration and cooperation with other forces in the theatre. These commanders also overcome their egos to create synergy of efforts. This is what Lt Gen J F R Jacob and

Air Chief Marshal P C Lal did to achieve spectacular results in the Eastern theatre in 1971. Lt Gen Sagat Singh and Group Captain Chandan did the same in making 4 Corps operations so successful.

Unfortunately, such examples were very few in 1971. The Southern and Western Command operations suffered from disjointed operations due to poor character-centric values. We will elaborate on these with examples from the Indian past. Back in 1947, one of the most celebrated officers of the Indian Army, Lt Gen Thakur Nathu Singh, made a very unflattering observation on the stock of Indian officers in comparison with the British Officers, 'I have not met a single British Officer who lacks national pride and I have not met a single Indian officer who takes pride in his country.'

In 1986, Gen K Sundarji on taking over as Chief of Army Staff wrote a semi-official letter to all officers. Here are some of his observations on the officer class as a whole (in 1986). 'Living in glass houses. Developed a yen for five star culture and ostentation. Being a gentleman (cadets in the military academy are addressed as 'gentleman cadet') does not mean Westernisation and becoming a poor imitation of a "white sahib".' R K Anand in his book *Assault on Merit The Untold Story of Civil Military Relations*, published in 2012 brings out a number of cases involving three/four star generals equivalent in the three services. Some of these officers had gone to court, approached political leaders on their promotions/postings. Several of these officers have gone to the extent of saying, 'I am better than him then how can you promote him over me.' Unfortunately, the courts and even the political leaders did intervene, corrected the 'anomaly'/pandered to the unreasonable arguments of the officers concerned.

Either way, it does not augur well for the military as an

institution. In March 2021, the Indian Prime Minister while addressing the Combined Commanders Conference (Kevadia, Gujarat) nudged the commanders to indigenise their processes, procedures and culture rather than focusing only on the doctrine.

Humanity: A soldier by nature must exhibit human values to friends and foes. In ancient India there were terms of engagement in the battle that ensured appropriate treatment of the captured enemy troops. India set an example by keeping more than 90,000 Pakistani Prisoners of War (POW) after the 1971 victory in good condition for almost a year. Compare this with the inhuman atrocities inflicted by the Pakistani forces on their own countrymen in erstwhile East Pakistan. This became one of the major causes of Pakistani defeat. Again in WWII, the Germans killed Russian civilians who greeted them (as these civilians were fed up of atrocities from USSR's totalitarian regime). The end result was that sentiment turned against the Germans. In Vietnam, the US forces behaved in the most diabolic manner against the Vietnamese population. The super power lost the war. In the 1956 100-hour war, the IDF was asked not to take any prisoners because speed of operations was critical and they did not have enough resources to cater to the POWs.

The IDF did not kill even a single Egyptian soldier on capturing the position. They let these soldiers flee to safety across the Suez Canal. This attribute becomes a campaign winning factor in counter-insurgency operations. This aspect becomes most relevant in addressing internal turbulence either due to externally abetted terrorism or internal turmoil due to poor administration/political bungling. Indian military has been subjected to these tests within the country on a number of occasions.

Cognitive Ability: This involves the analytical acumen to see through the chaff and read the situation with bare minimum inputs. The fog of war makes it difficult to make sense of available information. Besides the enemy too adds to the confusion with his acts of deception and perception management. On the other hand, the time to take decisions is at a premium. This is where the inherent intellect of the commanders and acquired wisdom through experience add up to enable military leaders to take good decisions within the limited time available.

In the 1965 war, the General Officer Commanding 11 Corps wrote to his Army Commander (Lt Gen Harbakhsh Singh) that all the infantry units of 4 Infantry Division need to be disbanded as the men were deserting. Harbakhsh met the GOC 4 Infantry Division and his subordinate officers. His cognitive ability suggested to him that the Division had enough fight in it if they were properly launched into battle. It was the same division and the same infantry units who stopped the famed Pakistani armoured division in its tracks and destroyed a bulk of their tanks in the battle of Asal Uttar (3 Cav helped them in this role). In 1971, Lt Gen J F R Jacob could visualise Dhaka as the only objective for the Eastern Command while others (Army Chief and the government) were content with capturing enough territory to send back the refugees. J F R Jacob was proved right.

Courage: This has moral as well as physical dimensions. At the moral level it is courage to give professionally correct (and not politically correct) advice during the process of collective decision making or accept own mistakes and take corrective actions. At the physical level it involves taking calculated risks with adequate precautions without jeopardising the conduct of battle or operations. In the 1948 operations against Pakistan, the senior Indian commanders could have prevailed over the political leadership to continue the operations till the entire Indian territory was recovered.

India had the resources and time to do so. There were Generals like Nathu Singh who could tell the Prime Minister what they felt was strategically correct. But the number of such generals was below the critical mass. A similar situation existed from 1959 to 1962. Except for Gen Thimayya and Lt Gen Daulat Singh there were not many generals who could prevail over one of the most disastrous decisions by the political leadership. In the 1965 operation, Lt Gen Harbakhsh Singh (Army Commander Western Command) found that most of the officers (battalion commanders and above) lacked physical courage and magnified the risks. Compare this with the examples we have seen in the IDF operations in 1948-49, 1956 and 1967. At the senior levels the commanders are expected to set examples to their command because courage like morale is contagious.

Learnability: The art and science of war has been changing at a very fast pace. It is almost impossible to ensure successful conduct of war based on the knowledge and skills acquired in the last war. Every war and every situation in a war is new and requires a fresh application of tacit knowledge. Indian Armed Forces have not shown any propensity for learning either from their own mistakes or from the environment.

The concept and functioning of Forward Air Controller (FAC) was operationalised during WWII. The Pakistani Forces used this in supporting their ground forces in 1965. The Indian Forces had not devised proper communications and procedures for such close air support in this war. By the time of the 1971 war, Air Chief Marshal P C Lal had made special efforts to prepare these teams based on his experience in the 1965 war. The FACs wherever deployed were most effective. Unfortunately, the ground forces did not deploy enough of these, even though the IAF had made enough young pilots available for the FAC.

It must be remembered that fighter pilots are precious for any air force. Letting them go unutilised is extremely wasteful to say the least. In Shakargarh, the ground forces had no role for the IAF after four days of war. As regards learning from others, we virtually copied the Information War doctrines made by the US Department of Defence after the first Gulf War. Later, the US Forces moved on and changed their Information War Doctrines whereas our IW Doctrines remain the same. Incidentally, the first war doctrine made by the Indian Forces was in 2005 almost six decades after Independence. Even this doctrine was based entirely on quotes from foreign generals. Our training institutes can change all this.

A natural query that emerges from the above discussion is: How to ensure the above attributes among the leaders and the soldiers at all levels? We may be tempted to assume that training establishments, adequate incentives and hygiene factors for the military organisations will achieve the above aim. However, the solution is not that simple. Daniel Kahneman in his best-selling book, *Thinking, Fast and Slow*, recollects his experience during his military service in the IDF. He spent some time attached to a unit that selected candidates for officers' training on the basis of a series of interviews and field tests. The validity of the ratings based on these was rather poor.

If we extend this argument further, the correlation between performance during training and performance on the battlefield would also be weak. According to training and development theories, organisational performance is a function of two factors. First, the aptness and rigour of training for the anticipated task and second, the organisational capabilities to absorb the newly trained talent in the team. Thus, the team itself needs to keep growing along the learning curve to absorb and exploit high calibre talent. If this does not happen, no amount of training will improve the organisational performance.

The five attributes that we have discussed above need to form part of the training and testing schedule. Once the trainees join their respective units, the above attributes must be reinforced in the routine functions they have to perform. In other words strength of character, humanity, cognitive ability, courage and learnability must be respected, recognised and incentivised attributes in the work place. If the units thrive on mediocrity it will not be able to sustain high calibre talent. Either the talented youngsters will succumb to the mediocrity of their peers, or bide their time for better opportunities. Thus, what happens in the units and regiments is critical to carry the desired attributes of jointmanship. We have had tri-service training institutes like the NDA, Defence Services Staff College, and the National Defence College. These have not helped in bringing even a modicum of jointmanship in the Indian Armed Forces. We have seen the gaps. The training institutes need to identify some more gaps between what exists and what is desired and formulate their training accordingly.

★★★

Epilogue

> The Process that has already begun, needs to be transformative in approach and nature. There will be some friction that is natural in such a statusquoist environment. But that will be a very small cost to pay for these big ticket military reforms.

Though the government tabled the Bill on 23 March 2023, when the Indian Parliament was in a polarised mood, gearing up for the next general elections in 2024, giving scant attention to 'mundane' subjects like military reforms, the media and especially the military think tanks came alive with the subject. It emerged from these media reports that the government was serious on this subject. Some reports suggested that the regional theatre commands will be established as early as August 2023. As it turned out this was too optimistic.

Meanwhile, there were indications that the three services are coming on board on some common understanding of the structure, command and control envisaged in these reforms. There are also reports that, 'there will be no job losses' as a result of these reforms. Also, there are some rumours of rotational appointments of regional commanders between the army and the air force implying that a regional theatre command will be headed by an army general and air force air marshal in rotation.

At the junior level (Major, Lt Cols and equivalent), officers of the three services are being posted to sister services for indepth understanding of the way each service functions. All these are welcome steps. However, this does not touch even the tip of the iceberg. Organisational structure plays a limited role in enhancing institutional performance. Given our legacy as a nation and that of our military derived from British leadership and guidance in 1947 while retaining the English culture, 'British Indian Armed Forces ethos' and operational dynamics (as exhibited in the wars India fought since 1947), the reforms need to go deeper than the 'number of generals', 'who-commands-whom' and cross posting of officers. We need to go back to our roots and then work out desired outcomes in the context of the military as an institution in the present geopolitical environement and transformed internal narrative. Since we are looking at the 'desired outcomes' from the military it is important to analyse the inputs, environment (internal and external), and the process that will have controllable and uncontrolled variables.

Let's concentrate first on the outcome. The military as an institution must synergise its resources to achieve the desired end state (decided in consultation with the political leadership) in the shortest possible time with minimal cost and collateral damage (to both ourselves and the adversay). Consider liberation of Bangladesh, Balakot air strike, surgical strike across Uri as examples. In order to achieve these war time objectives, the armed forces need to remain in a constant state of readiness. This would involve real time information, accurate and realistic interpretation, pre-planned responses with adequate flexibility to change course as the conflict progresses. As citizens of this nation, each and every member of the armed forces need to set highest standards in strength of character, commitment to the nation, apolitical behaviour, selflessness, prudence and honesty. By and large, the Indian Armed Forces have been the most respected institution in the country. If properly launched with clear mandate and adequate (at times even inadequate) resources, the Indian military has delivered, though a more stringent analysis will reveal that they could have done far more.

The inputs or the raw material for achieving this outcome includes the people, wisdom, knowledge and skills, material resources, economic strength and national morale. The most complex component of this input is 'people'. It is also the most valuable asset that can achieve unimaginably high results if properly nurtured (processed). These 'people' when converted into soldiers—that includes the leadership at all levels—need to have attributes where strong bonding with the civilisational values (as enshrined in the Constitution, ancient epics and folklores), strength of character, motivation to serve the nation and mental robustness top the list.

These attributes must exist in the psychological make-up of the new entrants. The induction and training processes can only refine these attributes. The Agnipath scheme launched by the government is expected to meet this challenge. Military knowledge and skills, mental alertness to adapt, capability to exploit technology, and learnability are aspects that can be addressed in the training establishments and within routine functions in the units. The bulk of the training process needs to be based on a 'transformational' approach as against 'transactional' pay offs and penalties. Most modern armed forces follow and propagate a transactional approach. This approach would entail more pay, lifelong entitlements, comfort factors even during war, higher standards of living, social exclusiveness and so on.

While a nation must give the best possible incentives to its soldiers, global experience indicates that these incentives do not create good soldiers and leaders in war. Shivaji's forces excelled on frugal resources. They defeated their mighty adversaries with their speed, simplicity, commitment to the cause and sheer endurance. Shivaji's forces seldom had tents. He himself used to sleep on the ground in open fields. They had simple dresses, good horses and could ride twenty miles on a raid and come back after accomplishing the mission in a single day. With this simple approach, Shivaji built a brave and victorious force.

The same force under the Peshwas (after Shivaji's death) got used to comforts and wanted to return to luxurious tents after a day out in the battle. Their defeat in the third Battle of Panipat (1761) was a direct consequence of this luxurious lifestyle. Similarly, Maharana Pratap in the Battle of Haldighati subsequently outwitted the Moghul Emperor and remained unbeaten. Maharaja Ranjit Singh of Punjab could keep even the British at bay during his regime.

While addressing the aspects of desired quality of men and the leaders in joint regional commands, we need to dig deep into the way our legendary kings and ordinary soldiers functioned during this glorious period and adapt the traits from that period to the present day. Another aspect relevant with regard to quality of soldiers is their 'number'. Careful analysis of major wars fought by Indians in the past would indicate that numbers seldom matter. In the epic battle depicted in the *Mahabharat*, the winning side had a million soldiers less than the side that was defeated. Babur had fewer forces than his adversary Ibrahim Lodhi in the first Battle of Panipat. The Germans and the Israelis were always outnumbered by their respective adversaries. They won most of the campaigns from 1939 to 1943. The Israelis on the other hand never lost to their Arab adversaries. Even in the

Yom Kippur war, the Israelis turned a likely defeat into a face-saving stalemate.

Weapons, finances and knowledge matters in a war, but so many other factors also affect it. Brigadier Desmond E. Hayde MVC, makes a very subtle observation in his book *The Battle of Dograi* . 'The difference between Patton and Sherman tanks or 105 mm and 25 pounder artillery guns besides the difference in quantum of available ammunition would erect more debilitating psychological barriers in the minds of commanders than in the fighting troops.' Successful military commanders know how to synergise these resources during war. The idea of regional joint commands is based on this dictum of creating synergy in application or use of resources.

The process: The entire range of military reforms leading to tri-services regional or theatre commands would involve three major phases—jointness, integration and theatrisation. The first two will have some overlap while the third phase, involving the establishment of theatre commands in given regions should preferably succeed after completion of the first two phases. We need to look deeper into each of these phases to understand the complexities of reform. Former Air Chief Marshal Arup Raha in *Force in Statecraft: The Indian Perspective* says mere creation of posts and organisations is no longer acceptable in the process of 'transformation' unless it can produce the desired outcomes. We discussed some of the envisaged outcomes earlier. But the most critical suggestion here is to use 'transformation' (what the former Air Chief meant was perhaps using a transformational as against a transactional approach). Given the current steep pyramid structure, an appraisal system based on 'ticket punching' (and, at times, boss management) compensations and entitlement based carrot-and-stick approach transformational approach though highly required will be a huge task. The current transactional approach is based on social exchanges (which the politicians and business heads employ through freebies, financial incentives and so on).

A transformational approach involves inspirational and motivational means (leadership) that align the individual objectives and goals with that of the group, organisation and the nation. This approach if followed properly will produce capable leaders at all the levels—from the top (theatre command) to the bottom (team leader). If we wish to be absolutely objective in our assessment, then we must admit that the current military organisation in India needs to cover a substantial distance to reach this paradigm. But the need definitely exists.

The environment in which the process will be operationalised has two facets. The internal environment of the armed forces and the external environment in the country—the political milieu, bureaucracy and the people. In a transformational approach to reforms, both these environments (internal and external) will pose serious challenges. General Cariappa, the first Commander-in-Chief of the Indian Army was known to be more British than the British themselves. Our warfighting, military thinking, tactics and operational inertia mimic the British Indian Armed Forces. Almost all our training and development of men and officers is based on a transactional approach. Individual performances through courses, appraisals, postings etc are rewarded with lucrative positions and financial benefits. Jointness or synergy in operations entail flat organisations. The Indian Armed Forces (as also most of the other armed forces) have long and steep hierarchies. In the Indian context, we are still very conscious of our positions (rank, appointment, material possessions). 'I am better than you' and 'mine is better than yours' become the undercurrents of organisations where the members are constantly competing for the next rank or a better position.

The external environment basically comprises of the political leadership, bureaucracy and people at large. We have seen how the political leadership addressed this issue in the beginning. The situation at present is far better. Another concern among the military officers pertains to precedence as also rapid promotion to higher ranks in other 'comparable' services, such as the police, Central Armed Police Force and even the Indian Armed Forces. In purely academic terms, these comparisons and consequent feeling of victimhood are misplaced. But in a real world situation @ the feeling of deprivation needs to be addressed.

Once the theatre commands are introduced, it will still take a long time before these reforms mature to their full potential. The process of transformation of the internal and external environments will have to continue for several years if not decades.

★★★

Appendix

Agnipath Scheme

Global Perspective on Manpower Planning in Indian Armed Forces

The expectations from men and women for the armed forces are generally the same in all modern militaries—recruiting the right people with the right age profile and intellect for the right-sized armed forces that has cost-effective maintenance. Different countries face challenges in doing this on a number of counts.

The common denominator in this quest is to get young, tech-savvy people with high levels of common sense and learnability. Modern armies are smaller in size with very high level of adaptability, with a flatter, organisational structures that can adapt to rapid technological and societal changes. At the same time, recruits need to be nationalists with a high degree of motivation since it has been seen that contractual armies such as the US military contractors and the Russian contract mercenaries do more harm than good.

Different Countries, Different Challenges

Three countries are actually in the midst of war right now. These are Israel, Russia, and Ukraine. These three countries have to address issues based on their indigenous culture, population, economic strength and severity of their conflicts. Israel with its small size and population of 9.1 million has a military strength of 0.17 million and has a very small growth rate of 0.51 per cent per annum, which is below the minimum replacement rate.

Israeli armed forces are composed of a very small regular military with very high strength that gets mobilised during war. Israel follows the policy of conscription where every able-bodied man or woman (with very few exemptions) is expected to undergo compulsory military training of 18 months followed by embodiments whenever called upon—from once in two years to once in four years. These embodiments are regular features in Israel to keep the reserve force ready. Culturally, Israelis try and avoid general mobilisation unless the threat to the nation is real. So far, they have seen wars in 1956, 1967, 1973, 2016 and now. Israel has been able to keep a ratio of one to four for its regular to reserve forces. It is only the regular forces that are entitled to pension. Others neither clamour for nor get any pension.

Even during the mobilisation period, the reservists get less than the professional forces as pay, while allowances and other perks remain the same. Israel has also been able to keep the average age of their soldiers between 24 to 26. Even their commanding officers are around thirty to thirty-two years old.

With a per capita income of more than $ 57,758, Israel is a rich country and can definitely afford a larger armed forces. It appears that an average Jew does not find a career in the military attractive unless the country is at war! They have much better job opportunities and better remunerations in non-military professions.

Russia with a population of 140 million and a standing military of 1.3 million should not have a problem in getting the right quality and recruits for their forces. However, they have a cultural hurdle of 'hazing,' the term used for mental and physical harassment bordering on torture, that makes their military service very unattractive. Desertions are quite common in the Russian military. With a negative population growth rate of -0.15 per cent, and a not very strong economy (per capita GDP of $ 15,482) they have still managed to keep the average age profile of their soldiers within 26 years.

Russia definitely faces cultural problems in recruiting an adequate number of soldiers in their forces and this problem will aggravate in the near future given their negative population growth, average economic growth and seemingly endless war scenarios.

Ukraine has been involved in intense war with Russia for more than two years, although conflict has been ongoing since a decade. It too has a negative population growth (-7.45 per cent), a population of just 36 million and a military force of 0.9 million. Their military is overaged, since they do not have a policy of conscription like Israel and China. They were recruiting even old men and women aged 50 and above into their forces. Only very recently has President Zelensky given in to pressure from the military for recruiting younger men and women in the age group, 25 years and above. Ukraine by normal European standards is poor with a per capita of $ 4,003.

Four Countries in Operational Readiness

These countries include China, India, Pakistan, and Taiwan China, India and Pakistan have adequate population of young people who can be recruited into their military forces. China has legislated conscription in its constitution since 1950. With a population of over 1.4 billion and a standing military of around two million, they have been able to create an entirely volunteer armed forces. Even the first war fought in Korea was with a completely volunteer armed forces. They have undertaken four military reforms since 1950 that involved creating an officers' class, getting better qualified people into the military, downsizing the strength of military personnel and creating a strong culture of Information and Communications Technologies (ICT) enabled armed forces based on the tenets of an Information war.

The average age profile of the Chinese military is 24-26 years. With an over $ 15 trillion economy and GDP per capita income of $ 12,598, China has a strong economy to support a large standing military force. Despite this, China has had two rounds of reduction in the number of their military personnel. At the same time, China has invested heavily in capital expenditure on creating an impressive modern arsenal for their armed forces.

India like China, is endowed with a large population with a large number in the millennial and generation Z category. With a population of over 1.4 billion, it is not difficult to maintain a standing military force of over 1.4 million in terms of population and availability of young people. Given the popularity of the Indian military, all recruitment calls are highly oversubscribed. But this is where the bright side ends.

India faces three major problems of recruitment for their forces. First, the terms of engagement since the seventies have made India's military over-aged (above 32 years) and it is now filled with older soldiers. Second, India spends a large chunk of its defense budget on revenue expenditure such as salaries and pensions. Third, by all standards, India is still a very poor nation with a GDP per capita income of $ 2,389 despite the fact that it is also the fastest growing economy for the past few years and an attractive destination for foreign direct investment.

With about 80 per cent of the defense budget spent on salaries and pensions, India can afford very little capital expenditure on defense. The Indian Government has taken up a new initiative called Agnipath in June 2022.

Pakistan, too, has a large reservoir of young population for its armed forces. With a population of over 2.4 billion, they find it easy to maintain a personnel strength of 6.5 million. However, they face a problem of their own creation. The demographic composition of their forces—around 71 per cent of Pakistani soldiers—is highly skewed in favour of Punjabis from the Pakistani province of Punjab. Efforts are ongoing to reduce this imbalance. Second, there is a large-scale infiltration of religious fundamentalists and Jihadis in their forces. Third, ethnic sectarianism lowers the professionalism of the Pakistani armed forces.

It is unlikely that the Pakistani armed forces will achieve their desired egalitarian composition based on capabilities and merit. Incidentally, the Pakistani armed forces have never won a war as their army is deeply politicised.

Taiwan is yet another country at the brink of war with a very big nation. It is a rich country even by European standards with a GDP per capita income of $ 34,431. Taiwan has legislated conscription that makes it compulsory for every young male born after 2005 to serve in the armed forces for a minimum of one year. They maintain an active military of 169,000 and a reserve force of 1.66 million (almost ten times the active force). Taiwan has a low population growth of 0.13 per cent that is much below the required replacement rate. They face a demographic crunch to maintain a large army both on account of availability of suitable young people as well as a resource crunch of maintaining a rapidly ageing non-productive population. They are likely to move from a conscription-based military to a small and all-volunteer armed forces.

There is another group of nations that includes countries like the US, Japan, France, Germany, Netherlands and the UK who have been passively involved in global conflicts and hence are wary of fallouts on their soil.

These countries typically have a policy of keeping the average age profile of their soldiers between 24 to 26. These are rich countries with meagre populations and less than replacement rate of population growth. Military service is not very attractive in these countries. Some of these countries follow some model of conscription ranging from compulsory military service of less than a year to around two years and their emphasis is on a lean but effective military aided by a high tech weapons system and tech-savvy soldiers. The US has, however, not used the conscription law since 1973 after the Vietnam war.

India launched the Agnipath scheme to modernize the manpower profile of its military. India has some major advantages for maintaining a sizeable and modern armed force in an economically viable manner. It has a readily available young population with a cultural inclination to join military service, and a high level of technological adaption rate among the young with their digital skills. Plus, it has a rapidly growing economy. In spite of these advantages, the manpower planning in its defense services suffers from critical deficiencies. First, the average age profile of the armed forces is around 32 years (some reports have even placed it at 37 years). Second, the terms and conditions of engagement have resulted in a very heavy percentage of military expenditure on salaries and pensions. And third, recruitment in the land forces is based on region, castes and quotas. This eliminates any probability of creating an egalitarian land force based on pan-India merit.

Entry-level tests are more biased towards brawn as compared to the requirement of skilled, intelligent young people who can fight a modern, technologically driven war. Let us analyse how this situation was created.

Till 1965, the men in the Indian Army were recruited for 15 years. This included seven years of compulsory service followed by eight years of reserve service that was not mandatory. Thus, a soldier could leave after seven years of military service if he was willing to forego pensionary benefits. Those who chose to serve for full length of compulsory and reserve service were entitled to pension. According to Laxman Behera of the Observers Research Foundation (ORF), around 65 per cent of soldiers used to leave after the compulsory service, not waiting for entitlement of life-long pension. Thus, just over three to four soldiers out of ten were receiving pension till as late as the seventies. With this ecosystem, the average age profile of a soldier in the Indian Army was around 24 to 26 years.

To get over the need for frequent recruitment drives to fill the vacancies created by 65 per cent of soldiers leaving the army, the government made a policy where every soldier was to serve for 17 years and was entitled to pension after 15 years of service. Thus, hundred per cent soldiers recruited in the army were eligible for pension. The result was that the average age profile of the army jumped to 32 years by the early eighties and the pensionary budget ballooned especially after the grant of one rank one pension, a long-standing demand by Indian servicemen that was implemented from 2014.

Military brass were the first to realise the dangers of an ageing army. Shekhar Gupta in *India Today* in 1989, quotes top military brass on the alarmingly high teeth to tail ratio of 8,829 compared to 1,274 in China and 2,307 in Pakistan. This ratio depicts the number of men per combat soldier who either cannot fight due to old age or are not required to fight due to their job profile. Thus, for every soldier in an actual combat job, there is a long tail of 8,829 men.

Gen T N Raina was the first to order a committee in 1977 to suggest suitable measures to correct these anomalies. Later, a committee headed by Lt Gen K Balaram (then Vice Chief of Staff) was formed to suggest a course correction. The committee's recommendations came in 1985 and the estimate committee of the tenth Lok Sabha was informed in 1992-93 that a new policy framework for manpower planning in the defence forces had been finalised. But it took three decades to bring out a new policy to remove the anomalies in manpower planning.

The essential aspects of this new initiative address three major aspects. First, it gives a pan India egalitarian composition to the personnel in the armed forces, based on online exams open to all in India. Second, it aims to reduce the salary and pensionary burden on the exchequer. The new inductees, called agniveers, will receive six months military training with a central military training institution followed by specialised training with technical training centres of each arm or service. After four years of military service, 25 per cent of agniveers will be retained based on an all-India performance-based merit list and 75 per cent will be demobilised.

Eventually, the Indian administration will reduce the cost on pay and pension by more than Rs 15,000 crores during the next twenty years, according to Laxman Behera of ORF. At the same time, the age profile of 24-26 years will be achieved in the next ten to fifteen years. The financial package for those who are being demobilised is reasonably attractive, and stands at Rs 4.76 lacs per annum for the first year and Rs 6.92 lacs paid out for the next four years, with a 30 per cent contribution to sevanidhi, with an equal amount paid by the government. After four years, the agniveer will receive a total of Rs 11.71 lacs. During active service, each agniveer will be insured for Rs one crore.

To further assure those who are likely to be demobilised after four years, the government has reserved job vacancies in the Ministry of Home, MoD, Ports and Shipping, Education, and in the Governments of Assam, Haryana, UP, and MP. This initiative, like so many other long-awaited reforms, has been a cause of social turmoil and political resistance in India. Nonetheless the plan has been implemented.

Conclusion

By the summer of 2024, two batches of agniveers have already been inducted into the three services. Women candidates have also joined this stream. The training centres found these agniveers to be intelligent, smart, dedicated and quick to learn the required skill or knowledge. The units where they were posted found them very effective and matched the regular soldiers who had joined the armed forces as per the old scheme. The enthusiasm among the aspiring agniveers is reportedly, very high.

For the Indian Air Force, for each vacancy, there were 250 applications. For the Army, this ratio was one to fifty. This was due to our high unemployment rates among school pass outs and the traditional pride in serving the nation.

A more objective assessment can, however, only be made when the first few batches of agniveers are demobilised and absorbed in the non-military job market and in the reserved vacancies earmarked for them. Even then, it would be more prudent to fix the loopholes in the scheme, rather than scrap it.

★★★

Bibliography

Introduction: India's Journey in an Era of Extreme Inertia

https://history.state.gov/milestones/1945-1952/asia-and-africa
Decolonization of Asia and Africa 1945-1960

French, Patrick (1997), *Liberty or Death India's Journey to Independence and Division*, Harper Collins India. ISBN 8172233280

Sareen, T R (2020), *INA and Subhas Chandra Bose: Through Japanese Sources,* Life Span Publishers and Distributors, ISBN 9788194458838

Lt Gen S L Menezes (1999), *Fidelity and Honour: The Indian Army from the Seventeenth to Twenty First Century,* Oxford University Press, New Delhi, ISBN 0195650476.

Maj Gen V K Singh (2022), *The Contribution of Jubbulpore Mutiny to India's Freedom: Did the INA also have a Role?* KW Publishers, New Delhi. *ISBN 97893949150804.*

MJ Akbar (2011), *Tinderbox: The Past and Future of Pakistan,* Harpers Collins Publishers India. *ISBN 9789350290392.*

Shashi Tharoor (2016), *An Era of Darkness The British Empire in India,* Aleph, *New Delhi. ISBN 9789383064656.*

https://www.vifindia.org/article/2022/august/30/freebie-debate-and-kautilyas-arthashastra

https://theunbrokenwindow.com/Development/MADDISON%20The%20World%20Economy--A%20Millennial.pdf

Chandra, Bipin et al, (1988), *India's Struggle for Independence,* Penguin Books India. *ISBN 9780140107814.*

Sumit Sarkar (1983), *Modern India 1885-1947* Macmillan, New Delhi ISBN *0333 904257.*

Durga Das (1969) *India From Curzon to Nehru & After.* Collins London.

https://www.vifindia.org/article/2022/january/05/India-1952-1976-and-2014-2021

Lt Gen Harbakhsh Singh VC, Padma Bhushan and Padma Vibhushan (2000), *In the Line of Duty: A Soldier Remembers.* Lancers Publishers and Distributors, New Delhi. *ISBN 8170621062.*

Major General Sukhwant Singh (1981), *India's Wars Since Independence Defence of the Western Borders,* Volume Two, Vikas Publishing House. *ISBN O706912772.*

Major General Lachhman Singh Lehl, *Missed Opportunities, Indo Pak War 1965.*

Maj Gen Rajiv Narayanan, *India's Theatre Commands: The Drivers, the Challenges and the Way Ahead;* USI Strategic Year Book 2021, Vij *Books ISBN 978939091748-8* .

Air Marshal Anil Chopra, Shalini Chopra (Edited) (2021), *The 1971 Indo-Pak Air War Reflections and Projections.* KW Publishers Private Ltd New Delhi, in association with Centre for Air Power Studies New Delhi. *ISBN 9789391490096.*

The Kargil Review Committee Report (1999), *From Surprise to Reckoning.* Sage. ISBN 0761994661.

https://www.google.com/search?q=appointment+of+Bipin+Rawat+as+CDS&rlz=1C5CHFA_enIN1014IN1014&oq=appointment+of+Bipin+Rawat+as+CDS&aqs=chrome..69i57j0i22i30j0i390i650.3458317j0j15&sourceid=chrome&ie=UTF-8

https://www.mod.gov.in/sites/default/files/Lt-General-Anil.pdf. *Appointment of Gen Anil Chauhan the current CDS.*

The Basics of Nomenclature

https://mod.gov.in/sites/default/files/AR8.pdf *Annual Report Ministry of Defence 2007-08.* (Basics about the three services explained).

https://idsa.in/system/files/jds/jds_9_1_2015_VijaiSinghRana.pdf 'Extending Jointness in Indian Armed forces' *2015.* (This explains the terms used in joint theatre commands).

https://apps.dtic.mil/sti/pdfs/ADA432870.pdf Noel Sporles *and Alex Yate, Historical Study for Operational Command Resource for Researchers.* Australian Government Department of Defense,

Review of Literature

https://newsonair.com/2021/06/24/decoding-indian-armed-forces-theatre-command-system-the-synergistic-integration-of-army-navy-and-air-force/ Abhinandan *Sharma 24 June 2021.*

https://www.hindustantimes.com/india-news/theaterisation-to-take-number-of-years-says-army-chief-general-naravane/story-fVgTOGc3yeAd8YylR0OKXO.html

https://indianexpress.com/article/cities/delhi/theatre-commands-only-after-defence-strategy-and-higher-body-gen-naravane-8351453/

http://www.indiandefencereview.com/spotlights/lost-opportunities-in-operation-parakram/ Brig Gurmeet Kanwal, *13 December 2011.*

https://www.orfonline.org/expert-speak/theater-commands-prospects-and-challenges/ Shauryavardhan *Sharma 03 Feb 2021.*

https://timesofindia.indiatimes.com/blogs/jay-speak/theatre-commands-a-borrowed-concept-why-is-the-politico-military-establishment-so-determined-on-forging-ahead-with-it/

https://theprint.in/defence/what-are-military-theatre-commands-and-why-does-india-want-to-switch-to-them/690487/ Snehesh Alex Philip 06 July 2021

https://www.ia-forum.org/Files/BNMWSM.pdf

https://data.worldbank.org/indicator/MS.MIL.XPND.GD.ZS

https://www.statista.com/statistics/266892/military-expenditure-as-percentage-of-gdp-in-highest-spending-countries/

https://theprint.in/opinion/indias-theaterisation-being-driven-by-a-1930s-mindset-cant-treat-iaf-as-artillery/689273/
Air Marshal Anil Chopra

https://www.orfonline.org/expert-speak/defence-budget-2023-24/
Aditya Bhan

https://www.idsa.in/issuebrief/Defence-Budget-2023-24_170223

https://www.orfonline.org/research/indian-defence-procurement-righting-the-ship/

http://164.100.47.193/Refinput/New_Reference_Notes/English/16122020_155303_1021205239.pdf *Recent Defense Procurements by India*, Lok Sabha Secretariat New Delhi, October 2020

https://data.worldbank.org/indicator/NY.GDP.PCAP.CD

https://www.vifindia.org/article/2021/february/02/air-defence-command-some-salient-points-and-imperatives

https://idsa.in/system/files/jds/14-2-2020-achieving-jointness-in-war-asingh.pdf Ashish Singh

https://www.britannica.com/event/Battle-of-Quebec-North-America-1759

https://www.financialexpress.com/defence/indias-command-structure-of-theatre-commands/2332320/ Brig Kuldip Singh(Retd)

https://indianairforce.nic.in/history-timeline/(Official site of the IAF).

http://www.dodccrp.org/events/7th_ICCRTS/Tracks/pdf/083.PDF (Dr Noel Sporels in consultation with other Western authors.)

Major General V K Singh. *Leadership in the Indian Army: Biographies of Twelve Soldiers.* Sage India ISBN *0761933220.*

https://www.claws.in/publication/nathu-la-september-1967-and-galwan-valley-june-2020-lessons-and-future-strategies-for-india/

Gurmeet Kanwal and Neha Kohli (2018) *Defence Reforms a National Imperative.* IDSA, Pentagon Press. *ISBN 9789386618344.*

https://www.orfonline.org/series/26-11-a-decade-after/Maj Gen (Retd) Rajiv Narayanan *India's Theatre Commands: The Drivers, the Challenges and the Way Ahead.* USI Strategic Year Book 2021,
Vij Books ISBN 978939091748-8

http://www.indiandefencereview.com/news/the-concept-of-theatre-command-in-the-indian-context/ Gp Capt A K Sachdeva July-Sep 2021

https://idsa.in/system/files/jds_1_1_psdas.pdf (Journal of Defence Studies)

Col(*Dr.*) Rajneesh Singh (2020), *CDS and Other Reforms.* Centre for Strategic Studies and Simulation United Services Institution of India, New Delhi, Vij Book India *ISBN 978-93-89620405.*

https://www.claws.in/theatre-commands-a-conceptual-approach/ Col Samir Srivastav 19 January 2021

https://www.orfonline.org/research/the-case-for-agnipath/ (Laxman Behera is an Associate Professor at the Special Centre for National Security Studies, Jawahar Lal Nehru University, New Delhi)

Gist of discussion with the scholars at CLAWS on 19 January 2022.

The *gist of discussion with scholars at CAPS on 8 February.*

Discussion with former Signal Officer in Chief Lt General Sabberwal, advisor to Gen Bipin Rawat

The Turning Point

https://www.britannica.com/event/Battle-of-Quebec-North-America-1759

https://ahec.armywarcollege.edu/exhibits/CivilWarImagery/cheney_vicksburg.cfm Official history Vicksburg battle by US War College (published in 2013)

CRMF Cruttwell (1936), *The History of Great War 1914-18.* Oxford: Clarendon Press.. (-*p.* 547).

John Connor (2019), *Someone Else's War Fighting for the British Empire in World War, I.* I B Tauris and & Co Ltd London, New York, ISBN 9781784532703.

https://history.army.mil/html/books/075/75-8/CMH_Pub_75-8.pdf

J H Anderson (1978) *American Civil War.* Nataraj Publishers: Dehradun.

Winston S Churchill (1958), *The American Civil War.* Cassel: London.

Ian F W Becket, *The American Civil War.* Alan Sutton Publishing Inc. ISBN 075090044.

https://www.britannica.com/event/Battle-of-Amiens

https://www.historyextra.com/period/first-world-war/ww1-fochs-grand-hundred-days-offensive-battle-allies-germany-france-armistice/ (Jointness in WWI)

Gordon Corrigan (2012), *The Second World War: A Military History.* Atlantic Books Main. ISBN 9781843548959.

John Keegan (2005), *The Second World War.* Penguin USA. ISBN 0143035738.

Brian Gardner (1961), *The Big Push a Portrait of the Battle of Somme.* Cassel., ASIN: B0000CL04U.

Liddle Hart B H (1978), *The North African Campaign 1940-43.* Natraj Publishers: Dehradun, Reprint 1983ISBN 8181580338

Gabriel A Richard, Savage L Paul (1981),*Crisisin Command Mismanagement the Army.* Himalayan Books. New Delhi.

Dixon Norman (1976), *On Psychology of Military Incompetence.* Jonathan Cape Ltd. ISBN 0224011618.

Wars in Ancient India

S Jaishankar (2020), *The India Way: Strategies for an Uncertain World* Harper Collins Publishers: *Noida ISBN 9789353579791.*

The Cholas Some Enduring Issues of Statecraft Military Matters and International Relations, P K Gautam; https://www.idsa.in/system/files/jds_7_4_PK-Gautam.pdf

A Study into the Ahom Military System in Medieval Assam .Nilam Hazarika;https://www.ijhssi.org/papers/v4(6)/Version-2/D0462017022.pdf

https://www.sanskritimagazine.com/kings-indraprastha-mahabharata/

https://www.vifindia.org/transcriptions-paper/2012/07/03/scientific-dating-of-ancient-events-from-7000-bc-to-2000-bc Saroj Bala, *3 July 2012.*

Shekhar Adhikari, 'Military Thinking of Ancient India' https://www.aninews.in/news/national/politics/an-outstanding-effort-to-recall-great-military-thinkers-of-ancient-india/

Ancient Indian Warfare;https://www.worldhistory.org/Indian_Warfare/

Weaponries During the Medieval Period of Assam; http://oaji.net/articles/2016/1707-1457180585.pdf

https://www.vifindia.org/sites/default/files/145812085-War-in-Ancient-India-1944.pdf

Girish Chandra Singh (2021), *Indian Art of War,* Sharda Pustak Bhawan Publishers and Distributors*:* Prayagraj ISBN 8186204342.

Jadunath Sarkar (1973), *Shivaji and His Times.* Orient Longman.

R D Palsokar (2003) *Shivaji The Great Guerrilla.* Natraj Publishers*:* Dehradun ISBN 818158003.

https://www.mapsofindia.com/history/battles/seleucid-mauryan-war.html

Indian Experience Post-1947

Maj Gen Kuldip Singh Bajwa (2003), *Jammu and Kashmir War (1947-48), Political and Military Perspective* Har Anand Publications. New Delhi. ISBN 8124109230.

Lt Gen S K Sinha PVSM (2007), *Operation Rescue Military Operations in Jammu and Kashmir 1947-49.* Vision Book Sixth Edition, ISBN 8170944988.

G (Edn) HQ Western Command for Army HQ New Delhi, *Selected Writings and Speeches from Officers of Western Command on Operations in J&K Immediately Prior to cease-fire.* Manager India Press*:* New Delhi.

USI Study; Lt Gen Vinay Shankar, Maj Gen GG Dwivedi, Air Marshal Bharat Kuma, Ambassador Ranjit Singh Kalha, Ms Bhavana Tripathi (2015); *1962: A View From the Other Side of the Hill.*

Vij Books India. ISBN 97893864464769.

Claude Arpi (2017), *Tibet: The Last of a Free Nation: India Tibet Relations, 1947-62 Part 1.* Vij Books India. ISBN 9789386457219.

Harbakhsh Singh, Lt Gen (1991), *War Dispatches: Indo Pak Conflict 1965.* Lancers International. ISBN 8170621178.

N Thapliyal, U N Thapliyal (2011), *The Indo Pak War 1965, A History* Nataraj Publishers: Dehradun ,Delhi. ISBN 9788181581570.

JFR Jacob, Lt Gen (1997), *Surrender at Dacca Birth of a Nation.* Manohar Publishers and Distributors: New Delhi. *reprint 2006 ISBN 817304189X.*

Mohammad Ayoob and Subramanyam, SK (1972), *The Liberation War* Chand and Co.

PVS Jagan Mohan and Samir Chopra (2013), *Eagles Over Bangladesh, The IAF in 1971 Liberation War.* Harpers Collins India. ISBN 978-93-5136-163-3.

Major Chakravarti Singh VrC (2021), *Cavalier in the Sky: Biography of Air Vice Marshal Chandan Singh MVC, AVSM, VC.* Maharaja Pustak Prakash Research Centre: Jodhpur. ISBN 9789383723669.

Sukhwant Singh, Maj Gen (1981), *Defence of Western Border Volume Two.* Vikas Publishing House., 0706912772.

D R Mankekar (2006), *Twenty two fateful Days: Pakistan Cut to Size.* Natraj Publishers: Dehradun. ISBN 8181580064.

Major General Hakeem Arshad Qureshi (2002), *The 1971 Indo Pak War A Soldier's Narrative.* Oxford University Press. ISBN 0195797787.

https://usiofindia.org/publication/usi-journal/air-operations-in-the-western-sector-during-1971-indo-pak-war/

Arjun Subramanaym (2016), *India's Wars: A Military History 1947-1971.* Harpers Collins Publishers India, ISBN 9789351777496.

Y M Bammi, Lt Gen (2002) *Kargil the Impregnable Conquered.* Gorkha Publishers: Noida. ISBN 8175253525.

Col Ashfaq Hussain (2006), *Witness to Blunder: Kargil Story Untold*/

V P Malik Gen, *Kargil from Surprise to Victory.* Harper Collins: Noida. ISBN 9788172236359.

The Kargil Review Committee Report (1999) *From Surprise to Reckoning.* Sage Publication ISBN 0761994661.

https://www.opindia.com/2021/02/nehru-himalayan-blunder-china-army-defence-expenditure-budget/

https://www.macrotrends.net/countries/IND/india/military-spending-defense-budget

https://www.macrotrends.net/countries/IND/india/gdp-gross-domestic-product

China and US Theatre Commands

People's Liberation Army Operational Concepts by RAND Corporation: https://www.rand.org/content/dam/rand/pubs/research_reports/RRA300/RRA394-1/RAND_RRA394-1.pdf

https://www.statista.com/statistics/1009819/total-us-military-fatalities-in-american-wars-1775-present/

https://www.usaspending.gov/agency/department-of-defense?fy=2023

Air Land Battle Doctrine

https://apps.dtic.mil/sti/pdfs/ADA202888.pdf

https://chinapower.csis.org/china-global-arms-trade/

https://www.globalsecurity.org/military/library/policy/army/fm/11-45/ch6.htm

IDF (1948 to 1973)

Chaim Herzog (updated by Sholmo Gazit (2005), *The Arab Israeli Wars, Wars and Peace in the Middle East.* Vintage Books, Aadivision of Random House: New York, ISBN *1400079632.*

SLA Marshall (1958), *Sinai Victory.* William Morrow and Company: New York.

Edgar O' Balance (1979), *No Victor No Vanquished The Yom Kippur War.* Natraj Publishers

Jeremy Bowen (2003), *Six Days: How the 1967 War Shaped the Middle East.* Pocket Books. ISBN 074344969.

Michael B Oren (2003), *Six Days of War June 1967 and the Making of the Modern Middle East.* Presidio Press, ISBN 0345461924.

Israeli Defence Forces' Defence Doctrine: English Translation August 12, 2016, https://www.belfercenter.org/publication/israeli-defense-forces-defense-doctrine-english-translation *(The original doctrine is in Hebrew. Harvard translated this into English with permission.)*

Noor Dahri (2022), *Israel Defence Force (IDF) Ground Forces , Operations Units & Command and Control.* Vij Books, India ISBN 9789393499745.

http://164.100.47.4/BillsTexts/LSBillTexts/Asintroduced/62_2023_LS_E315202331238PM.pdf (Lok Sabha notification introducing the Bill for Inter Services Organisations (Command Control and Discipline) Bill 2023

Seshadri Chari (2018); *The Saga of Israel From Nowhere to Everywhere.* Rana Rugna Seva Smriti, Sadan Marg, Mumbai

https://www.hindustantimes.com/india-news/triservices-missile-command-on-anvil-as-stand-off-weapons-era-dawns-101664767116679.html

https://openthemagazine.com/special/what-should-be-the-role-of-the-chief-of-defence-staff/

Col VS Yadav (2012), *Employment of Special Forces Challenges and Opportunities for the Future;* Centre for Joint Warfare studies Vij Books India: New Delhi. ISBN 9789381411285.

https://missilethreat.csis.org/country/india/

Alexai Arbatov and Vladimir Dvorkins (2014), *Outer Space Weapons Diplomacy and Security;* Knowledge World Publishers: New Delhi ISBN 9789381904947.

Arjun Subramaniam and Diptendu Choudhary (Edited) (2022), *Force in Statecraft: An Indian Perspective.* KW Publishers: New Delhi. ISBN 9789391490928.

https://indianstrategicknowledgeonline.com/web/C4I2SR%20for%20IA%20by%20Col%20Shantanu%20Dayal,%20CLAWS,%202010.pdf (ColShantanu Dayal on C4I2SR)

https://idsa.in/system/files/gkanwal_140214.pdf (Brig Gurmit Kanwal on C4ISR)

https://timesofindia.indiatimes.com/blogs/rakshakindia/right-choice-for-indian-army/?source=app&frmapp=yes (Maj Gen Anil Kumar Lal 18 May 2023)

https://raksha-anirveda.com/joint-pathways-transformation-of-the-indian-armed-forces/ Lt Gen Sunil Srivastava jointness through joint C4I2SR

https://www.macrotrends.net/countries/IND/india/military-spending-defense-budget

https://www.vifindia.org/brief/2018/december/12/optimising-defense-expenditure by Ashok Pathak

Ghosh A K (2013) *Resource Allocation and Management in Defence Need for a Framework.* Knowledge World Publication, ISBN 978-93-81904-45-9.

Behera Laxman Kumar (2016), *Indian Defence Industry: An Agenda for Making in India* Institute of Defence Studies and Analysis (New Delhi), Publication Pentagon Press. *ISBN 978-81-8274-905-4.*

https://www.google.com/search?q=India%27s+defence+export+in+2016-17&rlz=1C5CHFA_enIN1014IN1014&oq=India%27s+defence+export+in+2016-17&gs_lcrp=EgZjaHJvbWUyBggAEEUYOTIHCAEQABiiBDIHCAIQABiiBDIHCAMQABiiBNIBDDM0NDE3ODNqMGoxNagCALACAA&sourceid=chrome&ie=UTF-8 by Smriti Jain

https://www.vifindia.org/article/2022/september/19/indigenization-of-defence-production by Ashok Pathak.

Daniel Kahneman, *Thinking Fast and Slow* (2011), Penguin Random House UK. ISBN 978014103357.

http://www.terafiq.com/2017/05/gen-sundarji-letter-to-officers.html.

https://economictimes.indiatimes.com/news/defence/india-moves-ahead-with-creation-of-theatre-commands-for-integrated-war-fighting/articleshow/101078591.cms?from=mdr 18 June 2023.

Malcolm Gladwell (2021), *The Bomber Mafia: A Story Set in War. Penguin Random House UK, ISBN 9780241535868.*

Sanjay Badri Maharaj, *Nuclear India: From Reluctance to Triad,* Asia@War Series, Helion and Company Ltd, Unit 8 Amherst Business Centre, England, ISBN 9781914377044.

Bernard M Bass , Ronald E Riggio (2006), *Transformational Leadership.* Psychology Press*:* New York, London, ISBN 9780805847611.

JD Fletcher , PR Chatelier, https://apps.dtic.mil/sti/pdfs/ADA408439.pdf An Overview of Military Training August 2000 (US Institute of Defence Analysis).

Lt Gen Prakash Menon, Theatre Commands to Defence University: Why Indian security interests need a political push https://theprint.in/opinion/theatre-commands-to-defence-university-why-indian-security-interests-need-a-political-push/1262173/

https://pib.gov.in/PressReleasePage.aspx?PRID=1805368 12 March 2022

Sahana Singh (2017), *The Educational Heritage of Ancient India: How an Eco System of Learning was laid to waste.* Notionpress.com*:* Chennai ISBN 9781947586529.

R K Anand (2012), *Assault on Merit: The Untold Story of Civil Military Relations.* Har-Anand Publication*s:* New Delhi.

https://www.hindustantimes.com/india-news/parliamentary-committee-backs-bill-for-joint-services-commands-and-discipline-in-indian-armed-forces-101689965448785.html.

Principles of Jointness (Rubel)*:* https://apps.dtic.mil/sti/pdfs/ADA525717.pdf

https://www.valmiki.iitk.ac.in/sloka?field_kanda_tid=1&language=dv&field_sarga_value=1.

https://www.gitasupersite.iitk.ac.in/srimad?language=dv&field_chapter_value=1&field_nsutra_value=1&show_mool=1

Narendra Kohli (2021), *Ram Katha Abhyuday, Volumes 1 and 2.*

Diamond Pocket Books: New Delhi ISBN 9788128400032.

https://www.thesikhencyclopedia.com/historical-events-in-sikh-history/the-sikh-empire-1799-1839/army-of-maharaja-ranjit-singh/

https://www.britannica.com/biography/Ranjit-Singh-Sikh-maharaja

https://www.mha.gov.in/sites/default/files/table_of_precedence.pdf

https://theprint.in/opinion/by-no-stretch-of-imagination-can-the-military-be-compared-to-ias-and-ips-officers/84449/

http://www.indiandefencereview.com/news/iafs-squadron-strength-crystal-gazing-at-the-next-two-decades/

Sanjay Badri-Maharaj (2022) *90 Years of the Indian Air Force Present Capabilities and Future Prospects* Helion and Company: England ISBN 9781915070586.

DRDO Report 2022

Desmond W Hayde MVC (1991) *The Battle of Dograi* Second Edition Nataraj Publishers: Dehradun

Ronald Lewin (1981) *Rommel as Military Commander* Natraj Publishers: Dehradun.

Endnotes

A state of mind of doing the same thing over and over again and expecting different results. (Pp71 'The Dogmas of Delhi: Overcoming the Hesitation of History' in 'The India Way Strategies for an Uncertain world 'Harper Collins 2020)

*(Pp 25 The 1971 Indo Pak Air War Reflections and Projections, KW Publishers, Centre for Air Power Studies New Delhi, 2021, ISBN 97893914900906).

During the author's interaction with the Chief of Defence staff on 4 September 23, the CDS made an observation that the initial distrust and apprehensions are now things of the past. The discussion with scholars of CAPS was on 8 Feb 22.

The Inter services Organizations Bill 2023 passed by the Indian Parliament will resolve this issue.

Seleucus advanced with a huge army against India in 305 BC. The Indian soldiers were in fine fettle and their horsemen, chariot army and elephants were ready to inflict defeat on the invaders. A terrible war followed on the north-west borders of India. The Greeks could not withstand the onslaught of the gallant Indian fighters. The army of Chandragupta Maurya routed the invaders and Seleucus was forced to sign a peace treaty. Chandragupta Maurya, advised by Kautilya, presented his terms to the defeated army. Seleucus was forced to accept. By the terms of the treaty, Seleucus surrendered his territories in Afghanistan—Herat, Kandahar, and the Kabul valley—to Chandragupta Maurya. In return, he was presented a gift of 300 elephants. On Kautilya's advice, Chandragupta married the daughter of Seleucus, Helen. Seleucus also appointed Megasthenes as his ambassador to the Mauryan court. Megasthenes wrote a famous account of his stay at the Mauryan court in a book entitled Indica.

Reference.http://indiansaga.com/history/magadha_seleucus.html (accessed on 21 January 2024)

In October 1831, Ranjit Singh met with British officials regarding the disposition of Sindh province (now in southeastern Pakistan). The British, who had already begun to navigate the Indus River and were eager to keep Sindh for themselves, prevailed on Ranjit Singh to accept their plan. Ranjit Singh, however, was chagrined by the British design to put a cordon around him. He opened negotiations with the Afghans and sanctioned an expedition led by the Dogra commander Zorawar Singh that extended Ranjit Singh's northern territories into Ladakh in 1834.

Reference https://www.britannica.com/biography/Ranjit-Singh-Sikh-maharaja (accessed on 21 January 2024)

During the author's interaction with the CDS on 4 September 2023, the CDS observed that the concerned officers are on board and there is no ambiguity in the conceptual framework of jointness in the Indian Armed Forces.

Gen Anil Chauhan, the CDS has been at the helm while implementing the Aginpath Scheme. He visualises three major advantages from this scheme particularly for the armed forces (as explained by him on 4 September 23). First, the commanding officers will have a choice in selecting the type of men and women they prefer in their respective organisations (out of the selected lot that are given to them. Second, the nation will have well-trained and soldiers as reserves who can be called at short notice should there be a need. Though most military scholars believe there is no scope for long wars in present times, but then the Russia-Ukraine war has been continuing for more than two years and there is no sign of the war coming to an end soon. Third, the Agnipath scheme will allow the army to move beyond region and caste-based recruitments in times to come. If the Air Force and the Navy can have caste/region-independent recruitment, then, so can the army. Surely there are other rallying points for motivation.

Appendix

Massoglia Anna and Forest Julia (August 2023) *Defense Contractors Spent Big in Afghanistan before the US left and Taliban took Control*; https://www.opensecrets.org/news/2021/08/defense-contractors-spent-big-in-afghanistan-before-the-us-left-taliban-took-control/?__cf_chl_tk=0dv2t13JlW3g-6pmamalGnDyXsL9HNd5paSQKRi3iVDA-1719554346-0.0.1.1-4073

Knickmeyer Ellen (24 June 2023). *The mercenary chief who urged an uprising against Russian generals has long ties with Putin*; https://apnews.com/article/russia-ukraine-prigozhin-wagner-profile-e1939a58f216551b1a20157cc3803085

Ministry of Defence Press Release (14 June 2022); https://www.pib.gov.in/PressReleasePage.aspx?PRID=1833747

Radhakrishanan R K (15 June 2022), *Army Veterans Point Out Flaws in the Agnipath Recruitment Scheme*; https://frontline.thehindu.com/dispatches/army-veterans-point-out-flaws-in-agnipath-recruitment-scheme/article65529422.ece

Behera Laxman Kumar, Kaushal Vinay Kumar (16 August 2023), *The Case for Agnipath*; https://www.orfonline.org/research/the-case-for-agnipath/

Sharma Roopashree (4 November 2022), *Indian Army Recruitment Pattern: Check Syllabus and Latest Exam Pattern*; https://www.jagranjosh.com/articles/indian-army-agnipath-recruitment-syllabus-and-latest-exam-pattern-1656577234-1

Tri Raj (19 May 2023), *Indian Army Tradesman 8th Pass Syllabus*; https://www.embibe.com/exams/indian-army-agniveer-tradesman-8-pass-syllabus/

Gupta Shekhar (updated 21 October 2013, first published 28 Feb 1989), *India Today* 'Age Factor Becomes Worrisome for Indian Army'; https://www.indiatoday.in/magazine/special-report/story/19890228-age-factor-becomes-worrisome-for-indian-army-815803-1989-02-27

Hemmler John (September 2023) *Military Recruitment Across the Globe*; The Netherlands, Germany, Japan and France https://dsm.forecastinternational.com/2023/09/15/military-recruiting-across-the-globe-the-netherlands-germany-japan-and-france/

Hlusky Andries (15 February 2020), Military Recruitment in the US, China and Russia https://globalpolicyinsights.org/military-recruitment.php accessed on

Mishra Sukriti (19 October 2022), (*Law Beat*), *'Average Age of Below Rank Armed Forces in India Higher than Global Average*; Agnipath Seeks to Evolve Young Combat Force: Centre to HC; https://lawbeat.in/news-updates/average-age-below-rank-armed-forces-india-higher-global-average-agnipath-scheme- 24seeks#:~:text=The%20Central%20Government%20has%20pointed,the%20average%20age%20of%20Armed

Strashkulych Anhelina (16 May 2024), Ukrainaska Pravada, *'Old Men Belong Here How Ukraine Armed Forces Have Become 40+ age army and Whether Lowering the Mobilization Age will Affect Combat Capability'*; https://www.pravda.com.ua/eng/articles/2024/05/16/7455980/

Countries in World by Population (2024), Worldometer; https://www.worldometers.info/world-population/population-by-country/

Active Military Manpower by Country (2024); https://www.globalfire-power.com/active-military-manpower.php#google_vignette

GDP per Capita per Country (2023); https://www.worldometers.info/gdp/gdp-per-capita/

Gross domestic product (GDP) per capita at current prices in Taiwan from 1988 to 2024 with forecasts until 2029; https://www.statista.com/statistics/727592/gross-domestic-product-gdp-per-capita-in-taiwan/

Chad D Guzman (6 January 2023); Taiwan is Extending Conscription; Here is how its military compares to other countries; https://time.com/6245036/taiwan-conscription-military-comparison/

Mazza Michael in Global Taiwan Institute (24 January 2018), Taiwan's Demographic Crunch and its Military Implications; https://globaltaiwan.org/2018/01/taiwans-demographic-crunch-and-its-military-implications/